elson

Careers For Life

Authors
Sean Armstrong
Denise King
Lee Wallace

NELSON
THOMSON LEARNING

Australia • Canada • Mexico • Singapore • Spain • United Kingdom • United States

NELSON
THOMSON LEARNING

Nelson Careers For Life

by Sean Armstrong, Denise King, Lee Wallace

Director of Publishing
Beverley Buxton

General Manager, Social Studies, Business, and French
Carol Stokes

Publisher, Social Studies
Doug Panasis

Executive Managing Editor, Development
Cheryl Turner

Managing Editor, Development
Karin Fediw

Project Manager
Norma Pettit

Developmental Editor
Alisa Yampolsky

Executive Director, Content and Media Production
Renate McCloy

Director, Content and Media Production
Lisa Dimson

Production Manager
Cathy Deak

Senior Production Coordinator
Kathrine Pummell

Design Director
Ken Phipps

Content Production Editor
Stacey Kauder

Copy Editor/Proofreader
Sandy Manley

Indexer
Noeline Bridge

Interior Design
Liz Harasymczuk

Cover Design
Peter Papayanakis

Cover Images
first row (left to right): © Bill Miles/CORBIS, CP PHOTO/Kevin Frayer, © David Young-Wolff/PhotoEdit
second row (left to right): © Ron Chapple/Taxi/Getty Images, © Jeff Greenberg/PhotoEdit

Compositors
Rachel Sloat
Pamela Clayton

Photo Researcher/Permissions
Indu Ghuman

Printer
Quebecor World

Acknowledgements
Thomson Nelson would like to acknowledge the ongoing input and guidance provided by curriculum directors and consultants in the Newfoundland and Labrador Department of Education.

ISBN-13: 978-0-17-630223-8
ISBN-10: 0-17-630223-9

Printed and bound in the United States
1 2 3 4 09 08 07 06

For more information contact Nelson, 1120 Birchmount Road, Toronto, Ontario, M1K 5G4. Or you can visit our Internet site at http://www.nelson.com

EXPERT ADVISORY PANEL:

Cesare DiDonato
Halton Catholic DSB

Dan Dopko
Waterloo Region DSB

Claire Harrison
CANDO Career Solutions Inc.

Lee Powell
Ottawa-Carlton DSB

Amber Scotchburn
Dufferin-Peel Catholic DSB

Myrna Tidd
Toronto DSB

Joanne Twist
Peel DSB

Lisa Vincent
Hastings & Prince Edward DSB

Program Assessment Consultant:
Damian Cooper

Anti-bias Consultant:
Ken Ramphais

Thomson Nelson Review Team

James F. Paul
Centre for Distance Learning and Innovation
Nova Central SD

Barbara Anne O'Keefe
St. Kevin's High School
Eastern SD

Valerie Sheppard
Mealy Mountain Collegiate
Labrador SD

Table of Contents

Getting the Most from *Nelson Careers For Life*

Asking the Right Questions

What is the big question that you think this course will answer? If you think it is *What should I be when I grow up?* you'll probably be disappointed. For one thing, that question is almost impossible to answer. You are, and will continue to be, many different things. You will grow, learn and change, and the world you live in will change. Can you really pick one occupation now and know that you will always be engaged and happy in it?

There are many better questions that this course answers—and, more important, there are many better questions that you will learn to ask yourself. Read through the unit titles:

- Why Am I Doing This?
- Who Am I?
- What Is Out There for Me?
- How Do I Get Where I Want to Go?
- How Far Have I Come?
- What Can I Expect From Here?

Asking yourself these questions will help you make good decisions about the direction your life is taking. Asking good questions will help you plan a career that really suits you—that takes into account your interests, abilities and values and the options that are available to you. Asking good questions will also help you adapt to change, and there will be a lot of change in your life. New questions invite new answers—they invite you not only to look for new information but to regularly assess what that information means to you.

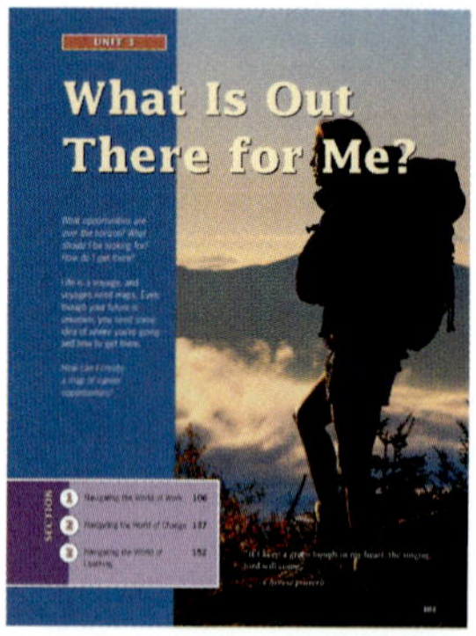

In short, this course is more about learning to ask questions than it is about answers. And the questions are about *you*. You are the subject of this course.

What You Can Expect

You will be participating in a decision-making and planning process that you can use throughout your life.

- In Unit 1, *Why Am I Doing This?*, you will learn about the knowledge and skills you will develop during this course. You will also try to answer the question in the unit title. You can be sure that many other people—the textbook authors, your teacher, your guidance counsellor, your teacher-advisor—have reasons why *they* think you should be doing this. But this course is about you—you need to have your *own* personal goals.

- In Unit 2, *Who Am I?*, you will gather information about yourself. You will learn how to express important things about yourself, and you will analyse your strengths and areas of need. You will think about who you want to become and you will work on skills that will move you toward that goal. Being able to acquire and analyse knowledge of yourself is essential for making good decisions about your life and career.

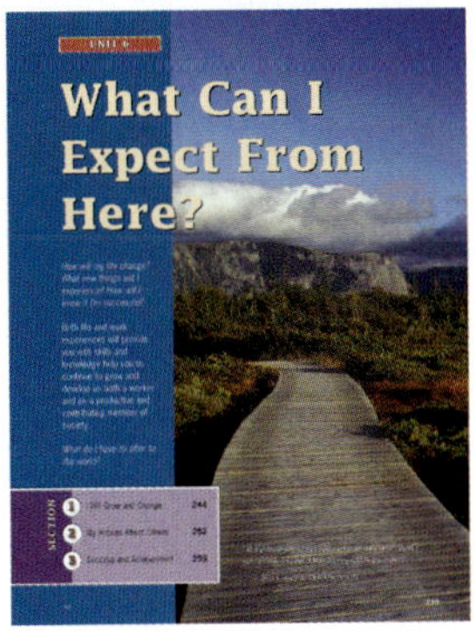

- In Unit 3, *What Is Out There for Me?*, you will develop the research skills you need to find out what learning and work options are available to you—no matter what your interests and skills, and no matter where in your career you happen to be. You will learn what options exist now, of course, but you will also learn what questions to ask so that you can continue to acquire and analyse knowledge about the world around you in the future.
- In Unit 4, *How Do I Get Where I Want to Go?*, you will set specific career goals and articulate real plans to reach those goals. You will also create a set of tools to help you take advantage of work and learning opportunities.
- In Unit 5, *How Far Have I Come?*, you will reflect on the process so far and plan how to use that process in your future career planning.
- Finally, in Unit 6, *What Can I Expect From Here?*, you will consider your future beyond the classroom and learn how to deal with changes in both your personal and professional life.

The Course Content Portfolio and Employability Skills Portfolio

Throughout *Nelson Careers For Life* you'll find key activities to help you build your Course Content Portfolio and Employability Skills Portfolio. Activities that go into your Course Content Portfolio are identified with this symbol: ; activities meant for your Employability Skills Portfolio are identified with this symbol: . The Course Content Portfolio is a collection of charts, inventories, assignments and written pieces that illustrates the decision-making process that is the foundation of this course. The Employability Skills Portfolio includes résumés, cover letters, references, transcripts, certificates and awards. It is a useful tool through which you can demonstrate the acquisition of knowledge, skills, behaviours and achievements to a potential employer during an interview.

Why Use Portfolios?

Here's an example.

Patricia is a 20-year-old applying for her first full-time job. The application form asks her why she thinks she would be a good candidate for the job, and leaves a space big enough to hold four or five lines. Patricia has no idea how to write four lines about herself, or why she'd be a good fit for the job. She fills out the rest of the application, but she's unable to fill out this part of the application. So the application lies around in her bedroom until the application deadline passes.

If Patricia had built up a Course Content Portfolio and an Employability Skills Portfolio, it would have given her practice in writing about herself. She could have gone to the portfolios and found summaries of her skills and interests, with evidence drawn from her experience. She would also have found examples to help her relate her skills directly to specific job requirements. Looking over these pieces of work, she would have remembered the process she went through in developing them. She would have used this experience and the examples she had to fill out the job application.

Your portfolios are for you—to help get you started in career planning, and to give you some specific items you'll need. They're designed to help you learn how to manage your own career development, and to collect the information you'll require. They can help you bring together your thoughts on career planning, collect some of the materials you'll need to apply for jobs, and reflect on what careers and career planning mean to you.

Some of the items that go into your portfolios will be assessed. Getting feedback from your teacher will help you make your portfolios as useful as possible.

Frequently, throughout this course, you will be asked to work with the contents of your portfolio. You might, for example, redo an activity and compare earlier results with present ones. The general steps to follow are:

- *Reviewing*—Go over the work you've done.
- *Reconsidering*—Has anything changed, in your knowledge of yourself or of the world around you, since you last looked at this information? Is this still what is most important to you? If not, you can redo one or more activities that you completed earlier.
- *Summarizing*—Distill the old and new information down to what is most important. Write down the key points on a summary sheet.

Other Features of the Program

After the title page, each unit opens with a **unit overview**. You will find:

- a summary of what you will learn and do;
- an introductory activity based on interpreting visuals;
- a discovery activity that draws upon what you already know and think about the subject of the unit (it always goes in your portfolio).

Next you'll find a **unit story**. This is a piece of fiction that explores the main theme of the unit. You will always find an activity based on the story.

Each unit is divided into sections that explore different themes. The **section opener** includes:

- a description of what the section is about;
- a discovery activity.

Within each section there are profiles, case studies, questions, surveys and a variety of other activites. You will also find a number of **links** to useful print and electronic information.

Each unit ends with a **unit summary.** It includes questions and activities to help you review what you learned and did in the unit. The reflection activity refers back to the discovery activity in the unit overview. There are other reflection activities throughout the text.

UNIT 1

Why Am I Doing This?

Who am I going to be?
What am I going to do?
What kind of life will I have?

Some people have always known what they wanted to be. Others may have a dream, but they have no idea how to get there, or they're too shy to talk about it. Others may have no idea at all.

How do I figure out what I want, and then how to get it?

SECTION

"Big dreams cost the same as little dreams. Might as well dream big."

—*Elly Danica, Canadian writer*

Why Am I Doing This?

In this unit you will:

- discuss the purpose of this course
- use a model to make balanced decisions
- map out the roles you will play in your career through life
- assess who you are and how that affects your career
- identify changes in the world that will affect your career opportunities

Did you know that your career development process has already begun? It is a lifelong process that, among other things, involves your work, school and life experiences. Career development is about more than just selecting a job or occupation. It is about how work connects with the rest of your life roles and experiences. You have already made important decisions that are part of your personal career development—the extra-curricular or leisure activities you participate in, the school courses you choose, and your level of community involvement. All these choices will impact your future.

But I already have a part-time job, so why do I need to learn about all this? A **job** is only part of your career. Your **career** is the path you take to achieve both your personal and professional goals. Each person's career is unique.

Look at the following photos. Each scene depicts a work, school or life experience. How are the people using their experiences to further their career development?

This course will take you on a journey of self-discovery. Throughout this journey you will learn new things about yourself and the world of work, which will enable you to make positive school, work and life choices for an ultimately satisfying and rewarding career.

DISCOVERY

Using your experiences

1. Make a list of all your past and present activities and experiences that you think may have impacted your career development. Use the following list to get started:

    - any sports you play or have played
    - places you have travelled
    - any part-time jobs you have or have had
    - any awards you have received
    - your hobbies
    - your volunteering experiences

2. Next to each item on your list, list the ways it has impacted on your career development process. Keep this list in your **Course Content Portfolio**. We will refer back to it later.

Catherine's Story

When you were born, you couldn't make any choices. Growing up means gaining more and more freedom to choose. Sometimes that freedom can be very difficult, as Catherine discovered one evening.

"Catherine! Phone for you!" her father shouted upstairs.

"Okay, I've got it," Catherine shouted back. It was her best friend Renée. Catherine had been hoping she'd call. She couldn't decide if she wanted to go to the dance at the school in a couple of weeks. She wanted to talk it over with Renée tonight, so she started right in.

"I just can't decide," she said. "I mean, it could be fun. But if Tony and Dave aren't there"—they were two guys that Renée and Catherine spent lots of time discussing—"then it'd really be a drag. Is there any way we can find out if they're going?"

Renée didn't answer right away. "I don't know—I had forgotten all about the dance. Listen, there's something else I really need to talk with you about."

Immediately Catherine was all attention. "So what is it?"

"It's my parents," Renée began. "They're moving to Ottawa."

Catherine felt the bottom of her stomach drop. Her best friend, moving away? They'd been together since kindergarten. Last year, they'd helped each other over all the bumps of grade 9 at Crestvale Secondary. They'd talked to each other every evening. Often, Catherine's father had to tell her to get off the phone so he could use it. "When are you going?" she asked. Her voice sounded small to her.

"That's just it," said Renée. "I don't know if I *am* going. Mom's got a new job in Ottawa—a one-year contract. They're moving in a month, and taking Carmen with them." Carmen was Renée's eight-year-old sister. "But they said they wouldn't make me go if I didn't want to, especially if it was going to be just one year."

Catherine felt relieved, and then she wondered what that would mean. "I don't get it—so what would you do instead?"

"Well, I could stay at my uncle's place," Renée answered. "He lives on the other side of town, but I could still go to the same school."

Wow, thought Catherine. She knew which choice she wanted Renée to make. But this was about Renée, not about Catherine. "So what do you want to do?" she heard herself asking. "I mean, do you know?"

"That's the problem," Renée answered. "I don't know what I think. How do you make a decision this big? I mean, what if I decide the wrong thing? I don't want to move away from you and my other friends and go to a new school. Mom's contract may only be for one year. But if I don't go, I'll really miss my folks. Especially Carmen—I mean, I'd miss her if she were away for a whole year."

Catherine knew what a big deal that was. She didn't have a little sister, but when she saw Renée and Carmen together she really wished she did. They often had big fights, but even then it was obvious that they adored each other. "Wow," she said sympathetically, wondering what else she could say.

After a moment, Renée went on. "I get along with my aunt and uncle all right, but it's not like I really know them that well. What if I stay with them and hate it?"

"You could always move to Ottawa then."

"I guess," said Renée. "But I want to make the right decision the first time, you know?"

Catherine agreed. The whole point about making a decision was that you didn't want to remake it two minutes later. Herself, she had difficulty with things like deciding whether to go to the school dance. She could spend all afternoon trying to make up her mind whether or not to ask a friend to the movies. Last fall she had spent two months deciding whether to try out for the swim team. Finally, the decision had been made for her—she had put it off so long that the tryouts were over. If it was that difficult for her to make up her mind about swimming, how could she ever decide a question this big? She was just glad she didn't have to.

"So they just told me," Renée was finishing. "Just half an hour ago. I called you as soon as I stopped freaking out."

Catherine could believe that. She would freak out too. She thought carefully about what to say. "So how do you feel about it?"

"I don't know," Renée said. "I haven't had time to think."

"Well, here's what I think," said Catherine, discovering insight she hadn't known was in her. *Who cares about the dance*, she thought, *maybe I'll go, and maybe I won't.* "First of all, you can't make a decision this big without really exploring your feelings and thoughts, and what you know. And you've got to talk about every bit of it, with your mom and your dad. And with me, too. So start in—tell me what you're feeling. I've got the rest of the evening free."

ACTIVITY

About the story

1. Make a list of things that Renée may be considering as she thinks about her decision. What does Renée think, feel and know?
2. What other things might come up in Renée's conversation with Catherine, or in future conversations with her parents? (For instance, she may want to know about the school she would attend in Ottawa.) Add these to your list.
3. People have different ways of making decisions. Logical people think and analyse their way through a decision. Others rely more on their intuition—what feels right. Look at the list you created for question 2. Are more items about facts or about feelings?

I Always Have Choices

You probably have some choices coming up in your life right now. Maybe you have to make here-and-now decisions, such as:

- What courses should I take next semester?
- Should I get a part-time job?

Or maybe you're thinking about choices coming up in the future, such as:

- Do I want to go to college, university—or neither one?
- Should I move into a place of my own?

No matter what kind of decisions you face, your first step is to think about how to make good choices—choices that you will find satisfying, or that will head you in the direction you want to go.

To do this, you need to gather all of the facts, and all of the feelings, that are connected to your choices—that is, you need to make the choice *conscious*.

If you don't make thoughtful choices, you'll be drawn through life by the deliberate choices of other people. Do you really want someone else running your life for you?

DISCOVERY

Do you want to take charge?

This is probably not the first time that someone has urged you to take charge of your own life. This seems to make sense, but not everyone is comfortable with the idea. How comfortable are you, at this time in your life, with the idea of taking charge of your own life?

Make a copy of this chart, and mark the spot that shows where you are right now.

(Keep this sheet in your portfolio. It will be interesting for you to look at later, to see if you have changed your position.)

I want to be in charge. — *Don't bother me with this.*

Making Decisions

Profile: Maidena Welsh

Here is the story of one woman whose life went in a different direction because of choices she made.

Maidena Welsh had been working as a hairstylist for 10 years when she made the decision to stay home with her children. To supplement her income, she began babysitting in her home for friends. She enjoyed working with children so much that she started a community storytime reading program for preschool-aged children like her own.

When the only preschool in the region closed, Maidena was encouraged by friends and family to open a nursery in Come By Chance. After some reflection, she agreed to give it a try. She applied to the College of the North Atlantic to complete its Early Childhood Education program. Balancing family and work commitments, Maidena completed the course through distance education. She says, "It took a lot of discipline, support and encouragement, but I knew I could do it."

Operating from the basement of her home, Maidena opened her business in Come By Chance eight years ago. Since she was not eligible to receive any government funding for the start-up of her business, Maidena had to employ creative means to get the resources she needed. She used toys and books that her own kids had previously owned, and she accepted donations of items from family and friends.

Today, Maidena is operating a very successful preschool play group serving children from Clarenville to Carbonear. She has morning and afternoon groups comprised of 8 to 10 children. "It's the most rewarding thing I've done. Children have so much energy, and they are so forgiving. Seeing them learn new things makes me feel good, even on a bad day." As for her choices, she says, "Right now, I am with my kids until they leave for school. I go to work. I am home and finished work when they arrive home from school at the end of the day. It's the ideal situation. I am available for my kids, but I have a career, too."

Maidena says venturing into business for herself was a big risk. It takes tremendous support and foresight, and you can never depend on promises. "You need a good business plan and a backup plan, too."

ACTIVITY

Satisfying choices

1. Maidena made a conscious choice about her future. What do you think her goal was? What evidence is there to support your answer?
2. What do you think were the most important things Maidena had to learn about and do in order to start her business?

Making Positive Choices

As your life situation changes, you will be required to make many decisions in response to your evolving circumstances. Some decisions, like choosing your clothes for the day, will only have a short-term impact. Other decisions, like getting a part-time job, will have future implications, such as learning new skills and exploring future job possibilities. You need to decide which decisions and choices are important ones. *How* you make these choices is equally important.

If you are like many people, you make choices based on a mixture of logical thinking and intuition. When the mix is good, this way of choosing is known as **balanced decision making**.

ACTIVITY

How you make choices

1. Copy the diagram below onto a sheet of paper, and then mark the place on the line that represents how you tend to make choices. Are you at one end or the other, or somewhere in between?

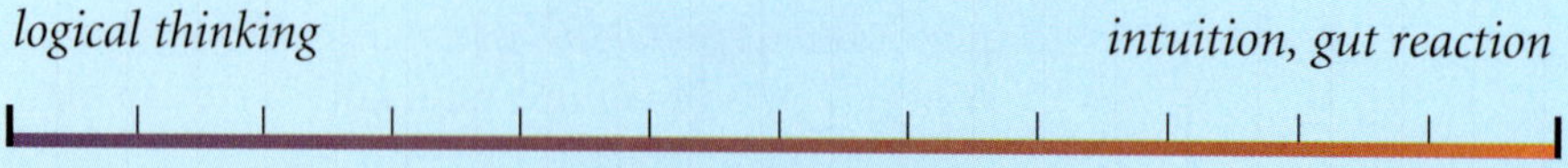

2. Now make five more copies of the diagram on the same sheet of paper and indicate how you would make a choice about:

a) what to do on the weekend
b) what courses to take next year
c) whether to get a summer job
d) whether to change your hairstyle
e) what to do after you finish high school

Moving Toward Balanced Decision Making

Ask Yourself:

Is this something I really want to do?

↓

Will this choice have any influence on my future goals?

↓

What effect will my choice have on my personal well-being?

↓

What are the possible alternatives?

↓

How will I implement my choice?

"... [T]omorrow's decision makers must become comfortable with contradictions and absurdity. They must be flexible, wary, optimistic, and magical. They must also be focused, aware, objective, and practical. They will learn to succeed by failing more; they will learn to make rules and to break rules; they will learn to respond creatively to change and to create change; and they will learn to plan and plan to learn."

—H.B. Gelatt, *Creative Decision Making*

Links

There are many decision-making models that people use to help them make good choices. One book, *Creative Decision Making: Using Positive Uncertainty*, by H.B. Gelatt, outlines a model that helps people make decisions in situations of change and uncertainty. Gelatt talks about intuition, and about our attitudes to making decisions.

Go to <www.careers.nelson.com> for information about other books on decision making and career development. Start a bibliography of background reading.

Jenny's Story

Jenny was working hard to get through high school, but every course was a struggle. Now, at the beginning of Level III, all of her classmates seemed to be well on their way with planning their futures. Some were leaving home to head to university or college, while others were heading to the mainland to find work. Still others were planning to stay home and find jobs, even if it meant working seasonally.

Jenny felt scared. She didn't have it all figured out. She was tired of everyone asking, "What are you going to do when you graduate?" or "What are you going to be?" She often wondered to herself, *What* am *I going to be?*

One night, Jenny's dad approached her about working part-time in the family business. Their restaurant was becoming increasingly busy, and he could use the extra help. Jenny wasn't really interested, but agreed to help her dad out.

Jenny was a natural around the restaurant. She really enjoyed the extra time with her dad and her conversations with the customers. Many often commented, "What's a young girl like you doing working here?" or "Shouldn't you be out enjoying yourself now while you're young?"

Jenny soon came to realize that she didn't have to figure out her future right away. Everyone's story is different. Her dad, for example, had opened the restaurant after the start of the cod moratorium. He had only ever known one way of life—fishing. Now he made the best fish and chips around! Her dad taught her that, although life is full of changes, there will always be opportunities presented to us. She decided that this job was one way for her to get some work experience, to interact with others, and to examine her strengths. It could also help her set some short-term goals. *Who knows what opportunity will be around the next corner?*

Reflection

"When one door closes, another one opens." What does this phrase mean to you? How does this relate to the career development process?

Feeling Good About Your Decisions

Feelings often have an impct on the decisions you make. When you are sad, you can make choices out of hurt and frustration. When you are happy, your energy and excitement may have an influence. Many of your choices will have an impact on your well-being, so it's important to use more than your emotions when weighing your options. For example, daily choices, such as the food you eat, the amount of exercise you get, the number of hours you sleep and how you react to stress can all have an effect on your well-being.

Being able to make positive choices when confronted with daily demands and stressors will positively impact your **well-being** and your **self-concept**. When you see yourself as a strong individual who is able to cope positively with life's demands, you will feel good about yourself. Having a negative self-concept can make you doubt your ability to make good decisions. Even though guidance counsellors or teachers can assist when making important decisions, having confidence in yourself goes a long way in making positive choices every day. It is important not to allow others to have a negative influence on your decisions.

Think for a second about how you respond to negative peer pressure. Are you able to stand up for yourself and tell your friends exactly how you feel? Do you give in to a friend's request, knowing that another option would have been better for you? How you choose to respond to life's challenges will determine your future success and happiness.

ACTIVITY

What impact will your choices have?

Consider the following situations and the choices you may have to make. Respond to each situation by indicating what you would do and the possible implications of such a choice.

A) Your parents are away for the weekend, and your friends are looking for something to do on Friday night. Someone suggests throwing a party at your place.

B) The formal is coming up, and your date wants to rent a limo for the evening. You would have to dip into your savings to pay your share.

C) Your best friend's band has its very first concert on Thursday night, and you promised to go to support the band. On Monday, your teacher tells you about a major exam on Friday morning that will require intense study.

Place your answers in your Course Content Portfolio.

Leaving It to Chance

Change Happens

You will have many choices and decisions to make throughout your life as the world around you changes. Sometimes recognizing and adapting to change is a smooth process. For example, you probably have many new teachers this year. Have you already identified their expectations and teaching styles? Whether you are ready for new teaching approaches or not, you will learn to adapt to such changes if you want to be successful at school. This is one example of change that you cannot control. What about the changes you *can* control? Sometimes when you are unable or unwilling to make choices, choices get made for you. If you leave things to chance, life may not always turn out as you would like.

Look at the chart on page 13. The chart contains random descriptions of what your future life could be like. These are arranged in five columns. Now, with a partner, take turns completing the following task:

1. Read through the six scenarios in the first column. Choose one of these for your partner and write your selection in your notebook.

2. Repeat this process for each column.

3. You should now have a five-part description of what your partner's future life might bring.

4. Share your choices with your partner.

Options for Next Year	After High School	After Post-Secondary	Family Life	Rest & Relaxation
take French and Drama	take a program to get high school equivalency, such as ABE	apply to college for advanced training in computer systems design, 2-year program	have 3 children, spouse works night shift	hang out at local café
take 2 technology courses	complete apprenticeship, 4 years	alternate unemployment with unskilled temporary jobs	get married, have 6 kids	learn new languages, travel
take 2 business studies courses	work in family hardware business	work for international business, marketing specialization	get married then divorced after 2 years	take up body building and painting
take all university preparation courses (including science and math)	obtain university degree in engineering, 4-year program	work for machine tool company	become single parent, one son, live with your parents	ride your motorcycle
take all workplace preparation courses	obtain college diploma, 3-year program	change jobs every 2 years	stay single, work abroad and leave friends and family behind in Canada	take up long-distance running
leave school after 16th birthday	go straight to work as a server	stay in family business for life	get married, have no children	design computer games and play them

Congratulations! Your life has just been decided for you. This is what your life may look like. *Would you prefer to leave your life to chance or to make your own choices?*

Reflection

Can you name three benefits of letting luck or other people decide your life for you? What are three drawbacks?

What are three ways you would plan your life differently from the way your partner planned it out for you?

My Choices Are About Me

Any choice you make is really about you, and depends on who you are. Your choices affect what you do, and what you will become. The choices you make depend on many factors—what's important to you, what options you have, what you know...

As you move through your life, you open the future by making choices, and in this way you build a life story.

How do choices, life stories and careers all relate to each other? What is a career, anyway?

DISCOVERY

What is a career?

What does *career* mean to you? Think about people you know or have read about, or about your own career dreams. Write a brief description, or a list of words that come to mind when you think about the word *career.*

My Career Is About Me

What Is a Career?

Your career is the sum total of your life experiences.

What's in a word?

The origin of a word tells us about its meaning. The word *career* comes from the Latin word *carrus*, meaning *cart*. Over time, the word came to also mean "the track the cart follows." So your career is both the cart carrying the events of your life and the track you're following. As the American career expert William Bridges says, "Think of your career as a journey that includes all the events in your life."

ACTIVITY

Name the pictures

1. Each of the pictures on this page represents a scene from someone's career. Describe what is happening in each scene. Use the diagram on page 15 as a reference.
2. Make a diagram based on roles you might take on later in your career. These might include:
   - friend
   - manager
   - helper
   - athlete
   - student
   - leader
   - organizer
   - musician
   - worker
   - parishioner
   - volunteer
   - artist
   - family member (child, sibling, spouse, parent, grandparent)

   Think of other roles to add to this list.
3. Which roles from question 2 do you have *right now* in your career?

Interview: Jerry Evans

How did your interest in art develop?
I was born in Grand Falls–Windsor, Newfoundland and Labrador, but my father's job took us to many areas of the province. We moved seven times before I reached high school, finally settling in the St. John's area. Each move was a big adjustment—I spent a lot of time by myself drawing. I think this may have been when the artistic seed was planted. My extended family also became much more important to me—it was at this time in my life that I became more curious about who I was and where I came from.

When did you first realize that art could become a career for you?
I did well in high school and was very lucky to have a great Art teacher who taught me many techniques in how to express myself visually. Both my teacher and parents encouraged me to pursue my interest and love of painting and drawing and to seek a career in the arts.

What sort of education helped to prepare you for this career?
The first step I took was enrolling in a commercial art course from what is now the College of the North Atlantic. I received my diploma nine months later. I was drawn to the fine arts so I left Newfoundland to attend the Nova Scotia College of Art and Design, where I graduated with a Bachelor of Fine Arts. I also earned a degree in Education from Memorial University and have been working in art-related jobs since.

How have you been able to transfer your skills to other creative areas?
Presently I'm learning the skills of filmmaking. For me it is just another means of expression, like my print-making or painting. I continue to make prints, paint, and express myself through other forms of art-making. There are many career opportunities available to those interested in the arts. One of the projects that interests me is film animation. I have been working on projects with Innu friends from Labrador and we now have an idea that involves animation of traditional Innu, Mi'kmaq, and even Inuit stories and legends. We feel that this would be a great way to record and share the stories of our First Nations people here in our region.

What are the challenges and rewards of your career?
It is very difficult at times making a living from your art. I have taken many different jobs over the years and luckily most were art-related. My career choice has taken my artwork and me all over North America and even to Europe. I teach and learn new skills at every opportunity. I will continue to make art as long as I am physically capable. It is a love and a career from which I shall never retire.

ACTIVITY

About Jerry Evans

1. Make a concept map to organize all of the things that Mr. Evans mentions as important in his career.
2. What other questions would you have asked Mr. Evans?

One Step At a Time

Career Building

A career is the story of a whole life, so you don't have to plan your career all at once. In fact, you can't. You will change, the world will change, and the choices you make will change.

But you should still plan choices that will eventually shape your career. Your interests, skills and talents will help determine your life story. Think about the general direction you want to go in, and start planning your next steps. There is an old proverb that says, "A journey of a thousand kilometres begins with one small step."

Sandra's Story

Sandra had loved books ever since she could remember. Fairy tales, picture books, suspense novels, biographies—she read books all through her childhood. She wasn't what you'd call a bookworm, though. She also loved to be around people, especially young children. She thought they were fun, and they made her laugh. She was also fascinated by how children develop and learn.

Sandra's interests and enjoyment led her to activities that helped her shape her career:

- She babysat neighbourhood children from the time she was 12 years old until she graduated from high school.
- Her favourite subject was English, but she also took courses about social issues, families and parenting.
- Several of her short stories were published in the school newspaper.
- She did volunteer work at her community centre in an after-school program.
- Several years in a row, she got a summer job organizing children's programs at her community centre.
- After high school, she got an Early Childhood Education certificate from college.
- She worked for two years at a day care centre.
- As well as caring for the children, she also helped with the office duties.
- Eventually she decided she wanted to pursue her interest in literature, so she completed a Bachelor of Arts degree at university.

Today, Sandra works as a buyer for a large bookstore. Her favourite part of the job is scouting out interesting children's books. "I still get to be around kids. Our store has a 'Reading Corner' where we read and do activities with groups of kids several times a week. I also get to see new materials from authors and publishers from all over the world." Sandra is currently writing her

own children's book. "Having one of my own stories in print has been a lifelong dream."

Sandra's career development journey began as a young girl. She identified specific areas of personal interest and made choices that increased her knowledge and ability in these areas. She knew she wanted a future that included literature and working with children. She made sure that her life experiences as well as her education prepared her for many such opportunities.

Like Sandra, you may already have areas of interest. There may be things you are passionate about or would like to learn more about. Having good **self-knowledge** and understanding will allow you to explore many career-related opportunities.

ACTIVITY

Know yourself

Copy this chart and fill in the three columns.

5 Things I Like to Do	5 Things I Do Well	5 Things That Are Important to Me
e.g., listen to music	*e.g., help my friends sort out their problems*	*e.g., fairness*

Keep this chart in your portfolio. We will come back to it later.

Make Your Talents Work for You

Now you have a better idea of what you enjoy doing and what you're good at. How can you use this knowledge to start building your career?

Without realizing it, Sandra was developing a career from the time she was 12 years old. In fact, by the time she had graduated from high school, she already had a résumé full of good **credentials.**

What are credentials? Experiences that make you better qualified to do a job, and that employers recognize as accomplishments. For example, if you were applying for a summer job as a lifeguard, a Bronze Cross would be one of your most important credentials, because it means that you have the specific swimming and life-saving skills that a lifeguard needs. But earning a Bronze Cross also demonstrates that you have self-discipline and tenacity, qualities that are valued by many employers. These qualities are credentials, too.

In Sandra's case, her credentials included all her volunteer, work and school experience, plus:

- a babysitting course run by her town
- St. John's Ambulance and CPR certificates required for her community centre job
- leadership skills built during the after-school program
- administration skills developed when she worked in the day care office helping the director

It is never too early to start developing good credentials that will help you as you move along in your career.

ACTIVITY

Collect your credentials

On a sheet of paper, make a list of the credentials you already have. There are many possibilities, such as:

- a Bronze Cross in swimming
- camping experience
- knowledge of another language
- volunteer activities
- a good grade on a school project
- experience in organizing a school event
- an executive position in a club
- physical fitness

Reflection

You have made a list of your current credentials—all the things that you already have going for you. Compare these with the lists you made on the Know Yourself chart (page 19). Do you see any connections between your current interests and current credentials? Can you identify areas where your credentials are particularly strong or weak?

My Choices Will Change

This book is about learning to make thoughtful choices that will shape your career and affect who you *become*. It's not about mapping a fixed route to a fixed goal, but about having flexible goals. As you change, the world changes, so your goals need to adapt.

DISCOVERY

How have you changed?

1. Think back to the interests, skills and preferences you had when you were eight years old. Copy the following chart and fill in the columns.

5 Things I Liked to Do When I Was 8 Years Old	5 Things I Did Well When I Was 8 Years Old	5 Things That Were Important to Me When I Was 8 Years Old
e.g., play checkers	*e.g., science projects*	*e.g., having many friends*

2. The chart that you created for Know Yourself (page 19) was about your interests, skills and preferences today. Compare it with the chart that you have just created in question 1. Circle or highlight things about you that have changed since you were eight years old. How much have you changed?

3. Your interests, skills and preferences have probably changed a great deal since you were eight. What does that mean for your future? Jot down a few ways you might change in the years ahead.

Change in the World of Work

Changing Technologies

Changes in the world—e.g., how countries are allowed to invest money and trade with each other, the age and size of the population, and technological change—mean changes in the workplace. To start thinking about change, complete the following activity.

ACTIVITY

What's next?

1. This chart shows how technology has changed some everyday items since 1900. Your job is to predict how much further technology can change these items. The first item in the chart has been forecast to the year 2025. Suggest how the remaining three items might change by then. *Let your imagination go!*

1900	1950	2005	2025
wood stoves	electric and gas stoves	microwaves propane stoves	laser cookware—pots that cook on their own?
wax cylinder records for gramophones	vinyl long-play records	CDs/DVDs	
hot-air balloons	propeller airplanes	jets space travel	
telegraphs	telephones	fax, e-mail, cellphone, video conferencing, web conferencing	

2. Brainstorm a list of other technological innovations that may change the workplace by the year 2025.

Effects on the Workplace

Is there a relationship between changes in technology and changes in the workplace? Consider these predictions:

1. Canadian workers will change occupations three or more times during their lives.
2. Changing technologies will demand that workers continuously upgrade their skills through ongoing education and training.
3. More and more people will work from their own homes.
4. Offices will shrink in size as workers only drop in for meetings and to use specialized equipment.
5. More Canadians will own their own businesses or become self-employed.
6. More companies will allow flexible hours and "family leaves" to ease stress on working parents.
7. More businesses will compete in international markets and need workers who can communicate in different languages.

We will look more closely at trends like these in Unit 3.

ACTIVITY

Consider the relationship

1. Refer to the chart of technological changes that you made in question 2 of the previous activity. Try to connect the changes on your chart to the predictions listed above.
2. Where you think a connection exists, write a brief explanation.

Learning About Change First-Hand

ACTIVITY

Interview the techno-pioneers

1. Interview someone over the age of 60 to learn how the world and the workplace have changed since the middle of the twentieth century. (See Interviewing Tips on page 25)

2. When all of the interviews have been completed, discuss the results in class. Make a chart like the following, with enough rows for all of your questions. In the Answers column, list the changes that you and your classmates have discovered.

Interview Summary	
Questions	Answers

3. If this many changes have taken place during the last half-century, how many changes are likely to take place during your career over the next half-century? What kinds? Name a few possible changes that come to mind.

Interviewing Tips

Most people enjoy talking about their lives. If your grandparents are available, their stories could be very interesting. Or you may have other relatives, friends of the family, or neighbours you could interview. If there is a senior citizens' residence nearby, you could ask if any of the residents would be willing to talk with you.

1. Go to the interview expecting to learn interesting things.
2. Be polite and patient.
3. Encourage the interviewee by asking questions you have prepared ahead of time, and by asking further questions based upon what you hear.
4. Before your interview, prepare a series of questions about topics that interest you. Here are some topics to consider when you are preparing your questions:

    - How have people's homes changed since you were a teenager? What appliances that are common in homes now did not exist at that time?
    - How have transportation and communication technologies changed?
    - When did you first see a television set, a jet airplane, a videotape recorder, a computer? What were the first versions of these machines like?
    - What was it like to be a teenager then? What were common leisure activities for teens?
    - How have the roles of men and women changed in society and in the workplace?
    - What work was most common in those days? How does this compare to now?
    - What changes have you seen in the way people work? How have offices, factories, farms and other places of work changed?
    - How old were you when you first started working?
    - How much money did you earn at first?
    - How much did various items cost?

    Add more questions that are of interest to you.

Links

Visit <www.careers.nelson.com> for links to information about change in society and how it affects your career opportunities.

Opportunities

Making Change Work for You

When change occurs, many people see only the problems it causes, but change can also be about **opportunities**. We can find the opportunities that change offers. By looking carefully at ourselves and the world, we will understand that a change is not a crisis, but a chance to do new things.

ACTIVITY

Opportunity hunting

1. For each change in this list, think of positive opportunities that could result.

Change	Possible Life or Work Opportunities
You graduate from high school.	*e.g., A chance to get out into the world and try my skills in new ways—a job, apprenticeship, college or university.*
You decide to leave home and get your own apartment.	
You get your first full-time job.	
You find out that your company has been bought out, and your job is gone.	
Your boss gets another job, and you don't like the person who's taken her place.	

2. Add to your chart any other large or small changes that you would like to examine, for example, something that has happened to you or to someone you know.

If you remain open to new ideas, it will be easier to handle changes in your life. You'll find that change can work *for* you, instead of *against* you.

Think of the giant panda. It only eats one kind of food (bamboo shoots), and only lives in one environment (the rainy mountainsides of southern China), so it's very vulnerable to change. It's not resilient.

Then think of the raccoon. It's clever, inquisitive, adaptable. It can eat almost anything and get along in most environments. If the world changes, it will adapt. It's very resilient.

Not Everything Changes

Constants

Maybe you are tired of thinking about change. Isn't there anything that holds steady in this world? Sure there is—our basic human needs and desires haven't changed over the centuries. Human beings have always wanted:

- good health
- people who care about us
- people we can care about
- work that's satisfying
- a healthy environment
- ideas that stimulate our minds
- things that make us laugh

Look at these photographs. Despite all of the changes, this is the same person from one photo to the next. Some things never change.

Reflection

In the activity How Have You Changed? (page 21), you looked at some ways you have changed since you were half your age, and thought about some of the ways you might change in the future.

Now, name some things about yourself that are not likely to change over time. These may include habits (e.g., keeping physically fit), personal values (e.g., honesty), beliefs (e.g., religion), and so on.

Key Terms

job
career
Course Content Portfolio
balanced decision making
well-being
self-concept
self-knowledge
credentials
opportunities

Use a concept map or another kind of graphic organizer to summarize the key ideas in this unit. Build on the key terms and add words, phrases and/or images that will help remind you of those key ideas.

Reflection

Go back to Using Your Experiences on page 3 and think about your experiences again. Have you thought of new ways that you hadn't thought of before? Add any new information to your list and return the list to your portfolio.

Questions

Knowledge/Understanding

1. **a)** Define "self-concept."
b) What factors do you think affect your self-concept? Explain.

2. Imagine that you have the chance to spend the next school year with an aunt and uncle in Australia. Illustrate how such a choice may or may not have a positive impact on your personal well-being and self-concept.

3. **a)** Define "career."
b) When does a career begin and end?

4. Research three examples of changes in the workplace in the past twenty years and give possible reasons for each of these changes.

Thinking/Inquiry

5. You considered information about many different things in this unit (*e.g.*, about social trends, about yourself). List the kinds of information you considered.

6. How will that information help you plan your career?

7. What other information might be useful? Create a list of questions that you would like answered to help you plan your career.

Communication

8. Use the information you gathered during your interview (page 24) to write a profile of the person interviewed. Imagine that the profile is to appear in the *Herald* as a promotion for a documentary that is to be aired that week.

9. Write a letter to Renée (pages 4-5) that will help her make her choice. Use what you've learned about decision making as the basis for your advice.

Application

10. What is the most significant change that's occurred to you in your life so far? Explain how this change has affected your ability to make decisions about your future.

11. Use Internet resources to begin bookmarking sites that can help you with your career development. Go to <www.careers.nelson.com> as your starting point. Use an electronic worksheet, or create a card file, to summarize information about each site.

Taking Stock: Your Portfolio

1. Review the contents.
2. Reconsider your initial responses.
3. Summarize the most important information.

UNIT 2

Who Am I?

How can I tell what I want to be? How do I know what kind of future I want?

The answers start with you—your likes and dislikes, skills and abilities, talents and personality. Who you are now will affect who you want to become. Who you want to become will affect what skills and interests you choose to develop.

How can I learn about myself, and start actively shaping the person I would like to become?

SECTION

"You must be the change you wish to see in the world."

—*Mahatma Gandhi*

Who Am I?

In this unit you will:

- assess your interests, skills, values and accomplishments using a variety of tools
- analyse this information to create a personal profile
- describe what influences have shaped you
- set broad goals that connect who you are with career opportunities
- explain how skills you have now are useful in various aspects of your career
- plan ways to build upon these skills

You know some definite truths about yourself—perhaps you are a sports fan, an art lover or a religious person. But likely you're not always sure about every aspect of yourself. Sometimes you have feelings that come out of nowhere. Sometimes, if you don't have an opinion of your own, you might take on the opinion of a friend.

Have you ever done a jigsaw puzzle? Sure, but have you ever done one without seeing the picture on the box? Putting together your own future may feel like doing a puzzle without a picture.

Who you are is a combination of many small bits of information. Each bit is important, but each one doesn't describe you totally. All the pieces need to be put together before you have a complete picture.

Take a few moments to look at the words on these puzzle pieces. Can you think of something about yourself that would correspond with each piece? Are there pieces missing?

This unit will help you assemble your puzzle. You are the only one who can answer the questions that are asked. The more pieces you fit together, the more you'll be able to see who you are.

This unit is also about who you will become. Thinking about your future, you can begin to make plans that will shape your future self. You may want to start developing certain skills. Career skills aren't only "hard" job skills, like knowing how to fix small motors or do CPR. Career skills also include "soft" skills, like communicating well or enjoying teamwork.

DISCOVERY

How well do you know yourself?

How well do you know yourself right now? What do you know, for example, about your interests, your skills and your personal characteristics? Copy this diagram and then mark the place on each line that best represents what you know about the different parts of yourself. Write a sentence to explain why you placed each mark where you did.

1. **Interests:** What I like to do.

My interests keep changing. — *I definitely know what I like to do.*

2. **Skills:** What I'm good at doing.

I may have skills I don't know about. — *I am very sure of my skills.*

3. **Intelligence:** How smart I am.

I'm OK, but not brilliant. — *I'm very smart.*

4. **Learning Styles:** How I learn.

I have trouble studying and remembering. — *I learn easily.*

5. **Personal Characteristics:** What type of person I am.

I can't get a "fix" on myself. — *I know the type of person I am.*

Keep this sheet in your portfolio.

Jake's Story

Thinking about who you are is an important part of planning a career. Once you have a better idea of who you are, you can think more clearly about where you want to go. Though it isn't always easy to know who you are, as Jake found out.

Jake kept thinking about what his Drama teacher always said: "You've got to reach inside yourself, pull out a real feeling and express it." Jake had lots of real feelings, but couldn't tell if one feeling was more *him* than another. When he talked to people, he could always see their point of view. But he couldn't always find his own opinion. This caused problems with his friends.

"I mean, can you believe it?" Kyle was saying. He and Jake were at Poppin' Pizza sharing a large with three toppings. "Can you believe Jen said that to me?"

Jake didn't know what to say. Kyle had been going out with Jennifer for two weeks, and he often complained about her. Jake knew that Kyle wanted him to say something like, "Yeah, that's really disgusting." But he just didn't feel that way. He could see that Kyle was upset, but he could see Jennifer's point as well. And in this case, she was right—Kyle was pretty self-centred.

"You listening, man?" Kyle said.

"Uh, sure," Jake said. "It's a bummer."

Just then, Kyle and Jake were joined by three other guys. There was a bustle as they moved tables together and gave their orders to the waiter. Jake knew these guys were cool. In fact, last year he had desperately wanted to be cool enough to hang out with them. Last year, he would have been thrilled to be seen sitting with them at Poppin' Pizza.

But now it didn't matter so much. He'd noticed that, from a distance, they all looked like Kyle. They wore the same brand names in the same colours. They seemed afraid to be seen in the wrong clothes, or to be heard saying the wrong things.

The problem is, Jake thought, *that I don't know who my friends are.*

His friends came from all over. He'd known Kyle since Grade 3. But he had other friends who were totally different. Like Ed, for example. He was really smart—Jake knew his own parents would be happy if he could get Ed's marks. Ed's hero was Stephen Hawking, the British scientist who probed the origins of the universe from his wheelchair.

But Ed was—well, it was like he worked at making people think he was weird, so he could pretend he didn't care. Kyle pretended too—that he didn't care about school. But he secretly did care. And secretly also, Ed did care what people thought of him. Sometimes it seemed to Jake that *all* Kyle cared about was what other people thought of him.

Jake knew that he wasn't like either Ed or Kyle. He was somewhere in between.

So where do *I fit in?* Jake asked himself, as he watched Kyle and his friends talk about last night's hockey game. He was worried about being a nobody.

"Be yourself. Don't be like other people," was what his parents said if he mentioned his feelings. *Be myself. That would be great advice,* thought Jake, *if I only knew who "myself" was.*

Kyle doesn't seem to have much doubt about who he is, he thought. *Neither does Ed. Maybe it's not Ed who's weird, maybe it's me—because I don't know who I am.*

Jake didn't have trouble in drama class, though. If he thought about it awhile, he could pull up almost any feeling and make it real. *Great! What does that make me?* he thought.

Jake thought about his father, mother, aunts and uncles. They all seemed to be sure of themselves. And his grandfather? Jake couldn't imagine his grandfather being unsure about anything! *He's 75,* Jake said to himself, *and his grownup children still do what he says!*

"Hey, Jake," Kyle said. "You see the game?"

"Yeah," Jake said.

"So what'd you think of that play?"

"Pretty amazing," Jake said, although he didn't know which play they were talking about. *Maybe figuring out where you fit in is something that happens when you grow up,* Jake concluded. The guys around him were laughing at some joke now, but Jake was getting more and more depressed.

He stood up. "Gotta go," he said.

Only Kyle waved goodbye. "See you," he said.

"Yeah, man," Jake said. But as he walked away, his confused feelings deepened inside him. *Who am I anyway? And how will I ever figure it out?*

ACTIVITY

About Jake

1. What is happening to Jake? How is he feeling? Why does he feel that way?
2. Do you think Jake's friends are having the same feelings?
3. What does "be yourself" mean?
4. What does "fit in" mean?

Who Am I Now?

- What am I good at?
- Where will I be happiest?
- What am I capable of?
- What, deep inside, is the strongest thing about me?

These are important questions that are worth examining every day. Answering these questions will give you information you need to plan your career. You will see what your strengths are—then you can build on them. You will see what your weaknesses are—then you can work on them. You will start to focus on the person you want to become. This process is called **self-assessment**.

DISCOVERY

What are you proud of?

1. Write a story about one thing you've done in your life that makes you proud. Everyone can think of at least one. It doesn't have to be a big thing. What is important is that you are proud of yourself for having done it.
2. Reread the story you have written, and list the qualities of the central person—you—in that story (e.g., kind, brave, conscientious).

Put your story and list in your portfolio. You will return to it later.

What Are My Interests?

Do What You Enjoy

What do you like to do? Do you have one main **interest**? Or do you have so many interests you can't decide which one to pursue first?

Either way, it's important to recognize what intrigues you, and then explore the career possibilities that it leads to. People who enjoy their jobs say that the work doesn't feel like work. Have you ever been so engrossed in doing something that you lost track of time? That's what happens when you enjoy your work.

But if you're bored, dissatisfied and unhappy with what you're doing, the reverse is true. You find yourself watching the clock, and time seems to crawl. You're thinking: *When is this going to be over?*

If you're bored, you end up in a vicious cycle:

- You're bored, so you don't do your best work.
- You don't do your best work, so you're not proud of what you've done.
- You're not proud of what you've done, so you lose enthusiasm for the work.
- You're not enthusiastic, so you're bored.

Nobody likes being bored and unhappy. Find out what you enjoy, and point your career in that direction. You'll have a happier, more satisfying future.

ACTIVITY

Survey your interests

1. Read each of the numbered statements in the Interest Sorter on page 36. Record the numbers of the statements that describe you best.
2. Reproduce the Interest Sorter Summary Chart on page 37 and, in the third column, record the statements that you selected in each category.
3. In which category did you choose the most statements? Think of three occupations that would suit someone with these interests. Do any of them appeal to you?

Keep the Interest Sorter Summary Chart in your portfolio.

Interest Sorter

1. I'd rather make something than read a book.
2. I enjoy problem-solving games and working at puzzles.
3. I like helping other people.
4. I enjoy reading and learning about new topics.
5. I like working with my hands.
6. I like being the leader in a group.
7. I prefer to know all the facts before I tackle a problem.
8. I like to take care of people.
9. I enjoy designing, inventing and creating.
10. I enjoy expressing myself through art, music or writing.
11. I would like a job where I could deal with people all day.
12. I like working with materials and equipment.
13. I enjoy learning new facts and ideas.
14. Co-operating with others comes naturally to me.
15. I like taking things apart to find out how they work.
16. I would rather work with machines than with people.
17. I can usually persuade people to do things my way.
18. I enjoy building and repairing.
19. I enjoy the research part of my projects.
20. I like interacting with people.
21. I enjoy thinking up different ways to do things.
22. I like hearing other people's opinions.
23. I enjoy learning how to use different tools.
24. I find it easy to follow written instructions.

Interest Sorter Summary Chart

Interest Category	Statements	My Statements
I'm a "hands-on" person. I enjoy using tools and machines, making objects with my hands, maintaining and fixing equipment and finding out how things work.	1, 5, 9, 12, 15, 16, 18, 23	
I'm a "people" person. I enjoy caring for and helping others, persuading people, working as part of a team, and leading and supervising others.	3, 6, 8, 11, 14, 17, 20, 22	
I'm an "information" person. I enjoy expressing myself through writing, music or art, doing experiments or researching, solving puzzles and problems, and studying and reading.	2, 4, 7, 10, 13, 19, 21, 24	

Using Interest Inventories

The Interest Sorter is an example of an interest inventory. An **inventory** is a tool for making a list. In an **interest inventory**, a quiz generates a list of your interests, and often matches your interests with related occupations.

Standardized inventories compare your results with a standard, which is created by analysing the results of a group of people who have completed the inventory. Usually this group is a large one chosen to represent the whole population or a particular age or group. Other kinds of tests and inventories, like skill and intelligence tests, can also be standardized. Is the Interest Sorter standardized?

There are many good interest inventories that can help you look at your interest patterns. Your teacher may have others that you can use. Many Internet sites also offer interest inventories. If possible, do more than one, because each inventory gives you a different way of looking at yourself. It is also worth doing them again each year, because you are changing constantly, and your results are likely to change as well.

Interpreting Your Interest Inventory Results

The most important aspect of interest inventories is the insight they give you into your patterns. For example, some people are happy if they like the top two or three occupations that are suggested for them by certain inventories. If they don't like the top few occupations, they get upset and say, "This is stupid!" Either way, they are cheating themselves.

Here are some hints for making good use of your interest inventory results.

First, take a quick look at all of the results.

Then pay close attention to what the results say about your interest patterns. Are any of the scores higher or lower than you expected? You may, for example, absolutely love drama, but your score for creativity and the arts may be disappointingly low. That is because you selected every question about drama, but didn't show much interest in music, dance or visual art, all of which are part of the same category. Are you creative, then? Definitely. Are there a lot of occupations in the arts that are suitable for your interests? Outside of drama, maybe not, but you never know for sure.

Now, if there is one, look at the complete list of occupations that go with your interests. You will probably dislike some of them. But what can they tell you about work that would fit your interests?

- If "minister of religion" shows up on your list, occupations such as social worker, counsellor, and other caring professions are likely to be also on the list. You may not be religious, but being a minister is one of many ways to help other people.
- If "weapons technician" shows up on your list, it doesn't mean that you should join the army. It could mean that you like hands-on technical work. Remember, it's the pattern that's important.

If you are still having trouble understanding your results, speak with your teacher or guidance counsellor.

Links

Some Newfoundland and Labrador schools use standardized interest inventories with students. Some of the most common are the *Strong Interest Inventory*, the *Jackson Vocational Interest Survey (JVIS)*, the *Career Occupational Interest Survey (COPS)* and the *Self-Directed Search*. Other inventories, like the Vocational Interest, Experience, and Skill Assessment (VIESA), are self-scoring. VIESA also lets you look at more than just your interests.

Many interest inventories, usually not standardized, are available on the Internet. Visit <www.careers.nelson.com> for opportunities to complete a number of on-line interest inventories.

What Are My Skills?

We All Have Skills

You can probably do many different things well. We all develop **skills** through a wide range of activities, not just in the classroom. Here are some other places where you can develop new skills:

- extra-curricular school activities
- hobbies and clubs
- sports
- part-time and summer jobs
- volunteer work
- leisure activities
- homemaking
- school-to-work transition programs
- after-school lessons or classes
- family and household responsibilities

ACTIVITY

Skill evidence

1. Read over the Skills Chart on page 40. For each skill category, add some more examples of things that demonstrate the skill.
2. Copy the following chart. Using a scale from 1 (least well) to 5 (most well), record in the second column how well you perform in each skill category.

Skill	Rating	My Example
Numerical	*e.g., 4*	*e.g., I worked part-time as a cashier*
Communication		
etc.		

3. Where you've given yourself a score of 3 or higher, use the third column to provide an example of a way you have used the skill.

Keep the results in your portfolio.

Skills Chart

Skills	Examples
Numerical	• estimate costs when buying things • measure ingredients in a recipe • calculate sports statistics • make a budget
Communication	• read the school newspaper • write an e-mail to a pen-pal • chat on the telephone • understand and follow directions
Leadership	• help plan a school dance • organize homework • coach a team • start a club at school
Sense awareness and use (of shapes, colours and sounds)	• enjoy an art show • enjoy a concert • decorate a bedroom • doodle when thinking
Problem-solving (to investigate, assess, analyse, test or solve)	• find out why paper keeps jamming in a printer • analyse why a friend is fighting with her boyfriend • assess why a friend is an impulsive spender • help the family solve a scheduling problem
Helping	• calm down a friend who has a problem • be a peer advisor • help care for a sick family member • volunteer at a community centre
Organizing	• keep school work neat • make a list of the day's tasks • use a planner or calendar • keep a stamp collection
Hands-on/technical	• use a computer • repair things at home • build models • sew a piece of clothing
Self-management	• set goals and meet them • be on time for appointments • have a healthy lifestyle • handle stress well
Creative/innovative	• write stories • make sculptures • design clothes • perform in a school musical

Reflection

Think of a situation in which you have to describe one of your skills (e.g., in a job interview, to convince a parent). Have a partner take on the role of the person you are trying to convince. Make your partner believe in you and your ability.

Links

Visit <www.careers.nelson.com> for opportunities to complete on-line skills inventories.

What Are My Abilities?

There Are Many Ways of Being Smart

What is intelligence? Do you often wonder how smart you are? If so, you probably measure yourself by the grades you get in school. If you do well, you figure you must be smart. If you don't, does that mean you're not smart?

Experts who study intelligence say that school "smarts" are only a small part of a much larger picture. School "smarts" can be measured by IQ (intelligent quotient). But IQ only measures how you handle verbal and math problems—and leaves out other entire areas of intelligence.

Many experts now believe that people have **multiple intelligences**—eight different kinds of "smarts." Each of us has some intelligence in all eight areas, but every individual has three or four areas that are dominant. These intelligences have a big influence over what we like doing and how we approach learning.

Many people suggest that there are even more than eight kinds of intelligence. The important thing to remember is that you can be "smart" in more than one way.

Knowing your multiple intelligences (MI) will help you better understand your strengths and make good decisions about your future.

The Multiple Intelligences (MI) Chart

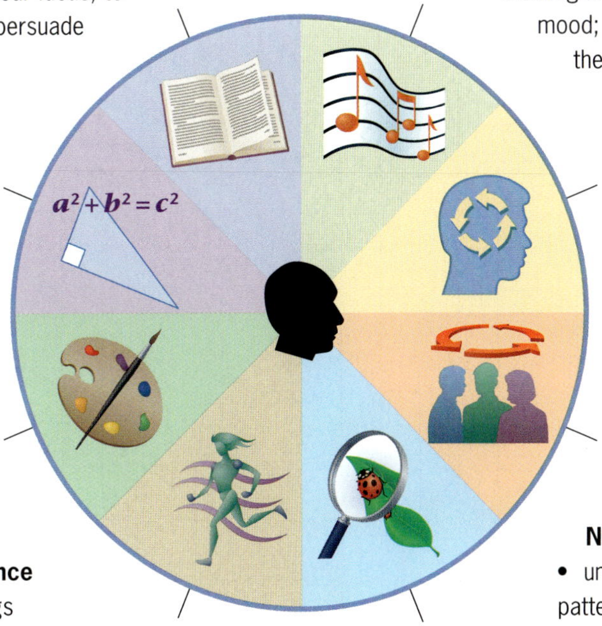

Verbal/linguistic intelligence
- using language to present your ideas, to express your feelings or to persuade others

Logical/mathematical intelligence
- reasoning, logical thinking; handling mathematical problems

Visual/spatial intelligence
- creating and interpreting visual images; thinking in three dimensions

Bodily/kinesthetic intelligence
- feeling and expressing things physically; doing hands-on work

Musical/rhythmic intelligence
- creating and feeling a rhythm to express a mood; detecting and analysing musical themes

Intrapersonal intelligence
(within the self)
- understanding your own interior thoughts and feelings in a very clear way

Interpersonal intelligence
(between people)
- understanding the feelings, needs and purposes of others

Naturalist intelligence
- understanding nature, seeing patterns in the way nature works; classifying things

ACTIVITY

What's your MI?

Take the MI Quiz to find out more about your talents, qualities and strong points.

1. Write down the heading for each "intelligence." Using a scale of 1 (not at all like me) to 5 (definitely me), record a number that best represents your response to each of the numbered statements.
2. Record a total score for each "intelligence." From your scores, list your top four intelligences.

Keep the results in your portfolio.

MI Quiz

Verbal/linguistic

1. I like puns and other wordplay.
2. I enjoy doing crosswords and playing word games like Scrabble™.
3. I remember things exactly as they are said to me.
4. I like to take part in debates or discussions.
5. I prefer long and short written answers over multiple-choice responses.
6. I enjoy keeping a journal and/or writing stories and articles.
7. I like to read.

Logical/mathematical

1. I work best at an organized work area.
2. I enjoy math and/or science.
3. I keep a "things to do" list.
4. I enjoy brainteasers and games such as Jeopardy™ and Clue™.
5. I like to ask "why" questions about issues and concerns.
6. I quickly grasp cause-and-effect relationships.
7. I am good at estimations.

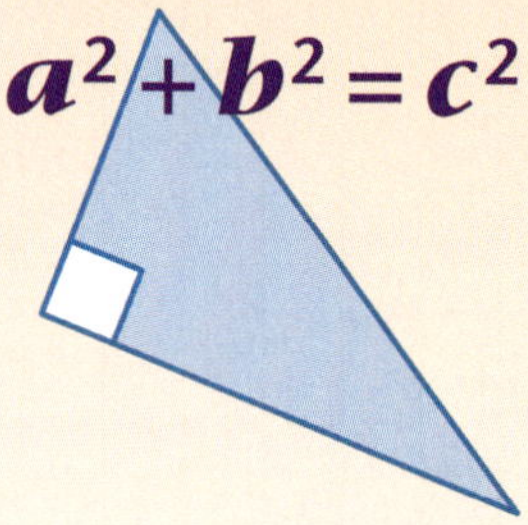

Visual/spatial

1. I understand what colours work well together.
2. I enjoy solving jigsaws, mazes and/or other visual puzzles.
3. I read charts and maps easily.
4. I have a good sense of direction.
5. I like to watch movies.
6. I have very vivid dreams.
7. I can anticipate the moves in a game plan ("hockey sense," "chess sense").

Interpersonal

1. I interact well with people.
2. I enjoy team sports rather than individual sports.
3. Being around people energizes me.
4. I like group activities better than ones I do alone.
5. I enjoy learning about different cultures.
6. I usually talk over my personal problems with a friend.
7. I enjoy sharing my ideas and feelings with others.

Intrapersonal

1. I am a private person, and I like my private inner world.
2. I have a few close friends.
3. I have strong opinions about controversial issues.
4. I work best when the activity is self-paced.
5. I am not easily influenced by others.
6. I understand my feelings, and know how I will react to situations.
7. I understand that I am responsible for my own behaviour.

Bodily/kinesthetic

1. I like to move, tap or fidget when sitting.
2. I participate in extreme sports (*e.g.*, sea kayaking, snowboarding, mountain biking).
3. I tend to touch objects to examine their textures.
4. I am well coordinated.
5. I like working with my hands.
6. I prefer being physically involved to sitting and watching.
7. I understand better by doing (touching, moving and interacting).

Musical/rhythmic

1. I play music in my head.
2. I make up rhymes to remember things.
3. It is easy for me to follow the beat of music.
4. I like setting songs and poems to music.
5. I keep time when music is playing.
6. I can hear an off-key note.
7. I feel proud of my musical accomplishments.

Naturalist

1. I have a collection (*e.g.*, shells, mugs, rocks, hockey cards).
2. I notice similarities and differences in trees, flowers and other things in nature.
3. I am actively involved in protecting the environment.
4. I enjoy digging for artifacts and finding unusual items.
5. I like planting and caring for a garden.
6. I enjoy fishing and tracking.
7. I learn best when I can go on field trips—outdoors, or to museums.

The Puzzle Grows

How is your puzzle coming along? Are you starting to fit some of the pieces together? Here's what you've done so far in this unit:

- You've learned about your general areas of interest.
- You've assessed your skills to find out what you're good at doing.
- You've taken the Multiple Intelligences test, and learned about your natural "smarts."

These bits of the puzzle are clues to your **potential**. Maybe, because you don't draw, you didn't know that you had a strong visual/spatial intelligence. Perhaps you never knew that fidgeting in class—a characteristic of people who have a bodily/kinesthetic intelligence—was linked to your ability to build things.

ACTIVITY

Your potential

Think of what you've learned about yourself. Ask yourself:

1. How do my interests match my intelligences?
2. How have my intelligences helped me develop my skills?
3. What skills would help me use my intelligences more?
4. Are there skills I already have that I could develop further?
5. How can I best build all these skills? List a few ideas.

Links

The theory of Multiple Intelligences is associated with Howard Gardner, a psychologist at Harvard University. You can learn more by reading his book *Frames of Mind: The Theory of Multiple Intelligences*. Visit <www.careers.nelson.com> for links to other related information.

How Do I Learn Best?

You Are Always Learning

Your career is about learning—the better you learn, the more successful you will be.

How you learn is directly related to your multiple intelligences. People with visual/spatial intelligence learn differently from people with a dominant musical/rhythmic intelligence. We all have our own **learning styles**. Take Mira, for example.

Mira's Story

Mira, now 22, dropped out of high school in Grade 11. "At the time, I thought I was just stupid because my grades were bad—except for math, which was always halfway decent. Otherwise, I figured I wasn't good at school."

As Mira got older, she realized she was, in fact, good at many things. Her job, for example. She worked at a factory, operating a machine that made bottles. She had a knack for spotting mechanical problems and fixing them. But she was bored, and she knew that finishing high school was the key to getting a more interesting job—like being Supervisor of Production in her factory.

When she went back to school, she took an MI test, and a learning styles test. "Both were a real eye-opener to me," she says. "My top three intelligences were visual/spatial, bodily/kinesthetic and logical/mathematical. That's why I always did okay in math. But the problem was with my learning style. I'm not a person who learns well when information comes at me in lectures in a classroom. I'm what's called a tactile learner. I need to do things with my hands to learn them better."

Mira now uses hands-on techniques that help her learn. "I write everything down. Sometimes I draw or build a model to help me remember things." She knows now that she shouldn't have jumped to conclusions about herself when she was 16. "I used to make beautiful bead jewelry and sell it. Now, I can see that bead-work was also hands-on work, and that this skill of mine is a special way of being smart."

ACTIVITY

What's your style?

1. Read each statement in the Learning Styles Survey below. Using the five-point scale shown, record the number that applies to you for each statement. Remember, there are no right or wrong answers in this quiz.
2. Copy the Learning Styles Summary Chart on page 47. Beside each statement number, write the number that you recorded for that statement in question 1.
3. Add up the points in each of the three columns. The column with the highest score indicates your most preferred learning style. But you may have another column that also has a high score. This indicates that you learn in more than one way. This is normal.
4. Complete the following statement: I am a ______ learner.

Learning Styles Survey

Scale:	5	4	3	2	1
	often		sometimes		seldom

1. I remember better from lectures with explanations and discussions.
2. I learn information more easily if it is written on the board.
3. I write down the information I read.
4. I use posters and models in the classroom.
5. I need verbal explanations of diagrams and graphs.
6. I enjoy working with my hands.
7. I enjoy making graphs and charts.
8. I can tell if two sounds match.
9. I remember best by writing things down several times.
10. I can follow directions on maps.
11. I do better at academic subjects by listening to lectures and tapes.
12. I like to play with coins, keys, pens or other objects when learning.
13. I learn to spell by repeating words out loud.
14. I prefer reading newspapers to listening to the radio news.
15. I chew gum or snack when I study.
16. The best way for me to remember something is to picture it in my head.
17. I learn how something works by taking it apart and putting it back together.
18. I would rather listen to a lecture than read the same material in a textbook.
19. I am good at solving jigsaw puzzles and mazes.
20. I grip objects in my hands while learning.
21. I prefer listening to the news on the radio to reading about it in the newspaper.
22. I prefer to get information by reading.
23. I enjoy classes with physical activity and movement.
24. I follow verbal directions better than written ones.

Learning Styles Summary Chart

	Visual	Auditory	Tactile
Statement	2.	1.	4.
Statement	3.	5.	6.
Statement	7.	8.	9.
Statement	10.	11.	12.
Statement	14.	13.	15.
Statement	16.	18.	17.
Statement	19.	21.	20.
Statement	22.	24.	23.
Totals			

Tips For Better Learning

If you're a:

Then, to improve your learning, you can:

Visual learner

1. Visualize yourself successfully performing a task.
2. Take notes. Write out everything.
3. Keep a journal of what you have learned.
4. Use charts, maps, notes and flash cards.
5. Make pictures of words, ideas and concepts in your head.
6. Ask your teacher to write on the board.

Auditory learner

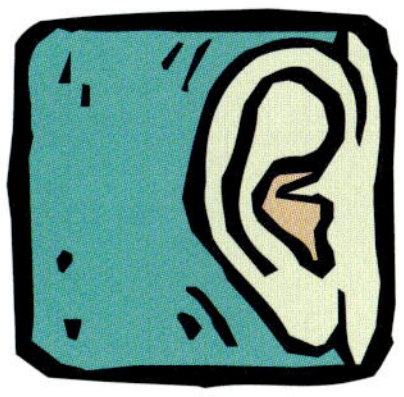

1. Tape lectures.
2. Read your notes or texts out loud.
3. Summarize what you have learned and tape yourself.
4. Explain to others what you have learned.
5. Make a song out of items you need to memorize.
6. Listen to music as you study (as long as it isn't distracting). Match words, ideas and concepts to musical themes.

Tactile learner

1. Take notes.
2. Underline or highlight important facts.
3. Make a scrapbook of what you have learned.
4. Act out a poem, story or historical event.
5. Walk through a series of instructions.
6. Build a model or draw a picture to illustrate what you are learning.
7. Create exercises or motions to match words and concepts.

What Are My Personal Characteristics?

Types of Personality

Who are you? What type of person are you? Many people, like Jake, have problems getting a "fix" on who they are. They feel different at different times. But experts have shown that, while all of us are individuals, it can be useful to think of people in terms of **personality types**.

Take Sam, for example. When he's involved in an activity, Sam prefers to take charge and get things done. No one does things quite like Sam does. But you probably know people like Sam. One of their characteristics is that they are organizers. This type of person takes on responsibility, saying, "Here is a good way to do it. Let's try this."

Your preferences are a key to discovering your **personal characteristics**.

ACTIVITY

What's your type?

1. Read the statements and personality descriptions in the Personality Sorter on page 49. Copy the statements that best apply to you.
2. Add up the number of statements for each personality type. The one(s) with the highest number of statements will indicate your personal characteristics.
3. Most people have more than one personality type. List the three types that best describe you.

Keep the results in your portfolio.

Links

In the early twentieth century, Swiss psychiatrist Carl Jung pioneered modern research into different types of personality. There have been many systems and theories developed since then. For example, the Kiersey Temperament Sorter groups people into one of four basic temperaments (Artisan, Guardian, Idealist, Rational) and then one of four subtypes within each temperament. John Holland, an American psychologist whose work is often integrated with career counselling, organizes personalities into six main categories: Realistic, Investigative, Artistic, Social, Enterprising and Conventional. And there are many others. Visit <www.careers.nelson.com> for opportunitites to complete on-line quizzes. Do more than one—these tools don't give you final or complete answers about yourself, but rather help you identify what you already know.

Personality Sorter

I'm an organizer/ manager type.	I like to make decisions. I like to take responsibility for things. I enjoy organizing and managing events. I like to lead group projects. I like assigning work to others. I say: "Let's do it this way."
I'm a social/helper type.	I like to explain things to other people. I enjoy helping my friends solve their problems. I like to work with others as part of a group. I like to encourage people to do things. I like to find out other people's opinions. I say: "How can I help?"
I'm a fixer/builder type.	I like to work with objects. I enjoy using tools and machinery. I like to find out how things work. I prefer to be organized when completing a task. I enjoy working with my hands. I say: "I can make this work."
I'm a creator/ innovator type.	I like to try new things. I enjoy using my imagination to solve problems. I prefer to use my own ideas. I enjoy being challenged by the unexpected. I like to do things differently. I say: "I have an idea."
I'm a doer/detail type.	I enjoy working at a steady pace. I like to be prepared before I start something. I prefer to follow a set of instructions. I enjoy finishing one project before I start another. I like a task even if it takes a long time to finish. I say: "Just give it to me and it'll get done."

Reflecting on Self-Assessment Tools

The four basic personality types

ACTIVITY

Typing personalities

1. Look at the cartoon above. How well does it describe personality types? Think of people you know who are like these people.
2. What are the legitimate uses of quizzes that classify people's characteristics? What illegitimate uses can you think of?
3. Which of the quizzes in this section gave you the results that seemed most true to you? Suggest reasons why this might be.

Reflection

Section 1 has been about developing self-awareness, an important step for your career development. Look back at all of the assessments you completed, both in this book and on-line. Were there any surprises in your results? How have the results influenced the way you see yourself now?

Who Can I Become?

In Section 1, you gathered information about who you are now. You put together the puzzle that gives a snapshot of you today. How will that help you plan a career?

First, knowing about yourself means that you can set career goals that really suit you. It also means that you can develop skills to achieve those goals. Who you are now is the basis for who you can become.

But information is not really useful unless you analyse it. In this section, you will look for patterns in that snapshot of yourself, and these patterns might suggest career directions. You will think about who you want to become, and with that goal in mind you will analyse your strengths and weaknesses.

What influences have made you the person you are? These will shape the person you become. You have a snapshot of who you are. Now this section will help you produce the video of who you would like to become.

DISCOVERY

Influences

List two personal achievements, two personal interests and two personal characteristics. For each item, describe an influence that helped shape you.

My Personal Profile

Analysing the Puzzle

So far, you have looked at your interests, abilities and skills, learning preferences, personal characteristics, and accomplishments. You have started to identify the patterns that connect these various aspects of you. Creating a **personal profile** can help make those patterns more clear. It can also help you connect who you are now with who you can become.

Hannah's Story

Hannah is a Level I student who is also taking this course. She has summarized the results of her self-assessment activities in Section 1, and has come up with the following:

Self-Assessment Category	Results of Activity	Comments
Achievements (What I'm Proud Of)	• *the volleyball team* • *my canoe trip last summer* • *my friendship with my best friend* • *being a good sister*	• *I'm not great at volleyball, but I tried out, worked hard and made the team.* • *I'm a natural canoeist!* • *My relationships with my friend and brother are important to me.*
Interests	• *1. people person* • *2. information person (a close second)*	• *I thought I'd be more of a hands-on person—come to think of it, though, the things I like to do almost always involve other people. (Maybe that's more important to me?)*
Skills	• *helping* • *leadership* • *communication*	• *I never thought of myself as a leader—it's not something I work at.* • *I should do this again and think of more examples. I think of myself as creative, but the examples in that category don't apply to me.*
Ways I'm Smart	• *verbal/linguistic intelligence* • *interpersonal intelligence*	• *No big surprises—I knew I didn't have a huge logical/mathematical intelligence! (Can I work on this? I wonder.)*
Learning Styles	• *visual*	• *I'm not sure this is right.*
Personal Characteristics	• *social/helper* • *doer/detail*	• *The doer/detail category doesn't seem related to my interest inventory.*

Hannah also looked through her portfolio entries from Unit 1, and her 5 Things I Like To Do list. Here's what the list looked like:

5 Things I Like to Do

- play volleyball
- be with my brother because the things he says amaze me
- talk with friends
- read books for my English book reports
- surf the Internet

When Hannah looked at the information that she had gathered about herself, she was amazed at all of the things she liked and dreamed about. She'd always thought vaguely about having a sports career—not as an athlete, she wasn't that good—but maybe she could work in a sports store, maybe even manage one.

After looking at the results of these quizzes, Hannah could see that being around people and working on relationships—even taking the lead—are very important to her. Whoever she became, she would have to make room for these aspects of herself.

ACTIVITY

Create a profile

1. Create a chart like Hannah's to summarize the results of the self-assessment activities you completed in Section 1. (Using a word processor will make your table easier to add to and edit.) Think about your individual results, and include comments that you think are important.
2. Look over the other self-assessment pieces in your portfolio, including the results of any on-line test you completed, and add relevant information to your summary chart.
3. In your chart, you have summarized many kinds of information. How does all this information connect? Find a creative way to illustrate the connections you see. Here are some suggestions:
   - a mind map
   - a mobile, a diorama or some other construction
   - writing (e.g., a short story, poem, play, or skit)
   - a performance (e.g., a song, skit, or reading of your work)
   - a computer program
   - an audio or video production

This activity allows you to use a variety of intelligences, so choose the approach that suits you best.

Reflection

Name one thing about yourself that you will certainly have to consider when setting any future goals.

My Values

An Analogy

Have you ever been hiking in unfamiliar territory? What would you need to get where you want to go? The essentials would be a destination, a compass and a good map.

Having skills and experience, good preparation and planning, proper equipment, food and emergency gear would also help, but the first three items are essential—*to keep you going in the right direction*. In the bush, you can't go in a straight line. You go up and down hills, over and around cliffs, through brush, across lakes, rivers and streams. Without a destination, a compass and a map you would get lost very quickly.

Life, too, requires preparation and planning, proper skills and tools. Because you are constantly being influenced by people and circumstances, you need to make good choices. You need to know where you want to go. To keep you on track, you need a life-compass and a life-map.

Your Values = Your Compass

Knowing what is *right* for you is important—but can you really say, at your age, what **values** are most important to you? Analysing the information you gathered in Section 1 should help you identify your values.

ACTIVITY

Your values

Decide how important each item on the list below is to you. Score each one using a scale of 1 (least important) to 5 (most important). Next, number them in order of their importance to you. For example, you may have four items rated 5. So which of these is the most important of all? Which is second-most? And so on. If you feel the list is incomplete, add other items.

- beauty
- generosity
- compassion
- competence
- creativity
- adventure
- independence
- security
- spirituality
- helping others
- leadership
- knowledge
- physical challenge
- sense of accomplishment
- recognition
- family
- helping the environment
- honesty
- influence, or power
- leisure
- money
- helping society
- popularity

These values are your compass. Your priorities may change, but the things that are really important to you now will probably be important to you in the future. So pay close attention to your values now, and let them guide your choices. If you don't pay attention to your compass, you get lost!

What Is Shaping Who I Will Become?

Influences

Some of the influences on your life-path will provide opportunities, and some will limit you. Some come from within, and some from outside.

Internal influences include your private values and attitudes. **External influences** come from your family, your friends, cultural or religious groups, and society's norms.

The Family You Come From

No influence is as great as that of your family. It's influence can be:

- positive—what a family encourages its members to do or think
- negative—what a family discourages its members from doing or thinking

For example, you may be expected to take over the traditional family business. Or your family may not want you to consider occupations that don't require a professional degree.

Family influence can be so strong that people aren't even aware of it. Or sometimes people react against family pressures, and go in the opposite direction.

Your career choices will be influenced by your social group and your cultural background. For example, a very powerful influence may be the desire to stay within your own community.

ACTIVITY

Family expectations

Make a list of the expectations that others have for you. Start with members of your family, then include other people in your life, such as teachers, friends and employers.

Profile: Dr. Roger Tabah

Even though his father is also a well-known surgeon, Montreal's Dr. Roger Tabah says there was never any family pressure on him to go into medicine. Rather, he received quiet encouragement for whatever he chose.

The only pressure was for Roger and his brother to go to university. "Our father had high standards for us, but all he wanted was that we become decent people, educated people, able to support ourselves. He expressed pride in me just because I was me, and it was the same with my brother."

Although Roger enjoyed science in high school, his first career interest was to do something in the foreign service. Languages were a bit of a tradition in the Tabah household—his father speaks French and a rusty but serviceable Arabic—and Roger spoke both French and Spanish. Today, he works fluently in either English or French, depending on his patients' needs.

It was in university that the change came for Roger, in the summer between first and second year. "That was the only time my dad pulled strings for me—he got me a summer job as an orderly, taking people to X-ray." It was a revelation for Roger. "I hadn't seen X-rays before. I started to look at them and the doctors would talk with me and show me what they saw in them. I found it fascinating—I realized the most interesting thing in the world to me was the inner workings of a human body."

It was that job that made Roger decide to become a doctor. At the end of the summer, he told his father. He remembers his father's response: "There was no pushing from him. He didn't get overly excited, he simply said, 'If this is really what you want to do, I'll support you.'"

As a medical student, Roger came to better understand his father and his work. After returning from overseas service with the Canadian army in World War II, his father had gone to the famous Sloan-Kettering cancer hospital in New York. Here he had trained to become one of Montreal's first cancer surgeons, a specialization into which his son would eventually follow him.

Today, father and son have grown closer, Roger says. "In many regards, I've become closer to my father in adult life than I was as a child. Today, we talk about interesting cases or particular problems I'm having. I really value his experience."

Charitable work is another area in which father and son have become close. Dr. Tabah senior has been awarded the Order of Canada for his work raising funds for the Cedars Cancer Institute over 35 years. Roger has been active in the Institute for more than 15 years now, as well as sitting on the medical advisory committee of Gilda's Club, an information centre for women with cancer, named in memory of comedienne Gilda Radner. Father and son also participate in a family foundation that raises money to pay for post-secondary education for those unable to afford it.

ACTIVITY

Interview

Interview an adult about how family influenced the choices he or she made in life.

Your Own Family

What if you decide to have your own family? How would that influence your career choices?

First of all, what about family responsibilities? How much extra money would you have to make to support your new family? How would having a family determine the work you did? What restrictions would be placed on the kinds of work you could look for, and where you could go?

It is difficult to think about these things at your age. However, if you had a family, it would be a central factor in all of your planning. What you wanted would have to change to fit the needs of your family.

Reflection

What are some other ways that having a family can influence your career choices? Return to the values list on page 54. How would you rank your values if you had a family? Would there be any changes in the numbers?

Your Peer Group

You've probably experienced **peer pressure**. Do you think it is difficult to avoid being influenced by peer pressure in high school?

Did you ever want to belong to a group so badly that you did things you didn't agree with? Did you ever say things you didn't believe because you wanted to fit in with people you admired? How about thoughts—did you ever think things that you didn't really agree with, or join in making fun of ideas or people you did agree with?

One of the strongest influences on you at this stage in your life may be your peer group—your friends, the group you hang out with, or even the general atmosphere of opinion in your class or school.

Your career choices may be so strongly influenced by your peer group that only certain career options appear possible.

Andy's Story

Andy lived in a northern town, with wild bush close by. Growing up, he loved to watch the forest birds and animals, and the changes of the seasons. He sometimes wrote short stories and poems for himself, about how the outdoors made him feel.

As a teenager he had other interests too, but he still loved to go out in the bush, and he still wrote in his nature book.

Andy was the only boy in his family. He wanted other males as friends, so he started to spend time with a group from school, even though he felt like an outsider, and always worried about how to fit in. He especially wanted to prove himself to Ray, the group leader.

One night the group was sitting around a fire, talking. Feeling comfortable, Andy started telling the group about how much he loved the bush. He even started reading out selections from his nature journals.

Someone in the group started laughing at what he had written. Then everyone started making fun of him, even Ray. Deeply ashamed, Andy stopped reading, and started making fun of himself also. To show the others that he completely shared their opinion, he took his journals and threw them on the fire. As they burned away, the talk gradually turned to other things.

But Andy remembered his shame, and hated whatever part of himself had betrayed those writings and feelings.

Several days later, he was talking with Ray. "You know, the other night?" Ray said. "I had to make fun of you too, or the other guys would have laughed at me. But you shouldn't have burned those things." Andy felt a little better because Ray seemed to understand, but he wished Ray and he had had the courage to resist the pressure of the group.

ACTIVITY

About Andy

1. Describe something similar that has happened to you or someone you know.
2. What should Andy have done? What would you have done in his situation?
3. What would you like to say to Andy? What would you like to say to Ray?
4. Andy's writing may have reflected his core interests. By stopping himself from expressing those interests, he might have thwarted a future career. Describe how that could have happened.
5. Make a list of positive ways in which your peers have influenced you.

Other External Factors

Chance: Chance plays a part in any life. You can fall into an occupation by chance, or by being in the right place at the right time. Alternatively, chance can prevent you from doing what you want.

Physical factors: If you don't look a certain way, for example, you'll never be a model. Whatever plans you make, you will have to consider physical factors.

Economic factors: Career choice is strongly influenced by financial status and the state of the economy. Everyone wants a job that pays well, but skills that are in high demand (today: technology and computers) will attract the most people. Of course, if everyone goes into computers, the demand will decrease. Another economic factor is the cost of training.

How Did You Get This Way?

How can you understand the external influences that are shaping you? And once you understand them, how can you do anything about them?

ACTIVITY

External factors

1. Make a list of examples in which the external factors listed above have affected your own or your family's careers.
2. Read Adesia's Story, below. Identify and guess at some of the interests, personality traits, intelligences and skills that make her career choice a good one.
3. Identify the external influences and conditions that affected the way Adesia made career decisions.

Adesia's Story

Adesia, now 25, is an environmental technologist. "I work for a firm of environmental engineers who help create environmentally friendly buildings. I carry out all sorts of tests, from how the building will affect the earth around it to what kind of air people will breathe when they work inside. I'm a detail person, so I like the detailed work."

But Adesia didn't always know what she wanted to be. "When I was a teenager I was really confused. I knew I liked science, but none of my friends did, so I didn't look in that direction."

Adesia graduated from high school and started a college program in journalism. Her family couldn't afford university, and her father thought that journalism would be a good choice, because her English grades had been high. "But I wasn't really happy," she recalls. "Then a girl in my journalism class told me about a friend of hers at another college who was taking an environmental technology course. It sounded interesting."

Her parents tried to dissuade her. "They didn't know what an environmental technologist was—it's a new occupation—so they couldn't figure out where I'd work or if I could even get a job." But Adesia did some research, and discovered that the training would put her in high demand. "That convinced them."

She shrugs. "My friends from high school still think it's boring, but I now have other friends in this field. We think it's pretty exciting to be helping the environment."

Seeing Myself in the Future

Possibilities

Imagining possibilities for yourself is one way of shaping your **career goals**. Who you can become is rooted in who you are now. The information about yourself that you gathered in Section 1, and the analysis you have done in this section, will help you see yourself in the future.

ACTIVITY

Visualize yourself in five years

Read and answer the following questions about your life in five years. Your answers can be recorded as a written description, a collage, a concept map, jot notes and pictures—whatever works for you. Add anything important that isn't covered by the examples.

1. ***Where:*** Where do I live? *For example:* my hometown, elsewhere in Canada, elsewhere in the world, in a city, in the country, in an apartment, in a house.
2. ***What:*** How do I spend my time? *For example:* What environment do I work in? How am I involved in my community? Do I have a full-time job? Do I have my own business? What field of work am I in? (General answers are fine at this point, *e.g.*, "with cars," "saving the rain forest," "anything with computers," "with people.")
3. ***How:*** What kind of lifestyle do I have? *For example:* How important are possessions to me? How much leisure time do I have? Do I commute? Do I travel on business?
4. ***Who:*** Who are the important people in my life? *For example:* Who are my friends? Do I see them often? Am I single or married? What kind of family do I have? Do I live near my parents and other older members of my family?
5. ***Why:*** What do I care about? *For example:* What sections of the newspaper do I read? Am I worried about education? health care? world politics? the environment?

Dreaming Now

Everyone may know that you like playing hockey, or shopping at the mall. But you may also have interests that you never share with anyone. Do you think your dreams for the future are just too wild and crazy? Well, dreams are another important influence. Dreams, too, can shape your career goals. The $10 Million Quiz can help you think about your dreams in practical ways. The sample answers will give you an idea of how to answer the questions.

ACTIVITY

The $10 Million Quiz	
If I won $10 million, what would I do?	• *e.g., travel and explore the world.*
Why?	• *e.g., I've never had the chance to travel, and have always wanted to.*
What does this say about me?	• *e.g., I have a desire for adventure and excitement.*
What does this say about my interests?	• *e.g., I'm curious about other people and places, and I want to explore the unknown.*
Does this answer give me career clues for my future?	• *e.g., I might like work that involves travel, or working with people from other countries.*
What kinds of occupations might suit me? (A guidance counsellor might be able to help.)	• *e.g., travel counsellor* • *e.g., teacher of English as a Second Language* • *e.g., international banker*

Remember Hannah?

Hannah (page 52) had trouble visualizing her life in ten years. She doesn't care where or how she lives—as long as her living situation has variety. She is sure that she wants to work with people, but she's not sure what occupation she will have—probably something without a fixed schedule. She sees herself being independent, with active hobbies. She will definitely want to travel (that's more important to her than possessions), and she won't be taking guided tours. She imagines having many friends, and a small family.

If Hannah won $10 million right now, she'd organize a mountain-climbing expedition for herself and a few friends, or buy a sailboat and navigate a crew around the world.

ACTIVITY

Career estimating

Hannah has come up with a list of four occupations she wants to explore:

- working with young people in a sports environment
- leading tours or expeditions (maybe bike tours in Europe)
- doing research or writing about sports
- working in retail sales (sporting equipment)

1. Why do you think Hannah came up with each of these possibilities?
2. Which of these four occupations do you think Hannah is best fitted for? Why?
3. Go back to your picture of yourself in the future. Check the "What" section on page 60. Can you think of new occupations to add there?

Where to From Here?

As Hannah does more research into her interests, she will need to find out about how she can qualify for certain jobs. You will find out about researching qualifications in Unit 3. For now, let's look at Hannah's inventory of skills for each job on her list:

Type of Work	Skills I Already Have
• working with young people in a sports environment	• I get along well with people. • I am a giving person. • I love sports and know a lot about them. • I have athletic ability and stamina.
• leading tours or expeditions (maybe bike tours in Europe)	• I get along well with people. • I have athletic ability and stamina. • I know about bikes, and am able to fix them.
• doing research or writing about sports	• I love sports and know a lot about them. • I am a good writer, and enjoy writing. • I get along well with people. • I am able to meet deadlines and follow schedules.
• working in retail sales (sports equipment)	• I get along well with people. • I know the product. • I have high energy. • I am good at communicating. • I have sales ability.

Hannah noticed that many of her skills were repeated in the various work areas. She made one list of all her skills, and then drew up another table, as follows:

Skills I Already Have	Where I've Demonstrated This Skill
• I get along well with people.	• I get along well on the volleyball team. • I enjoyed volunteering at the retirement home. • I just like talking with people!
• I manage my time well.	• I always helped to set up and take down camp on my canoe trip. • I always get my school assignments in on time.

ACTIVITY

Your work-related skills

Do an inventory of your own work-related skills, using Hannah's tables as your model.

SECTION 3

What Skills Will Help Me Become That Person?

In Section 1 you looked at who you are. In Section 2 you looked at who you think you will become. If the future "you" fixes cars, then you're going to have to develop car-fixing skills. If the future "you" opens a store, you'll need accounting and other business skills.

But your dream of who you will become is broader than just the work you will be doing. There are important general skills that will help you become more successful, no matter who you become. These include communication and time management skills. They are called **transferable skills** because they will be useful in all aspects of your life.

In this section, you will:

- look closely at some transferable skills
- decide which transferable skills you will need
- learn how to develop those transferable skills

DISCOVERY

Transferable skills

1. Brainstorm what skills you think would be transferable to any life or work situation (e.g., using a school planner, organizing your clothes, being adaptable to new people or situations, managing stress).Then create a class list of transferable skills.
2. Create a chart (like the one below) on which to list your own transferable skills. Copy the class list of skills into the first column, then complete the chart. Rate your skill level from 1 (low) to 5 (high). Leave space in each category (or use a computer), because you will be adding to your list.

Skills	Do I Have This Skill?	How Much Do I Want to Improve This Skill?	What Can I Do to Develop This Skill?
e.g., using a planner *keeping my clothes organized* *being adaptable*			

Transferable Skills

Profile: Andrea Peters

Andrea Peters has been hired as an administrative assistant for a large government project. The only specialized knowledge she has is of several common software programs.

Within weeks, everyone on the project—including the director—knows who she is. Her area of responsibility keeps growing. This is summed up in a funny way when someone puts a sign over her work area. It says, "Andrea Peters, President."

Andrea's an actress, doing this job to pay the rent. She has a university degree in French and music, and a three-year musical theatre diploma from Sheridan College. "It's a tough job," she says, "but I like the atmosphere and the flexibility. I can take time off for auditions and performances."

The job involves the usual administrative duties: word processing, photocopying and faxing, taking minutes at meetings, scheduling events, meetings and teleconferences, and general troubleshooting of all kinds. Andrea has to draw on her strong organizational skills to keep all the details together.

But it's her interpersonal skills that really shine, and this is where her training in drama becomes useful. "I don't have a problem talking to people, or with public speaking. I'm confident—that comes from acting and going to auditions. I'm not afraid of new situations. I'm a social person to begin with, but my drama training gives me an awareness of character and personality types."

The company picnic is an example of how Andrea's responsibilities have grown. Andrea had to plan a full afternoon of activities for 200 people on the last warm day of summer. Her employers wanted the picnic to be a "team building" event.

"I tried to keep the atmosphere as light as possible. I organized entertaining games that would get people involved. I brought my own personality and sense of humour to the job, and that's what made it work. The picnic was a huge success."

Andrea auditions whenever she can, but she has also discovered a new interest in the business world. "I like dealing with people and organizing things. I could be interested in an administrative or management career. I haven't changed my direction—I'm still going for acting—but I'm considering a career shift."

ACTIVITY

Spotting transferable skills

1. Why is Andrea so valued in her job? What qualities have enabled her to make such a positive impact so quickly?
2. List all the skills that Andrea brought to her new work. Where might she have acquired such skills? (Family, school, work, community activities.)
3. Compare this list to your own list of transferable skills (page 63). Add any of these skills that you feel you have to your list. You should review your list frequently.

Employability Skills

Transferable skills are like a "tool kit" for life and work. From every experience in your life, you will be constantly adding to this tool kit.

Take Meredith, for example. Her homework is always incredibly neat. Sometimes people call her a "neat freak," but she doesn't care. She likes to be organized about her clothes and jewelry, too. In fact, her room is the tidiest in the house! Her ability to keep things orderly was a skill that helped her build up a summer lawn-mowing business. Her clients liked how neat she left their yards. Meredith's organizing skills are part of her tool kit.

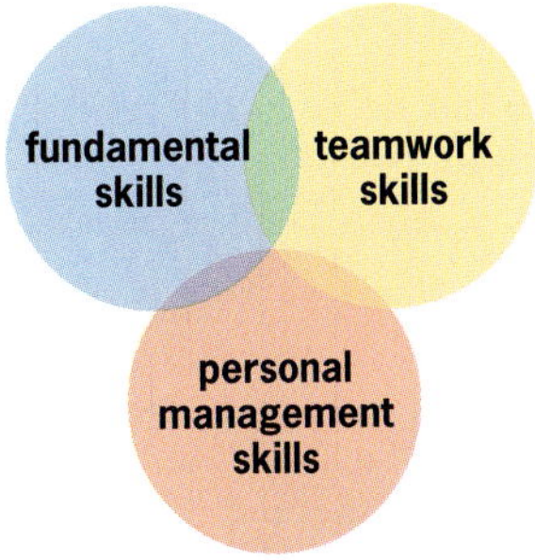

Do you have a skill like that? Something that helps you at school, and also gives you an "edge" somewhere else? The Conference Board of Canada calls these skills **employability skills**, and has organized them into three categories: fundamental skills, teamwork skills and personal management skills. The chart on page 66 lists these skills in detail.

ACTIVITY

List your skills

Does the list of employability skills feel overwhelming?

Go back to your own transferable skills list (page 63). How many employability skills do you already have on your list? Add any that are not already there. Complete columns two, three and four on the chart for these skills also.

This chart can be added to your **Employability Skills Portfolio**. This portfolio will be a useful tool to help you identify your particular skills and areas of need. It can be continually modified and used to help you develop your career goals. The Employability Skills Portfolio will be discussed in more detail in Unit 4.

Remember the credentials we talked about in Unit 1? Your transferable skills are also important credentials!

Links

The Conference Board of Canada is a nationally respected "think tank" that helps its members anticipate and respond to the global economy. Its members are Canadian business, government and public sector organizations.

You can find out more about the Conference Board of Canada by writing to them at 255 Smyth Road, Ottawa, ON K1H 8M7, calling them, or visiting their website. Go to <www.careers.nelson.com> for a direct link to up-to-date information.

Employability Skills 2000+

Fundamental Skills

You will be better prepared to progress in the world of work when you can:

Communicate

- read and understand information presented in a variety of forms (e.g., words, graphs, charts, diagrams)
- write and speak so others pay attention and understand
- listen and ask questions to understand and appreciate the points of view of others
- share information using a range of information and communications technologies (e.g., voice, e-mail, computers)
- use relevant scientific, technological and mathematical knowledge and skills to explain or clarify ideas

Manage Information

- locate, gather and organize information using appropriate technology and information systems
- access, analyze and apply knowledge and skills from various disciplines (e.g., the arts, languages, science, technology, mathematics, social sciences, and the humanities)

Use Numbers

- decide what needs to be measured or calculated
- observe and record data using appropriate methods, tools and technology
- make estimates and verify calculations

Think & Solve Problems

- assess situations and identify problems
- seek different points of view and evaluate them based on facts
- recognize the human, interpersonal, technical, scientific and mathematical dimensions of a problem
- identify the root cause of a problem
- be creative and innovative in exploring possible solutions
- readily use science, technology and mathematics as ways to think, gain and share knowledge, solve problems and make decisions
- evaluate solutions to make recommendations or decisions
- implement solutions
- check to see if a solution works, and act on opportunities for improvement

Personal Management Skills

You will be able to offer yourself greater possibilities for achievement when you can:

Demonstrate Positive Attitudes & Behaviours

- feel good about yourself and be confident
- deal with people, problems and situations with honesty, integrity and personal ethics
- recognize your own and other people's good efforts
- take care of your personal health
- show interest, initiative and effort

Be Responsible

- set goals and priorities balancing work and personal life
- plan and manage time, money and other resources to achieve goals
- assess, weigh and manage risk
- be accountable for your actions and the actions of your group
- be socially responsible and contribute to your community

Adaptability

- work independently or as a part of a team
- carry out multiple tasks or projects
- be innovative and resourceful: identify and suggest alternative ways to achieve goals and get the job done
- be open and respond constructively to change
- learn from your mistakes and accept feedback
- cope with uncertainty

Learn Continuously

- be willing to continuously learn and grow
- assess personal strengths and areas for development
- set your own learning goals
- identify and access learning sources and opportunities
- plan for and achieve your learning goals

Work Safely

- be aware of personal and group health and safety practices and procedures, and act in accordance with these

Teamwork Skills

You will be better prepared to add value to the outcomes of a task, project or team when you can:

Work with Others

- understand and work within the dynamics of a group
- ensure that a team's purpose and objectives are clear
- be flexible: respect, be open to and supportive of the thoughts, opinions and contributions of others in a group
- recognize and respect people's diversity, individual differences and perspectives
- accept and provide feedback in a constructive and considerate manner
- contribute to a team by sharing information and expertise
- lead or support when appropriate, motivating a group for high performance
- understand the role of conflict in a group to reach solutions
- manage and resolve conflict when appropriate

Work with Others

- plan, design or carry out a project or task from start to finish with well-defined objectives and outcomes
- develop a plan, seek feedback, test, revise and implement
- work to agreed quality standards and specifications
- select and use appropriate tools and technology for a task or project
- adapt to changing requirements and information
- continuously monitor the success of a project or task and identify ways to improve

School (Fundamental) Skills

Success At School

You already know what skills and habits will usually lead to success at school. You may or may not practise these **school skills**, but you know what is required.

Did you know that there's a strong relationship between the skills you need to do well at school and those you need to do well in the workplace?

ACTIVITY

Charting your school skills

Brainstorm a list of skills that you can use to be successful at school.

1. Make a four-column chart (like the one below). In the first column, write the skills from your list. Use a scale of 1 (low) to 5 (high) for rating yourself.

School Success Skills	How Much of This Skill Do I Have?	Evidence	Plan of Action (How I Can Get This Skill)
e.g., meeting project deadlines *participating in class* *giving class presentations* *researching* *taking notes* *solving mathematical problems* *reading and summarizing information*			

2. For any skill that you rated between 3 and 5, list evidence in the fourth column. If there is no evidence, you don't have the skill!
3. For any skill that you rated between 1 and 3, list methods you could use to acquire the skill or improve your skill level.

School Skills Are Transferable Skills

You've heard it a thousand times: "What's the point of staying in school? I'm not learning anything important."

But even learning that doesn't seem important today can help you acquire the skills that employers may want in the future.

Build Your Transferable Skills in School

Skills That School Can Help You Build	What These Skills Will Help You Do in the Workplace
Communication skills • giving class presentations • reading articles and books • writing essays, short stories and poetry	• prepare presentations • write clear and concise memos, letters and reports • speak well on issues • explain your ideas effectively • ask for help when required • communicate well with managers and co-workers
Teamwork skills • getting along with your friends • working with others on projects • participating in extra-curricular activities (*e.g.*, band, tennis, clubs)	• be a productive team worker • accept authority and supervision • view co-workers as equals • know how to be co-operative and share knowledge • get along with others
Time management skills • doing homework • meeting project deadlines • scheduling your day • getting to class on time	• get work done efficiently • be prepared for meetings • meet deadlines • plan schedules and set goals
Problem-solving skills • analysing information • understanding problems • defining problems • solving problems • applying results	• think analytically and clearly about issues • pinpoint problems • evaluate situations • identify risks • make informed decisions • find productive solutions
Organizational skills • taking notes • following written and oral instructions • keeping binders of information • following a schedule • setting priorities and goals	• keep a neat workplace • take care of equipment and tools • keep track of important details • handle interruptions well • organize activities to meet deadlines

continued

Skills That School Can Help You Build	What These Skills Will Help You Do in the Workplace
Learning skills • asking questions • reading information • using the library • researching information • joining activities and clubs	• think critically and act logically • learn from on-the-job training • upgrade skills as necessary • learn from mistakes • increase knowledge and productivity
Computer skills • keyboarding • word processing • using database programs	• be computer literate • use technology in the workplace • adapt to new technologies
Listening skills • attending classes • taking notes • visualizing what you hear • comprehending information	• understand what managers and co-workers tell you • help others with their concerns and problems • participate effectively in meetings
Creativity skills • learning how others have been creative • using your imagination • trying new ways to do things • looking at issues from a different point of view	• be an idea person • think of new ways to get the job done • create a positive work environment • increase motivation
Leadership skills • leading projects • being on sports teams • volunteering as a peer helper	• lead projects • manage people • coach others • help others reach their goals

And remember...

Every time you work on a class project, you're learning to communicate with others, work on a team, be a leader, use your creativity and help solve problems.

Every time you make a presentation in a class, you're learning to organize your ideas and information, speak effectively and persuade others.

Every time you work on an essay, you're learning about a new subject, doing research, managing your time, setting priorities, being creative and expressing your own point of view.

Every time you participate in a school activity, you're learning to be a team member, set goals and achieve objectives.

Every time you volunteer at a dance or fund-raiser, you're learning how to work with others, organize a project and get things done on time.

Employers speak out

"When we have applicants right out of high school with little work experience, we look for experience related to high school projects and presentations. Did the job applicant get up and give a speech in class? That counts for us."

—*Adrian Trepanier*, Human Resources Manager, Weyerhaeuser Canada Ltd., a pulp processing and lumber manufacturing company

"We know that students don't have much job experience, so we look for a good work record and good ethics even in high school."

—*Pat Chatelain*, Campus Coordinator, Human Resources, Syncrude Canada Ltd., a company that mines tar sands for oil

"We look for people who are active as volunteers in their schools and communities. We want to see lots of teamwork and life experiences."

—*Emily Loh*, Human Resources Administrator, Hughes Aircraft of Canada Ltd., a company that makes air navigation equipment and systems

ACTIVITY

Convince me!

You are going to sell your skills to a prospective employer:

1. From the chart on pages 68–69, choose five skills that you possess.
2. Using the chart, choose evidence that you possess these skills.
3. Prepare an oral presentation that explains how the evidence demonstrates the skills.
4. Convince your partner that you have the skills you claim to have.

Personal Management Skills

Wilton's Story

The alarm went off and Wilton groaned. He had been up late last night, trying to get his math done. He had also talked on the phone for an hour with one of his friends. He'd finally done the math, but that hadn't left much time for sleep.

He shut off the alarm, intending to get up, but dozed off until his mother woke him up again. "You're going to miss your bus!" At that, he was up like a shot and racing around getting ready. He just caught the bus, but he hadn't had any breakfast. He was wearing two different coloured socks. Very cool!

Seeing his friends on the bus and at school, he began to feel better. His girlfriend, Reena, said that she was really looking forward to going out tonight. His best friend, Stan, said he wanted to talk with him, so they agreed to meet at lunch.

During the last class of the morning, the teacher asked them to turn in their assignments. "Assignment! What assignment?" Wilton whispered to his friend Neil, who replied, "The one she gave us last week."

That hit Wilton like a punch. "Oh, man. I totally forgot about it!" He stayed after class to talk with the teacher, and managed to get an extension, but only until tomorrow. So much for going out on a date!

Reena was not thrilled at the news, and Wilton felt even worse. He wolfed down his fries and gravy and took off to see Stan, who was having problems with his girlfriend. He just needed to talk, but Wilton was having trouble listening. He had too many things on his mind already, including Reena. He couldn't concentrate very well.

Wilton survived the afternoon, though he came close to falling asleep in one class. Then it was time for basketball practice. Wilton loved basketball! He wasn't a star, but he was a good player. He also really liked his coach. After practice, the coach asked Wilton to talk to the team about an upcoming tournament. He agreed gladly, then wondered when he would ever find the time.

On the bus home, Wilton was a zombie, staring off into space. All he could think of was, "How am I going to do all this? I am so stressed!"

ACTIVITY

How skillful is Wilton?

1. Use a scale of 1 (low) to 5 (high) to rate Wilton's skills in the following areas:
    - time management
    - organization
    - stress management
    - maintaining a positive attitude
2. Choose one of Wilton's weak skills, and give him some friendly advice about how to work on it.

What Are Personal Management Skills?

Personal management skills are the ones you use *every* day to get yourself *through* the day. Many skills fall under this heading. In the following activities, you will focus on the same ones that you rated for Wilton.

DISCOVERY

How true are the following statements for you?

Use a 5-point scale to rate how true these statements are for you (1 = rarely true, 5 = usually true).

1. I get my assignments in on time.
2. I use my planner to schedule my time.
3. I can easily find the things I need.
4. I enjoy challenges.
5. I am cheerful when I'm doing household chores.

Time Management Skills

Putting the Right Things First

ACTIVITY

How you spend your time

Keep track of everything you do for one full school day. Use 30-minute intervals, and write down briefly what you did during each of those times. This may be difficult, but it will be worth it. You'll learn things about yourself you never knew—like where all your time goes! You will need this time analysis to do other work in this section. Keep it in your portfolio.

People who get things done are people who know how to manage their time. **Time management** means knowing the difference between *important* and *urgent*. Some activities are both. Some are neither. And some are one, but not the other.

Here's an example that illustrates the difference:

You're studying for a big test. It's urgent that you pass. That's what's important right now.

The phone rings. A ringing telephone sounds so urgent. You answer.

It's a friend, just wanting to chat.

Talking isn't as important as studying for the test. You could say, "Got to study, I'll call you back," but instead you talk for an hour.

Now what? You don't have enough time to prepare properly for the test, so you won't do as well as you wanted.

Something that sounded urgent but was not important—the telephone call—ended up overruling something that was urgent *and* important.

ACTIVITY

Important and urgent

Go back to your results from How You Spend Your Time on page 73.

1. For each 30-minute segment of your day, decide whether the activity was important or urgent. It could be both, or it could be neither. Write down the appropriate description next to each item.
2. When you have labelled each item, make four lists of activities, as on the chart below:

Important & Urgent	**Important**	**Urgent**	**Neither**
e.g., writing history essay for tomorrow	*e.g., writing résumé for summer job search*	*e.g., watching hockey playoff game*	*e.g., playing computer game*

3. Which category of activity received most of your time? Second most? Third? Analyse your use of time by answering the following questions:
   - **a.** Were there any important activities that did not get enough time?
   - **b.** If you could do it over, what changes would you make?

Making Time

Most people have difficulty finding time to do things that are important, but not urgent. These are often long-term goals, like building a relationship, getting in better physical shape, working on an assignment that is not due until next month, saving money, reading for pleasure, even getting enough sleep.

Here is an image to keep in your mind when important things aren't getting done. Think of a stream flowing by. Down the stream goes everything that is happening in your life. If you are waiting for the stream to slow down, you will have a long wait!

ACTIVITY

Stones in the stream

Make a list of important things in your life that are not getting enough of your time. Use the list for the next activity. Then keep it in your portfolio.

Think of a large stone as one of your "important" things. Place it in the stream. What happens? The stone stays where you put it. The stream has to change its course to accommodate the stone, not the other way around. *The important things will get done when you decide that they really are important and schedule them into your life.* The less important events and activities will flow around the important ones.

ACTIVITY

Placing stones in the stream

Take your list of important things that are not getting enough of your time. In your planner or calendar, schedule each of these *at least once during the next week*. Do it now. The rest of your activities will flow around them.

Every week, review your list, revise it and schedule in your important things. Make a habit of it.

Time Management Tips

- Spend time on important things before they become urgent.
- Don't be ruled by urgency. Never avoid important activities because of merely urgent tasks.
- Do important things early. Waiting until they're urgent will only increase your stress level.
- Number your tasks in order of their importance. Complete them in that order.

ACTIVITY

Time's up!

Think of an occasion when you didn't manage your time well, or when you were affected because someone else didn't manage their time well. Tell the story to a partner.

Organizational Skills

A Matter of Style

Being organized doesn't necessarily mean that you have everything arranged in a neat and tidy way, from your room at home, to your locker and notebooks at school, to your CD collection or your sports equipment.

Your organizational style is your own. Some people are natural organizers, and take pleasure in order. But those of you who aren't natural organizers can still learn to keep your lives organized in a way that works for you.

ACTIVITY

Are you organizationally challenged?

To identify your personal organizational problems, make a list of answers for each of these questions:

1. What kinds of things do you have trouble finding and why?
2. What kinds of things do you have difficulty remembering to do and why? (If you have trouble with this, your friends and family will be glad to tell you!)

If you are a person who never has trouble finding or remembering to do things, congratulations! For *your* lists, write down the strategies that you use to keep yourself so well organized.

The Basics of Being Organized

Having **organizational skills** means being able to do two things:

1. Knowing how to find something when you need it—your favourite shirt, your hockey socks, your pen, your homework assignment, something in your notebook.
2. Remembering to do something that you are supposed to do—your science assignment, being on time to meet your friend, something your boss asked you to do, buying a birthday card, early morning band practice, anything you promised your parents you would do.

As long as you can do both of these things, how you do them is up to you.

Be True to Yourself

If what you are doing works for you, keep doing it. If it doesn't work for you, don't kid yourself—do something different.

ACTIVITY

Your organizational consultant

The world is full of consultants, people who advise other people about how to solve problems. Right now, unless you're perfect, you need an organizational consultant. So ask someone to be your consultant, preferably someone who knows you well.

1. Your task, with the help of your consultant, is to find solutions to the problems you identified in the last activity. Make a chart, like the one below, and fill in the first three columns for each of the problems you have.

Problem	**Cause**	**Solution**	**Evidence of Using the Solution**	**Signature**

2. Now that you have solutions, you need to use them. Over the next week, actually use the solutions you have discovered. Present evidence to your consultant that you have done this. Enter the evidence in the fourth column of your chart, and have your consultant sign in the fifth column as a witness. Keep the chart in your portfolio.

3. If your consultant is also doing this activity, you can switch roles and become the consultant. You don't have to be an expert. It is always easier to advise someone else than it is to advise yourself.

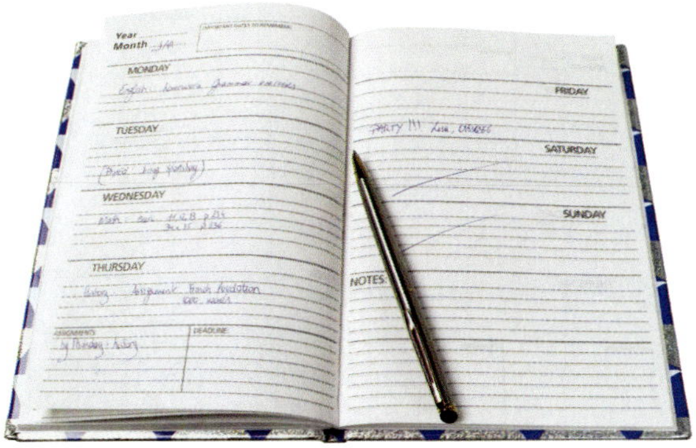

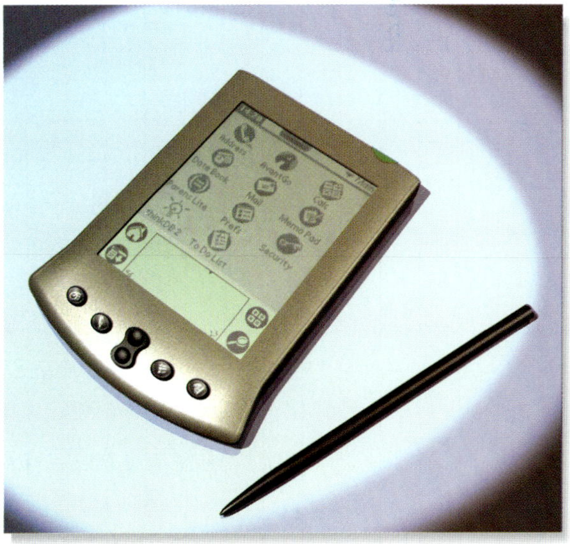

Recommendation: Use a Planner/Organizer

It's great for helping you remember what to do.

Stress Management Skills

A Balancing Act

Stress can help spur you on to do your best, but too much stress can interfere with your ability to do good work. Stress can even make you sick. So **stress management** is an important skill to develop.

Strategies for Handling Negative Stress

- ***Schedule your important activities.*** That way you know you are doing the most important things, even if you aren't getting everything done.
- ***Use a planner.*** It'll help you control your time.
- ***Keep a budget.*** It'll help you manage your money.
- ***Talk with parents, a guardian or other responsible adults for support.*** That's what they're there for.
- ***Have a support network of friends.*** That's what they're there for, too.
- ***Keep a journal to help organize your thoughts and feelings.*** If you can write your private thoughts on paper, they might not feel so stressful.
- ***Listen to music that makes you feel good.*** We all have different tastes. Find music that works for you.
- ***Participate in physical activity.*** The benefits are huge: you reduce the physical effects of stress, think about something else, enjoy another aspect of life, etc.
- ***Use breathing techniques, yoga, visualization and/or meditation to help you relax.*** Deep and regular breathing can help. (Your physical educational teacher might know some breathing exercises.)
- ***Eat a healthful diet.*** A bad diet increases stress, and can make you sick.
- ***Get plenty of rest and sleep.*** Nothing is more basic than this. If you're not getting enough rest, everything else seems worse.
- ***Use responsible decision-making skills.*** What decisions do you need to make? How can you demonstrate responsibility for those decisions?

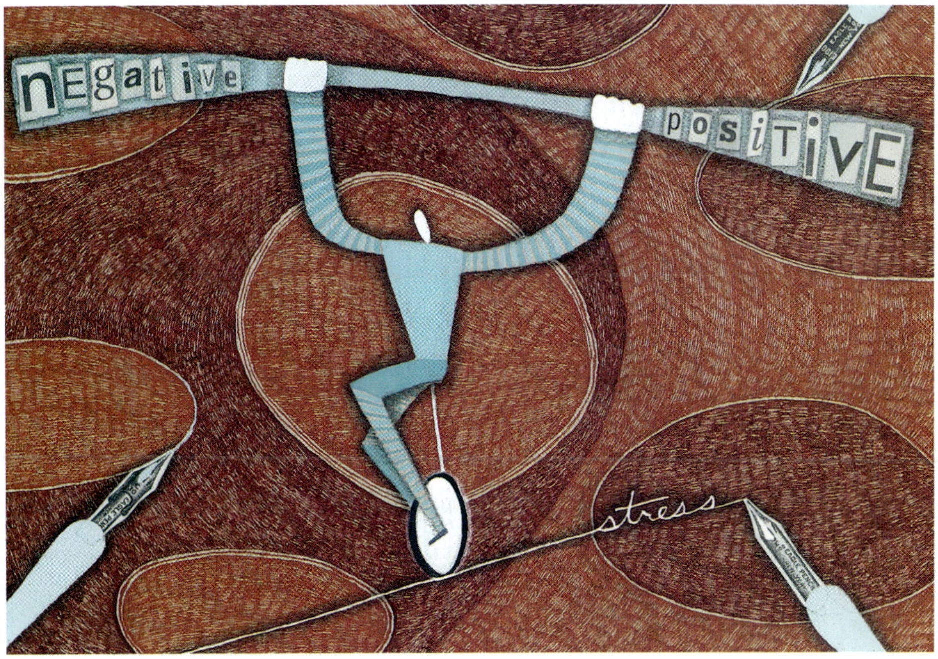

ACTIVITY

How's your stress-balancing act?

Everyone experiences stress. Think of an occasion when you felt an uncomfortable amount of stress.

1. In the centre of a piece of paper, jot down words that describe how you felt and put a circle around them.
2. Now choose the strategies (page 78) that you think would have worked in the situation you've charted, and connect these to the central circle.

What Do Some Stress Balancers Say?

Madeline, age 15: "I talk to my best friend, Celia. Not that she can always solve my problems, but just talking about them helps."

Reg, age 17: "I have to get out of the house and do something—like play some basketball with one of my friends, or ride my bike. It seems to help me let off steam."

Yee, age 14: "I turn music on as loud as I can and lay on the floor and listen. I know it's weird, but it works."

Carly, age 13: "I have an Internet pen pal who lives in Japan. We've never met, but I write everything to her. Then she writes back to me about all her stuff. Her world's really different than mine, but it's amazing how well we understand each other."

When Positive Skills Become Habits

Driving on Automatic

A **habit** is something that you do without thinking. Musicians practise so much that they don't have to think about where to put their fingers when they play. In the middle of a football game, a player doesn't have to think about the proper technique for blocking or tackling.

The more you do something, the more automatic it becomes. If that's a good "something," you've developed a positive habit.

Make a list of good things that you would like to turn into habits. You will probably find some on your list of important things that don't always get done. Then keep doing them consciously until you do them automatically.

Try this: Do whatever task you have set yourself *as if you really like doing it.* That's right, pretend; act the part. If you can do that for ten minutes, you will probably find that you don't dislike the activity as much, even if you really didn't want to do it in the first place. Try it. You will probably surprise yourself. Before long, it will become a habit and you will just do it. No big deal, but a big payoff!

Links

Stephen R. Covey's best-selling book, *The 7 Habits of Highly Effective People,* is an excellent guide to positive habits and other personal management approaches. There is a version written especially for teens by Covey's son Sean, called *The 7 Habits of Highly Effective Teens.* Go to <www.careers.nelson.com> for related information.

Work Habits of Effective People

1. ***Don't procrastinate!*** If you have to do it anyway, you might as well get started when you have time enough to get it done.
2. ***Keep a positive attitude.*** The right attitude is extremely important—ask any athlete. Keep focused on successful completion of the task.
3. ***Don't think the worst.*** If you think you will fail, it will only create a wall of fear that will make failure much more likely.
4. ***Set clear goals.*** Think about what you want, and what needs to be done. Be specific. Figure out a timetable with realistic goals at each step.
5. ***Set priorities.*** Make a list.
6. ***Break tasks into manageable chunks.*** Big projects feel overwhelming. Break them into manageable chunks. That's what professional project managers do.
7. ***Get organized before you start.*** Have all your materials ready before you begin a task.
8. ***Commit yourself to doing the task.*** Perhaps write yourself a contract.
9. ***Remind yourself.*** Write reminders to yourself, and put them in conspicuous places like on the TV, refrigerator, bathroom mirror, front door, etc.
10. ***Reward yourself.*** Celebrate, pat yourself on the back, smile and enjoy the completion of even the smallest of tasks. Don't minimize your accomplishments.

Words of Wisdom

Q: How do you eat an elephant?

A: One bite at a time.

ACTIVITY

Promoting good habits

Choose any transferable skill and create a promotion to encourage people to turn that skill into a habit. Consider the following:

1. Who is the intended audience?
2. What form should the promotion take to reach that audience (is it a brochure, a poster, a broadcast public service announcement)?
3. What tone should be conveyed, and how will that be achieved?

Make Self-Motivation a Habit

When people write about "unmotivated" teens, they mean that teens don't do what other people want them to. You can be highly motivated, though—to do what *you* want to do!

What other people want you to do may be really important, or could be in the long run—school work, for example. Even **self-motivated** students have days when they really don't want to do their homework. The most highly motivated workers also have days on the job when they really don't want to work. If you can solve your motivation problems now for school, you will have another great transferable skill.

ACTIVITY

Mission not impossible!

Here is a challenge for your creativity. Pick one of the following scenarios and brainstorm, with a group, ways that you could motivate yourself to do what has to be done. Remember, being motivated means that *you want to do it.* No, it's not impossible!

Scenario 1

It's after supper. You have a big assignment due tomorrow. You have the background work done, but you have to put it all together so that it makes sense. You have enough time to get it done, but you can't get motivated. You are agitated; you can't sit still; you keep rearranging things; you phone a friend. You even offer to do some chores around the house. You do everything except get started. All you can think about is, "I really don't want to do this!" How do you get yourself to do the work?

Scenario 2

You are sitting in class, bored out of your mind. The teacher and the other students are talking, but you haven't a clue, and you don't care. It's not because you are tired or upset or preoccupied, you just don't want to be involved. How do you motivate yourself to participate?

Compare solutions with others in the class, and make a list of "survival techniques." The next time you are in one of these situations, try the techniques. It isn't easy, but if you can do it, you have a great skill! Keep your motivation survival skills in your portfolio.

Reflection

Go back to page 71 and reread Wilton's Story. Do you have any new advice that you could give to Wilton?

ACTIVITY

Re-evaluate your personal management skills

Rank each of these statements from 1 (not at all true for me) to 5 (very true for me):

- I work effectively under pressure.
- I know how to handle stress.
- I know how to keep myself healthy, and I do it.
- I manage my time effectively by completing homework.
- I manage my time effectively by meeting project deadlines.
- I manage my time effectively by scheduling my day/month/year.
- I manage my time effectively by getting to class on time.
- I seek opportunities for personal growth.
- I try to evaluate my personal strengths and weaknesses.
- I take initiative at school and on the job when necessary.
- I avoid unacceptable behaviour in school and/or at work.

What's your score?
45-55: Are you sure you answered truthfully?
30-44: You're doing a good job of self-management.
20-30: Keep up the good work.
Less than 20: You may want to spend more time thinking about this section.

Reflection

Which personal management skills do you need to develop? With the picture of who you want to become in mind, explain how developing that skill will improve your chances of doing what you want to in the future.

Communication Skills

Who's Really Listening Out There?

Talking with a friend is a great joy, but it has to be a dialogue—two people sharing their thoughts and feelings. You know people who only communicate in monologues—they talk, you listen. This isn't very satisfying for you.

Listening is one of the least developed skills in our society. To prove this, listen to a conversation in almost any group. While you're listening, and watching people in the group, ask yourself:

- Is each person really listening to what everyone else is saying?
- Is each person relating what he or she says to what has been said by someone else?
- Are they talking *with* each other or *at* each other?

Active listening is an important skill. It encourages others to talk to you in a way that ensures that you understand well what they're trying to say. This means really listening—not just with your ears, but with your whole body and mind.

If you've been in a peer counselling, peer mediation or conflict resolution group, you probably have learned this and some of the other **communication skills**. If so, you can help others in your class, and the practice will help you improve your own skills.

ACTIVITY

Body language

Do this activity with a partner, sitting back to back. It will seem strange, but don't turn around:

1. Take turns telling each other about something that really interests you. Take about a minute each. Pay attention to how you are feeling, both when talking and listening. When you've both had a chance to talk, turn around and share how you felt. What was missing?
2. Now, do the same exercise, except face to face. Continue the conversation from before, or start a new one. Again, take turns and pay attention to how you feel this time as talker and listener. After you have both talked again for a minute, share your experiences. How did you feel this time, compared to when you were back to back?
3. What did the listeners do that made the talkers feel that they were really listening? Make a list of body language that encourages communication. Make a second list of body language that discourages communication.

Active Listening Skills

Let's think about Wilton again. Imagine him talking to his friend Stan.

Wilton: "I have a ton of things to do today! Not only do I have to do my regular homework but I have this assignment I had forgotten to do. I got an extension, but only until tomorrow, so I can't go out with Reena. Now she's mad at me! And I told the coach that I would talk with everyone on the team about our tournament. This is too much!"

The following chart illustrates a number of active listening skills that Stan could use in this situation:

Skill	Description	Stan's Response
Reflecting	Repeat back to the speaker what you think you heard, using basically the same words.	"This really is too much."
Paraphrasing	Put what you heard into your own words, and say them back.	"You really do have a lot to do. And it doesn't help that Reena's upset."
Clarifying	Ask for more details.	"How long do you think the assignment will take?"
Reflecting Feelings	Identify the emotion of the speaker and express it.	"You must feel frustrated."

Stan may not seem to be doing very much with these responses, but he is doing two things: encouraging Wilton to keep talking, and letting him know that he is *really* hearing what he has to say.

ACTIVITY

Understanding what is said

Work with a partner again, sitting face to face. Take turns being the talker and the listener.

1. One of you starts by telling the other about something good that is going on in your life. Keep it brief, about 20 to 30 seconds.
2. The listener's job is to think of different responses to what was said, by using each of these techniques: reflecting, paraphrasing, clarifying, and reflecting feelings. The talker's job is to help the listener do this. Write down your responses.
3. When you have finished, switch roles and do it again.

Practice Makes Habits

Practising active listening skills will probably feel awkward. Like any new skill—in sports, music or anywhere else—it doesn't come naturally unless you practise enough for it to become a habit.

Talking So People Will Listen

"Nobody listens to me," says Jenna. "Really. Even when I have something important to say, nobody ever listens. Maybe it's me, but I don't know. Everyone has a million things to do. Sometimes I wish the earth would stop for just one second."

Do you ever feel like Jenna? You go to talk to your dad, but he has work to do. Or you call a friend, but she has to study for a test. Jenna's right. People are busy. They each have responsibilities and pressures. So getting people to listen to you takes skills.

We are not talking about typical conversations here. These are tips for getting people to listen to you when it is important. The same techniques are useful in different situations: at work, at school, at home or with your friends.

Talking Tips

1. ***Watch your timing:***

   Make sure it's not a bad time for the people you want to have listen to you. If they're distracted, they won't be good listeners. If you aren't sure, check it out: "I know you are really busy, but I need to talk to you. If now isn't a good time, when would be?"

2. ***Get their full attention:***

   Ask for it if you have to. Do it nicely, but be assertive: "Dan, I really need your full attention."

   Prepare ahead of time:
   - What is the best way to start?
   - What will you say? Practise the words to yourself.
   - What will you do if it doesn't work out the way you want?

   Be assertive:
   - Assertive means standing up for yourself, and stating your case. It does not mean being aggressive.

3. ***Use "I messages":***

   "I messages" are statements that begin with your own opinions or feelings. These messages are particularly important when you are unhappy or upset with someone. Starting with "you" sounds like blaming, and puts the other person on the defensive. Someone who feels defensive is not going to be a good listener. Check the box on page 87 for the "I Message" formula.

4. ***Keep your cool:***

   It may be difficult if you don't get what you want, but if you lose your temper and lash out, what are the chances of getting a hearing next time? On the job, it could get you fired.

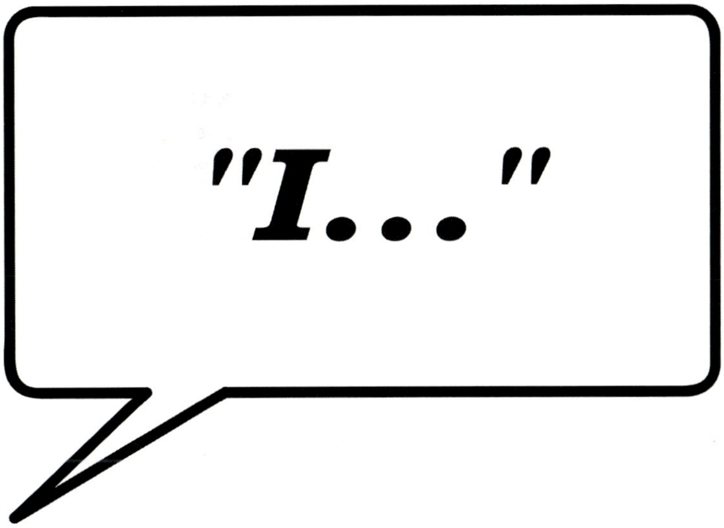

The "I Message" Formula

Practise using the formula as it is stated here. Then put statements in your own words.

"*I feel* ... (upset, disappointed, unfairly treated, discriminated against…)
… *when you…* (what the other person does that bothers you)
… *because* … (give your reasons)
… *and what I want you to do is…* (how you would like the other person to act)."

ACTIVITY

Ask for something

This is a role-play for teams of two. One of you be the employee, and the other one be the supervisor.

Scenario 1: You are scheduled to work next Saturday, but something has come up that you really want to do. You know the store is short-staffed right now, but you want to get the day off. How do you ask for it?

Scenario 2: You are unhappy about something your supervisor has done or said. You aren't sure if the supervisor knows how offensive it was to you. You would like to make sure that it doesn't happen again.

The employee chooses one scenario, and then talks to the supervisor.

The supervisor should make the employee work at asking, but not too hard. Use the Talking Tips on page 86.

When you are finished, talk about the situation, and what the best approach might be in real life.

Now switch roles, with the employee this time using the other scenario. When you are finished, talk about the best way to deal with this issue in real life.

Reflection

Think back to the picture you created of who you hope to become (page 60). Will developing good communication skills help you reach your goals? Give specific reasons why.

A Matter of Attitude

What Do You See?

A friend hands you a partially filled glass of water. If someone asks you how much water is in the glass, would you say it is half full or half empty? How you respond to that question is a reflection of your attitude. Your **attitude** is how you look at life. It will affect how you interact with others, how you respond to stress and success, and how you deal with the changes and opportunities in your life.

The Glass Is Half Full

Maintaining a positive attitude is an important factor in determining your future success and happiness. Think for a minute about all the tests and assignments you do right now. If you fail, do you work harder the next time? Or, do you simply give up and accept that you can't do it? A negative attitude sets you up for stress and defeat. If you accept that something is too difficult or overwhelming, it likely will be. This is called a **self-fulfilling prophecy**.

Having an optimistic attitude allows you to see the positive in any situation. Seeing the glass as half full rather than half empty allows you to recognize both possibility and potential. Recognizing opportunity allows you to progress and move forward.

Think Positively

Thinking positively means believing that something good will happen, even in negative situations. Individuals who think positively are generally more successful, self-confident, motivated—and healthier. Confidence helps ensure that you achieve your goals. When you're confident, you're willing to work hard and persevere through any challenge. Motivation is also increased, since positive thinkers believe that good things can and will happen for them.

Positive thinking can also have a tremendous effect on your health. When you are able to deal with stressful situations by thinking positively and engaging in positive self-talk, you often see the situations from a different perspective. **Self-talk** refers to the messages you tell yourself in any given situation. For example, if you try out for the school basketball team and aren't selected, do you tell yourself, "I'm no good at sports. I shouldn't have tried out anyway"? If so, you're exhibiting negative self-talk. A positive self-talker, on the other hand, would think, "Maybe if I work harder on my defensive skills, I'll make the team next year." When you are positive, others will enjoy being around you. You will receive encouragement and support and will be motivated to try your best at all times. Handling problems and difficult situations will also seem easier.

Are You Positively Charged?

Attitudes tend to lead to self-fulfilling prophecies. For example, if you think you'll never find a career that is "right" for you, you probably won't. But if you think that career planning is a great way to learn more about yourself and the hundreds of opportunities that await you in the world of work, you're well on your way to finding a fulfilling career.

Score yourself on the following quiz to find out whether you are "positively charged."

Scores

Mostly yes = 3 Sometimes = 2 Mostly no = 1

1. Am I friendly?
2. Do I refrain from complaining a lot?
3. Do I control my temper?
4. Do I feel well most of the time?
5. Do I keep my promises?
6. Do I readily admit my mistakes?
7. Can I be optimistic when others are disheartened?
8. Do I have a sense of duty and responsibility?
9. Do I speak well of others (*e.g.*, my teachers, coaches, employers)?
10. Do I follow directions willingly and ask questions when necessary?
11. Do I organize my work and keep up with it?
12. Is it easy for me to see the positive qualities in most people?

How Did You Score?

12–19 points: Mostly Negative

Maybe you should examine why you dwell on the "down" side. Low self-esteem or anger may be at the root of your negative energy. Are you being too hard on yourself? Or, perhaps you're not taking responsibility for your actions. Being negative about yourself is a self-fulfilling prophecy—that is, it can lead to self-defeating behaviours.

20–28 points: Middle Grounded

You are realistic and honest about what's going on with you. When you are confronted with an issue, you discuss it, deal with it, put it into perspective and move on. You are realistic and grounded: you don't wallow in the negative, but when it comes to new things, you are more conservative than enthusiastic. There's always room for you to grow—you might look for new challenges.

29–36 points: Positively Charged

You have a very upbeat attitude and you exude positive energy, which can be contagious. You are an optimist: you face the world with a smile, confident about yourself, your abilities and your interests. It's great to focus on the positive—but be careful not to "put on a happy face" when things aren't going well. Everyone runs out of self-esteem every now and then. You are a positive influence on others. Be yourself, and don't allow yourself to get drained by low-energy people.

Dealing With Criticism

Criticism is one of the most challenging aspects of communication with others. Your attitude will determine whether or not you accept criticism gracefully and grow from it, or whether you become defensive and close your mind to another's perspective.

Giving and accepting criticism is an essential skill that can be applied at school, in the world of work and in personal relations. **Constructive criticism** is criticism that is given in an attempt to help an individual grow and learn from an experience. For example, when professional athletes are in training, the coaching staff will often watch them at work, sometimes even videotaping their performance. Observations are then discussed with the athletes in an attempt to highlight aspects of performance that are not working and to offer strategies or suggestions for improvement. Such criticism, although focused on the negative, is actually meant to help the athletes experience more success.

When you have a positive attitude, your response to criticism will also be positive. Your mind will be open to suggestions and you will incorporate new behaviours into your daily life, at school, at work and at home. Having a negative attitude promotes defensiveness and closed mindedness when interacting with others. When friends or co-workers offer words of criticism, you may feel challenged and accused. This will affect not only your performance but also your relationships.

Offering criticism to others needs to be carefully considered. You should always keep in mind the positive aspects of a person's behaviour as well as the negative. Criticism should be specific and offer suggestions for improvement. The recipient of the criticism should not feel challenged or threatened, but rather should feel supported.

Links

Communication skills are recognized as among the most important transferable skills. There are many publications designed to help you develop these skills. Check your library.

Agencies created to help people with career development also support the development of communication skills. For example, the federal government includes a communication skills section on its WorkSearch website. Go to <www.careers.nelson.com> for a direct link to this and other related sites.

ACTIVITY

Dealing with criticism

1. Prepare a short paragraph (6–10 sentences) outlining what you feel are your most positive characteristics and strengths in terms of your communication with others. Share this paragraph with a friend.
2. After you have presented your paragraph, ask your partner for some constructive criticism on both your writing and presentation style. Make note of any suggestions.
3. Present your prepared paragraph to another classmate, keeping in mind the criticism given.
4. Write a short paragraph about this experience. Be sure to include how it felt to be criticized and to give criticism. Reflect on how giving and receiving criticism can help you when communicating with others.

Negotiating Skills

Working It Out

"Let's go see a movie," Jay said. His three closest friends were all at his house trying to decide how to spend Saturday afternoon.

Philip yawned. "There's nothing good on."

Mohammed, who was lying on the floor, turned over and started doing push-ups. "What about a bike ride uptown?"

"Oh, man," Marshall groaned as he watched Mohammed perform his fifteenth push-up. "Will you give up on that stuff? It makes me tired just watching you. Anyway, a bike ride would be okay, but my bike needs a new tire."

"What about calling Neil?" Jay said. "He's got that new computer game."

Marshall shook his head. "Neil's gone shopping with Judy for her Mom's birthday. How about that new video arcade?"

"Okay," Mohammed said, sitting up.

"Great idea," Philip said.

But Jay shook his head. "I hate that place."

Does this conversation remind you of anything? Maybe your family disagrees about when to watch television. Maybe your class project group is unable to decide who should do what.

We can't all agree, all of the time. But what happens when something has to get done and people aren't agreeing? One answer is **majority rule**, where more than half the people get what they want, and the rest lose. This is called a "win-lose" solution. It doesn't feel good to be on the losing side.

A better, but more difficult, way is to work toward agreement among all the members of the group. This is called a **consensus**, a unanimous agreement among a group of people. It is a "win-win" solution. Everybody wins; nobody loses.

Consensus Building

Jay and his friends are all bored, and nobody can figure out what to do. How can Jay and his friends reach a consensus? First, specify everyone's position. If you put it in a chart, it will look like this:

	Movies	Bike Riding	Video Arcade
Jay	yes	no opinion	no
Philip	no	no opinion	yes
Mohammed	no opinion	yes	yes
Marshall	no opinion	no opinion, but bike needs a new tire	yes

What this chart reveals is that there are two options with a definite "no" attached to them: going to the movies, and the video arcade. No one is totally against bike riding, and Mohammed is enthusiastic about it.

How can these friends build consensus about bike riding? Here is one possible scenario:

- Mohammed points out that there's a great bike riding trail they haven't tried.
- Jay has an extra bike tire in the garage; he suggests they fix Marshall's bike.
- Philip points out that it could be their last good bike ride before winter hits.
- Marshall likes the idea of getting help with his bike, so he agrees. Besides, he has heard that the trail is pretty neat.
- Mohammed says there's a good pizza place at the end of the trail.

Pretty soon, they're heading out the door with a plan of action that everyone has agreed to.

This group was keen to agree: they were friends and they wanted to do something together. But other factors also made it a win-win situation.

ACTIVITY

Saturday afternoon consensus building

As a group in class, examine how Jay and his friends reached consensus. Then answer the following questions:

1. How did it help the group that everyone made suggestions?
2. How did it help the group that no one gave up and left?
3. Do you think *how* they spoke to each other was important? When you answer this question, think about respect and the ability to listen.
4. What kind of "working it out" skills did Mohammed demonstrate? What about Jay?
5. How did mentioning the positive factors help to build consensus?
6. How was each boy's needs and wants met through the conversation? You know how Marshall's needs were met. Can you guess about the others?

ACTIVITY

Create your own win-win solution

Working in groups, your task is to answer this question and come to a consensus:

> *What is the best and fairest way for your teacher to assess how well each of you has learned and used the communication skills discussed in this unit, and give you each a mark for this section of the course?*

What answer did you agree upon? Why did you choose that method? What did you do within your group that helped you reach a consensus? Be prepared to report to the whole class on your discussions.

Here are two other terms often used to describe ways of reaching a consensus.

- A **negotiation** is a discussion designed to result in an agreement. Examples of negotiations would be: the United Auto Workers negotiating a new contract with General Motors, Israel and Syria negotiating control of the Golan Heights on their border, or you negotiating with the Vice-Principal about when you will serve your detention.

- **Conflict resolution** is a process designed to bring together people or groups who have disagreed and been hostile. Often there is a mediator involved, someone who is not part of the dispute, whose job is to help the others reach some agreement.

Mediators can be used in negotiations as well. Some schools have conflict resolution or **peer mediation** programs where students act as mediators to help other students work out their differences. Does your school have such a program?

Getting to a Win-Win Solution

- Use active listening.
- Find out what is really important to the people involved.
- Get the people to talk, and listen, to each other.
- Make sure everybody gets a say in the discussion.
- Look for solutions no one has thought of yet.
- Make sure everybody agrees with the solution.

Teamwork Skills

Teaming Up

Teamwork has become one of the most important elements of work today. It hasn't always been this way, though. Consider what happened at Lights Up Inc., a company that makes lamps and other lighting fixtures.

At Lights Up Inc., the people who made the light fixtures didn't talk to the people who designed them. The people who designed the light fixtures didn't talk to the people who sold them. Rather, the managers talked to each other. If one of the industrial engineers, who worked in Halifax, had a design problem that would affect the manufacturing process, which was done in a factory in Truro, he told his manager, who then brought it up at the once-a-week managerial meeting.

This system broke down for three reasons:

1. In the late 1980s, Canada went into a recession, and companies had to become more efficient, or they would go bankrupt. They realized that they didn't need so many managers. Why not just have the industrial engineer talk to the equipment operator?

2. Loosening trade barriers between countries meant competition from manufacturers around the world. Canadians saw other lamps and liked them. Lights Up Inc. had to adapt quickly in order to survive. The salespeople needed to let the industrial designers know right away what customers wanted. The company couldn't wait until the next week's managerial meeting.

3. Computerization meant everyone could now talk to each other through e-mail no matter where they worked, and the conversations could be as fast as any face-to-face meeting.

How does Lights Up Inc. run its business today? By having everyone work in teams. An idea for a new light fixture starts as brainstorming among a team of designers, salespeople and production workers. Problems that used to take weeks to solve get solved in a day. Each member of the team is able to understand the needs of other members. And, rather than having managers whose only job it is to oversee people, one member of the team is its leader.

There is almost no one in today's workplace who does a job in isolation. Each worker has to get along with people who have different ideas, attitudes, opinions and beliefs.

Teamwork skills are really a combination of interpersonal skills, communication skills and consensus-building skills.

ACTIVITY

Thinking about teams

You've probably been on a number of teams. Perhaps you've played on a sports team, played in a band or musical group, been part of a stage production, or worked on a group project for a class. These have given you teamwork experience, although you may not have thought much about it at the time.

Take a deeper look at teamwork. Write down your answers to these questions:

1. What do you like about doing group work in school?
2. What do you dislike about doing group work in school?
3. Would you like group work more if you could pick the people in your group? Why or why not?
4. If you could pick your own group, what personal qualities would you like your group members to have? Why?
5. Based upon your experience with group work in school, what do you think are the most important teamwork skills?

Keep this list in your portfolio.

Good Team Members

Your list of qualities for a good group member probably includes some variations of these three items:

- good attitude—fits in and works well with others
- can do the job—has the necessary skills and abilities
- will do the job—is reliable and can be counted on

ACTIVITY

Your teamwork skills

Now look at your own qualities that relate to working with others in a group.

1. Use a chart like the one below. In the first column, list all groups, teams, clubs or other organizations to which you have belonged. Leave some space beneath each one.
2. In the second column, write all the transferable skills that you have learned from being in that group.

Groups, Clubs, Teams, Organizations	**Transferable Skills I Have Learned From the Experience**
e.g., *ball hockey* *newsletter committee*	*e.g.,* *teamwork* *meeting deadlines*

Keep this chart in your Employability Skills Portfolio.

Group Dynamics

Why do geese fly in formation, instead of alone? Geese fly about 10 percent faster in formation, and up to 70 percent farther. Geese also share the lead. When the lead goose tires and rotates back into the "V", another moves forward as the leader. Also, when a weak goose drops out of the flight, a stronger goose drops back also, to help and protect it.

ACTIVITY

Synergy

Look up the word "synergy" in the dictionary. How does it relate to how the geese survive? How does it relate to your own teamwork?

Of course, human beings are more complex than geese. But when you work in groups, you have to contribute to the overall effort, and help others. In a band, a drama group or a sports team, everybody has a role to play. How does synergy relate to these groups?

Group dynamics have to do with the way group members deal with each other. Studying groups in action can tell us what works and what doesn't work in a group or team.

ACTIVITY

Fishbowl

Divide the class into two groups of equal size. Arrange the desks so that one group sits in a circle, facing each other, in the middle of the room. The second group sits in another circle, outside the first group. This arrangement is called a fishbowl. The inside group has a task to perform together. The outside group observes the inside group performing its task.

The task of the inner group is a "team-building exercise" designed to get the group members working together. Here is a simple one. Your teacher may have others from which to choose.

The Task:

Using index cards, create the tallest house of cards you can. You have 10 minutes. This is a contest.

Each member of the outer group is assigned one member of the inner group to observe. Each observer takes notes on what their person does and says during the activity.

After 10 minutes, measure the height of the structure and record it.

Now switch the groups around. The new inner group has the same task to perform, also within 10 minutes.

The new outer group observes, each member taking notes on the actions of the person they are assigned to observe.

After 10 minutes, measure the height of the new structure and record it.

Now debrief the exercise. Each group, in turn, gives their observations about the activities of the other group. Keep in mind what we learned about giving and receiving feedback. Answer the following questions:

1. What happened in the group that helped them to work effectively as a team?
2. What happened in the group that got in the way of their being an effective team?
3. From the comments, make two master lists, one with things that help a team to be effective, and the other with things that keep a team from being effective.
4. Compare your lists with the ones below. Add any that you think are needed on your lists.

   All class members keep a copy of these lists in their portfolios.

What Makes a Good Team?

- A clear goal. Everyone understands and agrees.
- High standards. Everyone giving their best.
- Strong leadership. Direction, encouragement, inspiration and support.
- Members supporting and helping each other.

Teamwork Means "All for One and One for All"

Every team is composed of individuals. For the group to function well, its individuals must be encouraged to give their best. So a good group is one in which individual members can:

Contribute ideas openly. How is the group ever going to get the best out of its members if they aren't free to offer what they have?

Stay focused. We can all remember times when discussion went on too long, or wandered far way from topic.

Feel free to ask questions. Have you ever figured everyone knew what was going on but you? A good group allows people to say: "Hold on a second. I don't get this." Chances are, you aren't the only one who doesn't understand.

Actively seek information and opinions. Be curious and active about learning new things.

Follow directions. Once a decision has been taken, all members work towards the common goal.

Solve problems. Each team member should feel free to contribute their unique skills and knowledge to deal with problems.

Leadership

The leader is concerned about the direction of the group:
Where do we want to go? Why? Are we still going in the direction we want? Do we need to change direction?

ACTIVITY

Leaders

1. Think of someone you know who is a good leader. It doesn't matter how old the person is, or what position the person holds. List characteristics that make that person an effective leader.
2. Discuss your list with the rest of the class, and come up with a master list of good leadership characteristics.
3. As a class, brainstorm a list of characteristics that would make someone a bad leader.
4. Assess your own potential as a leader based on these characteristics.

Leadership in Action

"The Outdoor Education program at our school included a spring backpacking trip. One of the best learning experiences was right at the beginning of the trip. We had to go up a steep trail to get on top of a ridge. Because the group included students with varying degrees of physical fitness and experience in the bush, it didn't take long before some of them, labouring under heavy packs they had never carried before, were lagging behind, while others wanted to rush to the top of the ridge. One of our ground rules was that if anyone lost sight of the person directly in front, we would stop the whole group until everyone was together again. Some of the more athletic members of the group got upset at the delays. They didn't need to rest. Others, however, caught on quickly and stayed behind to help and encourage those who were having a harder hike. By the time we got to the top of the ridge and looked out over the rugged countryside, most people understood. We were a team. We did things together. We succeeded together. The leaders were not the ones who were the fastest to the top."

—High School Teacher

Reflection

Go back to the chart of transferable skills you made in the Discovery activity on page 63. Add any further information that now seems relevant. Choose at least two skills that you want to work on, and create a plan for developing those skills.

In our earlier analogy of a hike in the bush (page 54), we talked about the destination, the compass and the map. The leader uses all of these to keep the team going in the right direction. Good leaders, however, are never so focused on the destination that they forget about the team members. If no one is following, you aren't leading.

Key Terms

self-assessment
interest
skill
multiple intelligences
potential
learning style
personality type
personal profile
values
external influences
career goals
transferable skills
employability skills
school skills
personal management skills
self-motivation
communication skills
attitude
self-talk
constructive criticism
teamwork skills

Use a concept map or another graphic organizer, to summarize the key ideas in this unit. Build on the key terms and add words, phrases and/or images that will help remind you of those key ideas.

Reflection

Find the activity How Well Do You Know Yourself? (page 31) in your portfolio and give yourself new ratings on each of the lines. Put today's date next to the new scores. Do you have a better knowledge of yourself now than you did when you first rated yourself on this exercise? Why or why not?

Questions

Knowledge/Understanding

1. Describe the purpose and use of self-assessment and standardized assessment tools in the career development process. Use specific examples drawn from your experience during this unit.
2. List ten skills that are important for your personal career development. Provide a specific example from your own experience to illustrate each skill and indicate two ways in which each of those skills can be further developed.

Thinking/Inquiry

3. Write a paragraph that summarizes the most important things you learned about yourself in this unit.
4. Make a list of five things you'd like to change or strengthen about yourself. What internal and external influences will help you make those changes?
5. Think of one learning experience that has had a significant effect on you. What knowledge did you acquire? What skills did you develop? What made the experience meaningful and memorable?

Communication

6. Choose a realistic recruitment situation (*e.g.*, you need a drummer in your band, you want a pen pal, you need people to work on the yearbook) and write an advertisement that explains that situation and outlines what skills and attitudes you would be looking for in a respondent. Give examples so your expectations are clear.

Application

7. With a group, design an activity that uses the fishbowl technique (page 97) to demonstrate effective communication skills. Observers should use checklists of these skills to focus their observations and provide feedback.
8. Go to <www.careers.nelson.com>. Complete the inventory provided and analyse the results.

Taking Stock: Your Portfolio

1. Review the contents.
2. Reconsider your initial responses.
3. Summarize the most important information.

UNIT 3

What Is Out There for Me?

What opportunities are over the horizon? What should I be looking for? How do I get there?

Life is a voyage, and voyages need maps. Even though your future is unknown, you need some idea of where you're going and how to get there.

How can I create a map of career opportunities?

SECTION

"If I keep a green bough in my heart, the singing bird will come."

—*Chinese proverb*

What Is Out There for Me?

In this unit you will:

- research and analyse information about work and learning opportunities
- match your skills and interests to different occupations
- assess the advantages and disadvantages of self-employment
- discuss your employment rights and responsibilities
- predict how change in the world at large will affect future opportunities
- identify effective ways of coping with change
- compare a variety of learning opportunities that suit your interests, skills and broad career goals

You have been offered a ticket to anywhere in the world. Where do you want to go?

You probably already have some idea about your destination. But wait—how much do you know about the rest of the world? Maybe there are destinations that you don't know anything about, and that you would enjoy much more. It's a big world—maybe you should do a little research. Maybe even nearby destinations have surprises in store for you.

In the same way, when you think "careers" you may think only of the ones held by people in your family, or your friends' families.

Look at these objects. Choose one, and list all of the people who had a hand in making it. Look beyond the obvious occupations. Are you surprised by possibilities?

Maybe you have a career destination in mind already, or maybe you don't. Either way, it makes sense to spend time researching the range of destinations that would suit you. Look beyond the immediate horizon.

DISCOVERY

Whisper

Think of an occupation that interests you, and whisper it to the person next to you.

Everyone in the class stands up, and the teacher calls out a list of common occupations. The person you mentioned your occupation to will sit down when that occupation is called. You sit down when your partner's occupation is called.

After the teacher has called out the list of common occupations, how many of you are still standing? What occupations haven't been called?

Write down all the occupations that you and your classmates mentioned. How many occupations do you think there are in Canada?

Julia's Story

Opportunity and change go together. The world is changing very rapidly, including the world of work.

If we continue the metaphor of your career as a voyage, storms are a distinct possibility. You need to be confident that you can weather the storms. That's a lesson Julia learned from her mother.

Julia was waiting for her mom to come home. Friday was a special night in her house: she was finished school for the week, and her mom was finished work. Maybe they'd go out to the corner restaurant for Chinese food, or order in a pizza.

They often had their best talks on Friday nights. Tonight Julia had a couple of things on her mind. Christmas was coming up. She knew there wasn't much money—there never was—but she hoped that her mom would be able to afford contact lenses for her, as well as get her a new outfit she'd been eyeing at the store. She could maybe ask tonight. The other thing was this boy in class: she thought maybe he liked her, and her best friend thought so too. Julia sometimes discussed things like that with her mother—not all the time, but it always felt good to know that she could if she wanted to, and that her mother would listen.

Julia had already done some of her weekend homework, and she had tidied up the place a bit for her mom. Right now, she was idly drawing on a piece of paper. Art was her favourite subject, and she was always designing buildings and interiors in her head. She was drawing a plan for the house she'd buy for her mom and her if she won a million dollars tomorrow.

She heard the elevator, and then her mother's key in the lock. Her mom came in, put her purse and bag down by the door, and turned to take her coat off. She looked tired, but she usually looked tired when she came home from work.

"Hi, mom," Julia called out.

"Hi, babe," her mother answered. She didn't sound very cheerful. Julia looked up, ready to give her a hug. "Give me a minute," her mother said. "I need to call your Aunt Julia." She picked up the cordless phone and went into her bedroom, shutting the door behind her. Julia was suddenly worried that something was wrong. Her mother always called Aunt Julia whenever anything was wrong.

Whatever it was, her mother was talking so quietly Julia couldn't overhear anything. She looked at the picture she had been drawing. It seemed silly now; she began drawing lines across it. The worst fear came into her mind—maybe her mother was sick. Thoughts of Chinese food were gone now. She didn't really need contact lenses—her glasses were fine.

Her mother opened the bedroom door. She laid the phone on the table as she sat down across from Julia.

"Mom?" Julia asked. Her mother reached out her hand. Such a strong hand it was, capable of doing so many things.

"Julia. I just had to talk to your aunt first. She's coming over. I got bad news at work. They're going to close the company and move all the jobs down to Tennessee. I'm out of a job January second."

Julia felt two feelings: shock, but also relief that her mother wasn't sick. "What'll we do?" she heard herself saying.

Her mother smiled a lopsided smile. "I'll think of something."

"But how could they do that, mom? You've been there for years, and you work so hard." It was true. Her mother even brought work home. Julia felt angry now.

"I know, baby," her mom said. "They decided they could get the work done cheaper in the States. Everyone in the Canadian operation is out on the street. But don't you worry. I'm still working until January, and then I'll get a month's pay after that."

"I hate them, Mom!" Julia burst into tears. How unfair it was!

"I know, honey. It's not fair. Come here." She took Julia's hand and drew her close. They hugged each other for a few minutes.

Her mother held her hand and smiled at her. "You know, I never intended to stay at that job forever, anyway. I always planned to get into marketing, and I've been looking around. I've already checked out some courses. I know I can get some retraining. And your Aunt Julia knows people I can talk to. So we'll be okay."

Julia thought this over. "Really, mom?"

"Yes, really," her mother answered. "I saw this coming, even though it's still a shock when it happens." She sighed, and looked around the kitchen. "In the meantime, let's get some food together so we're ready for your Aunt Julia."

Julia felt relieved. Her aunt was coming over. She'd have some ideas, and anyway, she had this knack of always making everyone feel better.

ACTIVITY

About Julia

It is difficult to be optimistic when faced with job loss, but Julia's mother manages to do so.

1. What has she done to prepare herself in case a change like this happened?
2. What can she do now that she knows she will lose her job?
3. Go back to Opportunity Hunting in Unit 1 (page 26). What positive opportunities did you write down for "your job is gone"?
4. How could these options apply to Julia's mom?

SECTION 1

Navigating the World of Work

Think about planning that once-in-a-lifetime-trip again. Would you plan a sports vacation? A relaxing trip to a beach? A safari? A learning experience? A return to your roots? A shopping spree? Whatever your choice, you would start researching destinations based on what you want out of the trip.

Similarly, planning your trip into the world of work, you should start with at least a general idea of what you want, and think about your destination. You should check out different maps to get an overall idea of where you are heading and what it will take to get there. And you should do plenty of research.

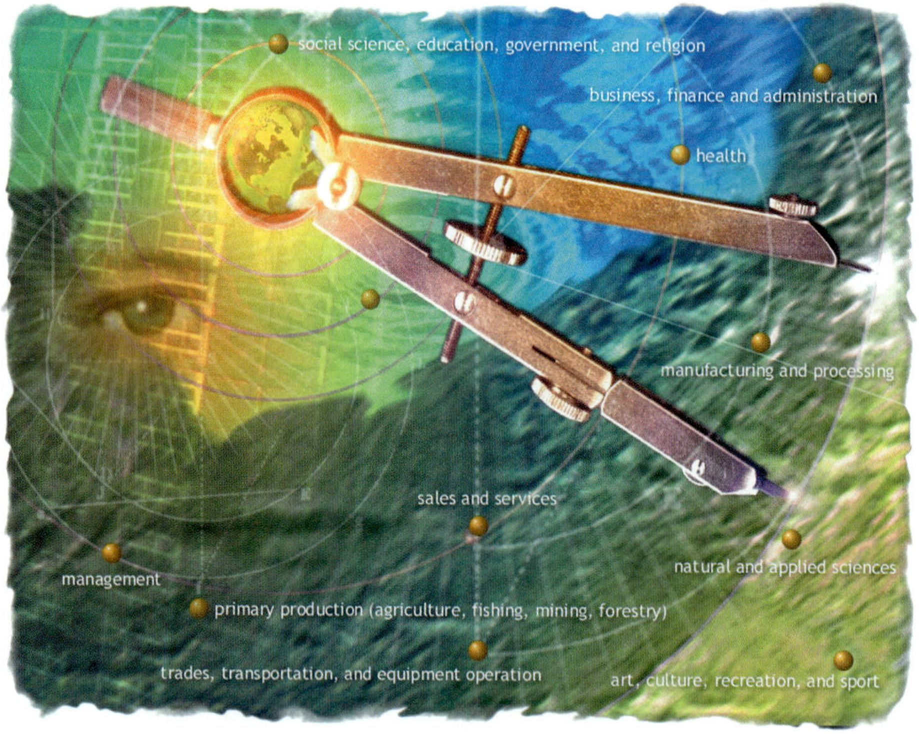

DISCOVERY

Where to research

You want to learn about the world of work. Make a list of possible resources you could use to find out more. Start with general categories ("magazine articles" or "the Internet"), and then think of specific organizations and people that you could contact.

Where Do I Start?

Focus on Yourself

There are thousands and thousands of occupations in the world. How are you going to break down your research into a manageable task?

Start with what you know about yourself. For instance, you could focus on a major interest. You could find out what kinds of work people who share this interest do. Maybe you have a passion for live performance. Look at the flowchart below; it shows you all of the jobs necessary for putting on a performance.

Links

Content of the flowchart and profiles on this page is reproduced from *The Spotlight's On*, a publication of the Cultural Human Resources Council. The CHRC has information about many cultural occupations, including jobs in media, publishing and broadcasting. Visit <www.careers.nelson.com> for a link to the CHRC.

Robert Marinier, Playwright

Robert's career began in high school when he discovered that he enjoyed acting and had a knack for writing plays. Although he later took specialized training in acting, Robert found that he was more a playwright than an actor. Robert says a playwright has to analyse and understand every dramatic device: "What's a character? What's dialogue? What's dramatic action? Why does a scene work in one play and not another? You need to know the answers." Interested in writing plays? "Get practice by acting and directing. See as many plays as you can. And, most of all, develop your storytelling skills."

Sheila Johnston, Education/Group Sales Manager, Grand Theatre

Sheila thinks of herself as a sales rep and a communicator, helping people to have an enhanced theatre experience: "When I promote a play, I study and research it and prepare an audience guide." Sheila learned the importance of audience relations as a ticket seller at age 16. "People were always asking me about the plays." She also developed a love of theatre as a place that is "exciting and always changing." In addition to building good communication skills and getting hands-on theatre experience "so you know the vocabulary," Sheila recommends "a university program that emphasizes reading and writing or a college diploma in public relations."

Playwright
Creates an original work for the stage.

Dramaturge
Works with playwright or director to further develop a script.

↓

Choreographer
Creates movement for live performances including dance, opera and theatre.

↓

Composer
Creates music for opera, musical theatre and ballet.

↓

Librettist
Creates a story and words for opera, musical theatre and ballet.

↓

Interpretive Performer/Artist
Performs the creator's work before an audience.

Agent
Markets the skills of creators and performers to producers and directors.

↓

General Manager/Administrative Director/Managing Director
Oversees the operations of an arts organization.

Controller/Auditor

↓

Artist Manager
Sells artist's performances to presenters and impresarios.

Marketing and Communications Manager/Director
Runs sales campaigns, develops spin-off products and oversees publicity staff.

Impresario
Brings live performances to many communities.

↓

↓

Artistic Director
Oversees the artistic direction of a performing company or theatre.

Costume, Set, and Lighting Designers

↓

Fund-raiser/Membership Director
Raises funds from individuals, foundations and corporate sponsors.

↓

Director
Interprets the creator's work and directs the performers and designers.

↓

Set Builder/Carpenter/Painter

Production Manager
Ensures that the work of creative teams is on time and on budget.

Warehouse Manager
Handles supplies of company's equipment and products.

↓

Stage Manager
Ensures the smooth running of performances.

Stagehand
Installs and moves scenery, furniture and props, and operates the curtain.

↓

Lighting Technician/Assistant

Technical Director
Oversees set design, lighting and sound.

Sound Technician/Assistant
Amplifies music and operates special sound effects.

↓

Make-up Artist
Provides appropriate make-up for performers.

↓

Wig Maker, Wig Dresser

Head of Wardrobe/Wardrobe Master/Mistress
Oversees maintenance of costumes during performances.

Dresser/Wardrobe Attendant

↓

Publicist
Markets the production to the public.

↓

Box Office Manager
Monitors availability of seating and oversees ticket sellers.

Ticket Seller

↓

Front of House Manager
Ensures audience's comfort and safety, and oversees ushers.

Usher

↓

Audience

Michael Leclair, Tent Master, Le Cirque du Soleil

Michael was a carpenter who fell in love with the circus. Today he manages a crew that puts up a Big Top holding 2,500 people. "We rig the tent by putting up ropes and cables, welding vinyl, inserting grommets, and customizing the tent for different apparatus." Michael says circuses are always looking for men and women to work as riggers. "You need good manual dexterity and a willingness to be on call 24 hours a day. You can't be afraid of heights." Attitude is critical. "Ninety per cent of this job is heart," Michael says. "It's intense work, mentally and physically."

Donna Gliddon, Theatrical Wig Maker

It usually takes one to two weeks of handcrafting to make a wig after researching and creating the style. "First, I build the wig's foundation on a wooden block the size of the actor's head," Donna explains. "Second, I fit it to the actor to determine the hairlines. After sewing in the hairlines, I knot the wig with human, yak or synthetic hair." Would-be wig makers should consider getting a hairdresser's licence and then "take specialized training in Britain or the U.S. or on the job. There's no program in Canada."

Is there a big demand for skilled wig makers? "Huge," Donna says. "I'm freelance and I work all the time."

Zaib Shaikh, Actor

Zaib always wanted to be an actor, and has a B.A. Honours in Theatre and Drama and a college diploma in Acting. "As well as auditioning for work, I'm learning to create my own opportunities." Zaib has co-founded a theatre company and received funding for a high school play about drinking and driving. "The skills I learned writing essays at university helped me write a good grant proposal." Zaib says actors need many other skills to survive: "Looking for work requires good organizational and time management skills. And, since you have to connect with directors and agents, you need great 'person' skills."

ACTIVITY

Finding the common threads

1. Read the profiles on pages 107 and 108, and make a list of interests, skills, characteristics and values that these people have in common. Which of these do you share?
2. Working with a group of people who share an interest of yours, write a list of all the occupations associated with that interest. How many can you think of?

Identifying Fields of Work

Mapping the World of Work

As you can see, there are many different jobs in the field of live performance. If you were interested in this area, it would make sense to look at the entire field, instead of just saying "I want to be an actor." You can do this kind of exploration because the world of work has been mapped into sets of related occupations or **fields of work**. This allows you to choose an area that interests you, and then discover all sorts of possibilities in it that you hadn't thought of before. And that helps you discover new opportunities.

Benefits of Exploring Fields of Work

- Many occupations within a field may suit your interests, abilities and characteristics.
- You may never have heard of some occupations related to your interests.
- New occupations are created all the time. If you focus on the field, you will hear about them.
- Narrowing your focus too soon means you might miss opportunities that could be great for you.

Kim's Story

Kim loved art in high school, and later completed a graphic design program at college. When she graduated she wanted to work with people, but she ended up working by herself in a cubicle. A friend suggested she apply for work at an insurance company as a salesperson. She got the job, and much to her surprise, she loved it. Kim has become a very successful insurance agent, and wouldn't trade it for anything!

John's Story

John decided in high school that he wanted to be an automotive mechanic. He focused all his energies on his studies and took all the math, science and technology courses that his school offered. John entered college with one goal in mind—to be an auto mechanic. During his first year, John struggled with the hands-on portion of the program. He did really well in his technology courses, but just couldn't get the hang of the tools and equipment in the shop. He had never really considered other options. He then decided to take some extra electronics courses as electives and eventually switched programs and became a successful electronics technician.

ACTIVITY

Keeping options open

1. What aspects of themselves did Kim and John pay too little attention to?
2. What training might have been more fulfilling for Kim?
3. What advice would you have given John while he was still in high school?
4. Ask some adults you know how they ended up with their occupations. Write a brief paragraph showing the path one of them took. Did this person keep options open when he or she was young?

The Sector Councils

A **sector council** brings together business, labour and other interests within a particular industry. There are more than 40 sector councils in Canada, including the following:

- Canadian Automotive Repair and Service Council
- Canadian Council of Professional Fish Harvesters
- Canadian Trucking Human Resources Council
- Cultural Human Resources Council
- Electronic and Appliance Service Industry
- Software Human Resources Council
- Petroleum Industry Human Resource Committee

Each council exists to inform the public about the work of its sector, how important it is for the economy, what opportunities exist in it, and how young people can choose a career in it. Many sector councils have career awareness materials (*e.g.*, booklets, brochures and CD-ROMs) that describe typical occupations in their sector. All of them provide information.

ACTIVITY

Sector research

Search the Internet (try the Human Resources and Skills Development Canada site), or contact HRSDC to find a list of sector councils. Choose one council, and find out more about the field of work it represents. Identify specific employers who are active in that sector. How can you find out where they are located, whether they are expanding, what their plans are for the future? Are there employers in your area of interest in this sector?

Unions and Professional Associations

Across Canada, people who do similar work are often organized into **trade unions** or **professional associations**.

The main purpose of a union is to provide a common voice in negotiating a contract or collective agreement for its members. This sets out the terms and pay rates under which union members will work for an employer, over and above the minimum standards set by provincial or federal labour laws. Unions have a leadership elected by the members, and each individual workplace has a local branch. Unions in Newfoundland and Labrador are grouped into provincial and federal associations, the Newfoundland and Labrador Federation of Labour and the Canadian Labour Congress.

A well-known union is the Canadian Auto Workers. Its 215,000 members are found not only in the auto industry, but also in industries as diverse as aerospace, mining and smelting, and hospitality. In addition to negotiating contracts, the CAW provides services to its members and is active on social issues that affect them, such as advocating on behalf of a national child care policy.

Professional associations are similar to unions in many ways, except that they tend to represent individual members of an entire profession. They present a common voice for their membership, establishing fee schedules and sometimes lobbying governments for legislative change. They also provide services for their members. The Newfoundland and Labrador Medical Association is a well-known example of such an association.

Professional associations are different from regulatory or governing bodies, which set the standards that individual members of a profession must meet, and give them licences to practice. Newfoundland and Labrador examples of regulatory bodies include the Law Society of Newfoundland and Labrador, the Newfoundland and Labrador Psychology Board, and the Institute of Chartered Accountants of Newfoundland and Labrador. Many other professions, such as nurses and registered social workers, are governed by similar bodies.

Links

Your school may have access to Internet-based programs that can help you research fields of work and occupations. If you search an occupation with *Career Guidance Resource Tool,* for instance, it will provide you with the mailing addresses and websites of related professional associations. Here are some organizations to start with:

- Newfoundland and Labrador Federation of Labour
- Newfoundland and Labrador Medical Association
- Newfoundland and Labrador Psychology Board
- Law Society of Newfoundland and Labrador
- Newfoundland and Labrador Teachers' Association

Visit <www.careers.nelson.com> for links to these and other organizations.

The National Occupational Classification

The **National Occupational Classification 2001 (NOC)** is a list that describes and classifies Canadian **occupations**. It provides descriptions for more than 520 occupational unit groups and about 30,000 individual occupational titles.

The information catalogued in the National Occupational Classification is available on-line. The data is also used by other groups. For instance, *Job Futures*, a reference tool published by the federal government, uses labour market data and the NOC to provide salary ranges for different occupational groups. And *Profile Desktop 2004*, a CD-ROM published by Nelson Thomson Learning, combines all the NOC information and *Job Futures* data in a searchable database.

The NOC classifies occupations in two ways: skill type and skill level.

Skill Type

Here are the ten major categories under skill type. Since most career materials produced in Canada refer to NOC categories and codes, these are the categories we will use when we are talking about occupational fields:

0	management
1	business, finance and administration
2	natural and applied sciences
3	health
4	social science, education, government and religion
5	art, culture, recreation and sport
6	sales and services
7	trades, transportation, and equipment operation
8	primary production (agriculture, fishing, mining, forestry)
9	manufacturing and processing

Skill Level

There are four basic skill levels:

- university degree (graduate or undergraduate)
- college or technical school training; apprenticeship training
- high school completion; on-the-job training
- short demonstration training (no formal education requirements)

These four levels are identified numerically:

1	professional
2 or 3	technical, para-professional, skilled
4 or 5	intermediate (semi-skilled)
6	labouring and elemental

These numbers represent a way of charting all occupations. For example, under NOC classification, an audiologist is classified as 3141. This means that it belongs in major skill type 3—health—with skill level 1, professional. The final "41" specifies the job more closely: "314" designates occupations in therapy and assessment, and the additional 1 points specifically to audiology.

Comparing Systems

Your public and school libraries probably use the Dewey decimal system for cataloguing nonfiction books. Can you see similarities between the Dewey decimal system and the way the NOC classifies occupations?

Your Guidance office may have copies of NOC publications. These include:

- *Occupational Descriptions*, which details more than 500 occupations
- *Career Handbook*, second edition, which links types of work with characteristics most common among people doing that work

ACTIVITY

Using the NOC

1. Choose an NOC field that interests you. Think of as many occupations as possible that fall into that category.
2. Go to <www.careers.nelson.com> for a link to the full **NOC** classification. Then answer the following questions:
   a) Which skill level has the most occupational groups? Which has the fewest?
   b) Which skill type has the most occupational groups? Which has the fewest?

Case Studies

Ursula
As a nurse, Ursula was always fiercely devoted to the welfare of the patients in her care. Now that she works as a *director of nursing* for a retirement home, she misses the daily contact with patients, so she tries to visit with the residents as much as she can.

Ian
More than just a *carpenter*, Ian can make almost anything with his hands. He has jobs booked six months in advance, but he's thinking of how he can move to a small town with his family.

Donna
As *pay and benefits clerk* for a community college, Donna is a central part of the administration. Whenever a difficult question comes up, someone says, "Ask Donna."

Amy
Amy has loved science since she was young, and she received high honours for her work in school. Today she does research as a *biologist* at a major hospital.

Brendan
A *graphic designer* for an advertising firm, Brendan works with high-end computers and large graphic display screens. He likes to call himself a "pixel pusher" or a "propeller-head," but that's because he's shy about calling himself an artist.

Ludmila
As an *audiologist*, Ludmila helps to test people's hearing and fit them for hearing aids. Her clients appreciate her sensitivity, patience and good humour.

Terry
Terry wasn't sure he wanted to be a *teacher* before he started. Today, he loves it. He's teaching Career Studies this year. It's a demanding job, but it has huge rewards.

Menno
Menno's family have been *farmers* for at least five generations. Menno has no doubt that it is the world's most rewarding occupation, and one that crosses all boundaries. To farm successfully, you have to know something about everything.

Swaminathan
Swaminathan works for a company that is a major supplier to the automotive industry. He makes a good living for his family as a *machine operator*, making plastic bumpers for cars.

Sue
There's no easy way to describe being a *police officer*. For Sue, one of the greatest rewards is thinking about the times she made a difference in someone's life.

ACTIVITY

Make a match

1. Which of the ten NOC occupational fields does each of these ten people represent?
2. What similarities can you see among their occupations?
3. Here is another list of ten occupations. Which person do you think is most suited to each of these occupations? Justify your decisions, and compare them with your classmates'.
   - **a)** long-distance truck driver
   - **b)** family doctor
   - **c)** minister of religion
   - **d)** electrical engineer
   - **e)** professional football player
   - **f)** regional sales agent
   - **g)** nickel miner
   - **h)** senior administrator
   - **i)** bottling-machine operator
   - **j)** securities analyst

Exploring Fields of Work

Choose Your Starting Place

Making good career decisions means having career goals. At this point, you are focusing on broad goals—fields of work that include a variety of occupations. Relate the knowledge you acquire about the fields to your own characteristics, but remember: you are changing, and so are the occupational fields.

How do you start exploring fields of work? First, think about what is most important to you. Is it most important to find work that fits your interests, abilities or other characteristics? Or is some other factor even more important? (You may need to refer back to the self-discovery activities in Unit 2.)

Starting With Your Interests

Your Situation	How You Can Start
You have only a vague idea of the kind of work you would like to do (*e.g.*, helping people).	Go through the lists of occupational fields and pick out the ones that relate to your interest. Sometimes, only part of the field is related to your interest, so look carefully.
You have a definite interest in a particular field (*e.g.*, health, which includes medicine), but you have no definite occupations in mind.	Find out whether there are any other fields that have similar characteristics to the one that interests you.
You want to check out the occupational fields suggested by the occupations in your interest inventory. (See Unit 2.)	Some interest inventories suggest occupational fields, while others list only individual occupations. Go from the occupations to the broader fields.
You have a strong interest in one occupation (or a few of them).	Discover that occupation's field, and check the whole field for similar occupations. It helps if you know why you like this occupation. Look for other fields that might also have these characteristics.

Starting With Your Abilities

What are you good at now, or what could you be good at in the future? What occupational fields relate to your strongest abilities and skills? Warning: there are usually more related fields than you think.

For example, if you have ability and skill in working with your hands, trades (7) is an obvious field, but health (3) may also be appropriate. Surgeons, dentists, hygienists and technicians all need "finger dexterity." There are technicians in many fields.

Starting With Other Characteristics

This approach is similar to starting with interests and abilities. Some examples of other characteristics might be:

- you really want to work outdoors
- your disability would make some work difficult or impossible
- you like to be in charge

Not all of the occupations within any field will suit you.

Links

On-line inventories will point you to fields of work that typically suit people with results similar to your own. If you didn't try any on-line inventories in Unit 2, this is an excellent time to do so. Go to <www.careers.nelson.com> for links to suggested inventories.

You may also want to use *Profile Desktop 2004*, a CD-ROM with simple inventories—all of which are in electronic form—that will direct you to specific NOC occupational categories. Ask your teacher or guidance counsellor if your school has this or other career-related software programs.

Using the Internet for Research

The Internet is a tremendous source of information about occupational fields, individual occupations and **jobs**. And learning how to search the Net successfully is another great transferable skill.

Internet Search Tips

- Add words to narrow the search:
  - entering "careers" leads to 852,000,000 sites
  - entering "careers" and "environment" and "Canada" and "Newfoundland" and "Labrador" leads to 80,100 sites
- Use more than one search engine (they vary).
- Bookmark your search results page so that you can find it again.
- Find out who maintains the sites you use (you want your information to be credible).

ACTIVITY

Finding fields of work

Now you can relate what is important to you to various fields of work. Use the NOC, information from the Sector Councils, the Internet, computer software, or whatever is available to you to choose fields of work to investigate.

Make a list of fields to investigate and, for each field, write down reasons why you chose it. (Be more specific than the ten NOC occupational fields.) Keep this list in your portfolio.

ACTIVITY

Field maps

Make a map for each of the fields of work that you selected in the last activity. Put the name of the field in the centre. Around it, write occupations from that field that relate to your preferences. Group similar occupations together. You decide which similarities to emphasize. These maps will be the basis of your later work, when you investigate the occupations in greater detail. Keep the maps in your portfolio, and add to them whenever you find more occupational possibilities.

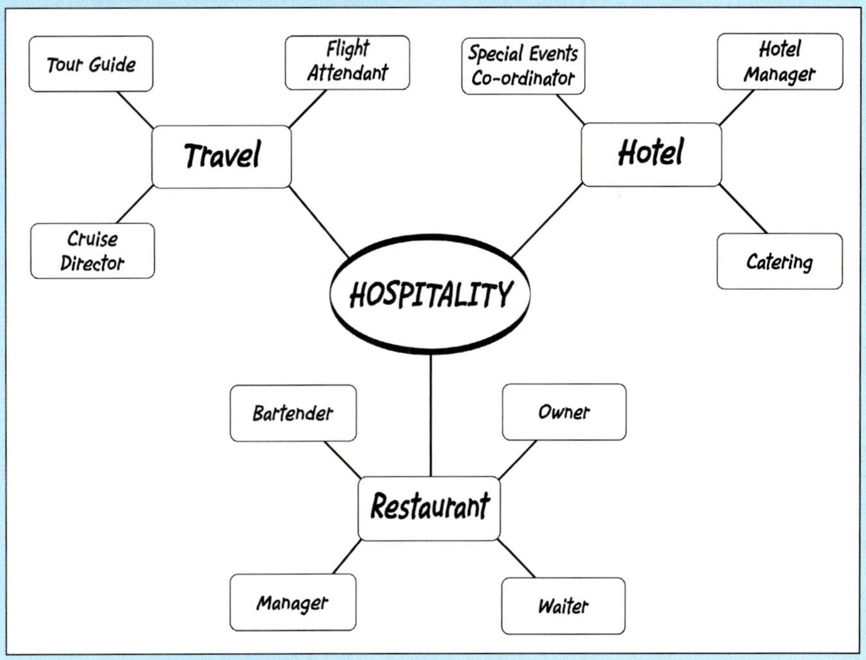

Reflection

Go back to Where to Research on page 106. Add any information that you did not include in your initial list.

Exploring Occupations

Local Opportunities

You can learn what opportunities exist in your community by visiting work sites, talking to people and participating in your community.

ACTIVITY

Create a contact database

This is an activity you can pursue individually or with a group. Set up a database using one of the common software programs available. For each example, list contact names, the name and address of the organization, the type of work it does, where you got the information and notes of what you found out. Make sure that you can search your database by individual name, organization name, and type of organization. Keep adding to this database as you work through this course, both as a class and individually.

The Information Interview

An **information interview** is a meeting, in person or by telephone, with someone who works in a field that interests you.

Be prepared.
The person you are interviewing will not appreciate having to answer really obvious questions, so be informed.

Start with a brief introduction.
You should know exactly what you are going to say when you request an information interview. Indicate who you are and what you're looking for—be simple, short and clear. For example:

"Hello, my name is Justin and I'm a grade 10 student at Valleyview High School. I understand that you create video animation. I am really interested in that as a future occupation. Could I please have 10 minutes of your time during this week so I can find out more about what you do?"

Not everyone will say "yes." If the answer is "no," you might say, "Thank-you. Could you recommend someone else? May I use your name when I contact them?"

Prepare your questions.
In this kind of interview, your job is to gather information. You're not asking for a job. Write down your questions before you start. And remember: you have *one* mouth and *two* ears, so listen carefully. Take notes. Some possible questions are:

- What happens during a typical work day?
- What do you like most about your work?
- Are there things you don't like about your work?
- What skills would I need to work in your field?
- What education would I need to work in your field? What specific training would I need? Where would I get it?
- How could I get started in a similar career path? Do you have any tips or strategies that could help me?

Be courteous.
Say thanks for your interviewee's time and help. If a telephone interview has gone well, you might ask if you can visit the person at work.

Follow up.

- Write down what you've learned.
- Add the person to your contact database.
- Organize your information and keep it in a special file so you can refer to it again.
- Make sure to send a thank-you note. It is polite, and the person is much more likely to remember you if you call again.

Interview Tips

It's always difficult to approach a stranger, but remember that most people like to talk about what they do. And most people like to help others.

If it's an in-person interview, make sure your grooming and clothing are right. As the saying goes, "You never get a second chance to make a first impression."

Remember names. All of these people become contacts in a network that can help you when you are looking for work later on.

ACTIVITY

Local employers

1. Choose an employer in your area to research. If it is a major employer, the annual report may be available at your local library, or perhaps you can get basic information over the Internet.
2. Create a set of information interview questions for someone at the company you have researched. Practise the interview with a partner.
3. If possible, contact someone at the company and conduct the interview. It may even be possible to arrange a class visit and conduct a class-wide interview.
4. Write a brief analysis of how well the interview went. List things that went well and things that you would change in future interviews.

Contributing to Your Community

Your **community contribution** experiences can help you to learn new skills, to meet people who can influence your career, to learn about yourself, to develop self-confidence, and to get credentials. Also, volunteering can help you test your evolving career goals by getting you involved in the world of work.

"I volunteered at CISM 89.3 FM—attached to the Université de Montréal. I started work at 5 a.m., and read through the daily papers. Then I had to write two news bulletins and read them on the radio. I volunteered at the radio station every Sunday for a year and a half."

—Jean-Patrick Balleaux, Montréal, QC

"I never really knew what social workers did. But through my volunteering experiences, and contact with social workers, I am now interested in a whole new field that I never knew existed."

—Jennie Onyett-Jeffries, Toronto, ON

Links

The quotes on page 120 are taken from the booklet *Be Part of Shaping Your Future*, developed by Volunteer Canada to help young people become involved in volunteer activities. Go to <www.careers.nelson.com> for a guided link to the website.

ACTIVITY

What can you learn?

1. What have these young people learned through their community contributions?
2. How could that learning affect their career goals?
3. Talk to someone who has done volunteer work. (Or, better yet, use your own experience.) What did they (or you) learn?
4. Brainstorm ideas for contributing to your community—individually or as a group. Keep in mind the opportunity for first-hand experience in an occupation of interest to you.

Exploring Through Job Shadowing

A **job shadow** experience is one in which you spend a day with someone who works in an occupation that interests you. You stay with the person, like a shadow, and observe the work that he or she does. It is a great opportunity to see what the work is really like.

Many schools offer a job shadow program. You may have participated in "Take Your Kids to Work" or some other program like that. You don't, however, have to wait for someone else to organize a job shadow for you. You can do it yourself.

ACTIVITY

Job shadowing

Prepare an action plan for arranging a job shadow.

1. Choose a person who does work that interests you, and complete a contact entry for that person in your database.
2. Research the company and the occupation thoroughly.
3. Prepare for your initial contact. Write an introductory statement and make a list of questions you need to ask.

Exploring Through Co-operative Education

Some high schools in Newfoundland and Labrador offer a co-operative education program. **Co-operative education** is an excellent way to earn school credits and get practical experience at the same time. You can find out about the occupation and about the realities of the workplace. The program consists of an in-class component and a work placement. High school co-op students are not paid for their work placements, but rather are awarded credits toward graduation. Such practical workplace experiences have proven invaluable to participants.

ACTIVITY

Co-operative education

Contact a co-op education teacher in your school or local area and find the following information:

1. How does the co-op program in your school work?
2. What are the benefits and any disadvantages of being in a co-op program?
3. What kinds of placements are possible for co-op students?
4. How much time is involved?
5. How would you be marked?
6. How do you apply for the program?

Exploring Through Work-Term and Internship Placements

Many college and university programs now require students to complete a work term or internship as part of their post-secondary education. Work terms and internships vary in length but can last up to a full semester, depending on the program of study. They are designed to give students practical experience in their area of study prior to entering the workforce. In addition to fulfilling program requirements, students may get paid. Upon completion of the required courses, students apply for placements within the community. Students are supervised and graded by their workplace supervisor. Many students get job offers from companies in which they had work-term or internship placements. When you are exploring university and college programs, investigate whether any such programs are available.

ACTIVITY

Work-term and internship placements

Research post-secondary programs that require students to complete work terms or internship placements. What would be the advantages of such an opportunity? Would there be any disadvantages? Keep post-secondary program requirements in mind when choosing your high school courses.

Working for Myself

Creating Your Own Work

Self-employment can take many forms: being a franchisee, doing contract work, freelancing, being an agent or distributor for a product or service. It can mean being a professional. Or it can mean starting your own business.

People often use the term **entrepreneur**. It means someone who starts an enterprise or business. It comes from the French word *entreprendre*, which means "to start, undertake or embark upon something."

DISCOVERY

Portrait of an entrepreneur

1. Why do people create their own work?
2. What are the most important characteristics of an entrepreneur?
3. Do you have to be "born" an entrepreneur?
4. What do entrepreneurs value more—financial success or personal accomplishment?
5. Are entrepreneurs big risk-takers?

Consider these questions:

- What is the purpose of a business?
- What is the goal of a business?

Entrepreneurs see problems that need solutions. Where others see a problem, they see an opportunity. The opportunity comes when they can develop a solution for the problem they have identified.

You could say that the *purpose* of a business is to solve a problem, and the *goal* is to make a profit.

Profiles: Young Entrepreneurs

Stefanie Konkin, 23, Whitehorse

By Carla Cook

After completing an honours degree in international studies, Stefanie wanted to use her skills in a positive and ethical way. She knew it would be economically viable to import handcrafted goods from developing countries, but she didn't like the exploitation of workers that often occurred in the process. So Stefanie created her shop, A Fine Balance Imports and Exports, to put her ethics into action. "I've travelled to Third World countries, and have seen how the global system is generally based on a socially irresponsible profit." Stefanie believes in "conscious capitalism," and her ethics may be why, in the first week her store was open, she almost sold out of stock. She buys direct from producers, and checks out the working conditions in person. She also puts 10 percent of her profits toward international development projects. "People just feel better when they're responding with a conscience to global issues," she says. She's also encountered many obstacles along the way. "Doing business in developing countries is pretty dicey. There are barriers that women entrepreneurs have to confront. You just have to be patient, keep going, and be prepared for anything to happen."

Ashley Feltham, 22, Goulds

Owning her own dance school is something Ashley has dreamt of since she was 11 years old. Ten years later, her dream became a reality when she opened the doors to *The Ashley Feltham School of Dance.* "I really felt I had a new approach and ideas on how to get children and adults more engaged and interested in dance." During her initial research, Ashley came across the Community Business Development Corporation (CBDC), which she credits for assisting her financially and supporting her through the start-up process. It seems fitting that the school should bear her name, as Ashley wears many hats as the school's only staff member, including personally teaching each of its 35 weekly classes. Offering all disciplines of dance, the school caters to both the young and young at heart, with its 250 students ranging from toddlers to seniors. Ashley likes to give her students as many opportunities as possible to showcase their skills. Students participate in a year-end dance recital and perform at various parades and carnivals around the city. Running the school is not without its challenges, however. "Being a business of one, you have to do everything, from cleaning to teaching and everything in between. But I love it and wouldn't change a thing!"

Dameion Royes, 26, Ontario
By Anne Pepper

Big It Up is not your typical corporate name. But then Dameion is not your typical business owner. Working with a team of 18 people from all over the globe, Dameion makes funky hats. "We're able to bring different ideas and innovations to the table, and that gives us a real edge," he says. "We have a very diverse market, from teenage girls who love our terrycloth bucket hats, to grandfathers who want sun protection." *Big It Up* actually started as a skin care product that Dameion developed. While promoting his product, he wore an old hat. "We put our own logo on the hat, and everyone started asking where they could get one." Dameion tracked down the hat's original maker and led the company down a new path. Now Dameion travels frequently to trade shows across North America, and his work seems to be paying off. The *Big It Up* label is available in Athlete's World, and on campuses in the United States and Canada. "When you start a business, the best education is just doing it. No classroom can teach you the intricacies." Regarding the unusual company name, Dameion explains, "*Big It Up* is Jamaican vernacular. It means to give respect."

ACTIVITY

Find out more

1. Imagine that you could interview one of the people profiled. Make a list of questions that you would like to ask.
2. Make a list of adjectives that describe these individuals. Can you think of anyone you know who has these qualities?

Links

The Canada/Newfoundland and Labrador Business Service Network's *Young Entrepreneurs Info-Guide* has many links to programs to assist young entrepreneurs. Go to <www.careers.nelson.com> for guided links to these resources.

Did You Know?

- Over 30 percent of young people between 18 and 35 rank becoming an entrepreneur as their profession of choice, ahead of traditional occupations such as lawyer, teacher or stockbroker.
- Approximately 30 percent of small businesses in Canada are owned by entrepreneurs under the age of 30.

ACTIVITY

The two sides of independence

The desire for independence is frequently given as one of the biggest reasons why people seek self-employment. What are the advantages and disadvantages of independence?

ACTIVITY

Interview an entrepreneur

1. Speak with someone who is self-employed. What do you want to learn about starting your own business? To prepare, use the information interview steps (page 119). Decide as a class what questions you will all ask. Here is a list of examples:
   - How did you enter the field you are in? What were your main reasons? What training or specific experience was necessary?
   - How many hours a week do you work? How much time off do you get? Are you able to take regular vacations?
   - How steady or reliable is business? How has it been over the past 10 years?
   - What are the advantages and disadvantages of running your own business?
2. When everyone in the class has finished their interviews, compare the results and draw some general conclusions about the advantages and disadvantages of being an entrepreneur.
3. Review the NOC categories to identify the fields that interest you most. Where would you find out about self-employment in these fields? What skill level do you need to be in business for yourself?
4. On a scale of 1 (low) to 5 (high), how would you rank your current interest in creating your own work?

Entrepreneurship: Myths and Realities

People sometimes have false notions about entrepreneurship. Here are some myths, answered by realities.

Myth	Reality
Entrepreneurs are born, not made.	You can learn to be an entrepreneur by learning a set of skills.
Entrepreneurs are gamblers, addicted to taking risks.	Entrepreneurs take calculated risks. They try to eliminate risk.
Entrepreneurs are independent.	Entrepreneurs may work independently, but they rely on many others—customers, suppliers, etc.
Entrepreneurs are motivated only by money.	Not true. They are also motivated by a desire for independence, and for fulfilment in their work.
Entrepreneurs undergo more stress than people in the traditional work force.	Different people find different things stressful. No one would deny the hard work that's involved.

Links

Junior Achievement is a non-profit international organization supported by businesses and individuals. Its purpose is "to inspire and educate young Canadians to value free enterprise, to understand business and economics and to develop entrepreneurialism and leadership." Visit <www.careers.nelson.com> for guided links to Junior Achievement programs in Newfoundland and Labrador.

Could You Succeed in Small Business?

This is a quiz for people thinking of starting their own business. It was developed by Human Resources and Skills Development Canada.

ACTIVITY

Could you succeed...?

Record the questions on pages 127–129 on a separate sheet of paper and answer each of them "yes" or "no."

1. **Do I have a burning desire to be "on my own"?**

Most entrepreneurs have a strong inner drive to strike out on their own. They like the idea of being their own boss, and not having to report to anyone.

"I've always had an independent streak, even when I was working in a large federal agency. I'm sure it was that independence that helped me decide to take the plunge and start my own business when I was let go. After three years, I still like the feeling of being in control."

—K.T., Ottawa, Ontario

2. **Am I confident that I can succeed?**

Successful entrepreneurs believe in themselves. They are optimistic about projects they undertake, and are good at motivating others and sharing their enthusiasm when pursuing goals. They are likely to say, "When I set my mind to it, I usually do well. I expect to succeed." or "I've succeeded in the past and I'll succeed now. I won't let a setback stop me."

3. **Am I willing to take calculated and moderate risks?**

Going into business involves taking a chance. You may have to push yourself beyond what is comfortable for you and try new things. Successful business people are willing to take risks, but they are also realistic. They gather as much information and support as possible before making a move. In this way, they build a safety net for themselves and decrease the amount of risk involved.

"Risk taking is an essential part of both initiating and operating a small business. Starting a business means having the willingness to risk losing the money and time put into it, so you must decide if the reward for success is great enough to take the risk. You must be able to continue taking calculated but sensible risks, such as investing more money or hiring new employees."

—A.S., Stephenville, Newfoundland and Labrador

4. **Am I a self-starter?**

Successful entrepreneurs believe that what happens in life usually depends on themselves. They are often described as "internal"—people who choose to do something based on their own interests and views. Because they believe that they control their own destiny, they refuse to be at the mercy of others or of events. As a result, they take the initiative in starting projects and getting ideas off the ground.

5. **Am I able to set long-term goals? Can I stick with them? Even if I'm faced with a difficult problem or situation?**

Successful business people are patient and determined. They have the ability to work toward a goal, delaying rewards until a future time, and persist even in difficult times. They understand that it takes time to build success—sometimes years.

"At first, it was frightening to realize that everything about the business—the problems, the solutions, my staff of two, its ultimate success or failure—depended on me. But I was determined to take anything on and to make the business work. My hard work and determination got me through the low points to where I am now. It was worth it."

—V.B., Winnipeg, Manitoba

6. **Do I believe that money is the best measure of success?**

If your only reason for going into business is to make money, it may not be enough to make you a success. The desire for money is not a prime motivation for most successful business people. Rather, they want personal fulfilment and enjoy doing their best. While money is important to them, it is as a means to do more, not simply as wealth and a way to gain prestige.

7. **Am I creative? Am I always looking for new approaches and ideas? Am I innovative?**

Entrepreneurs often have many ideas and a great capacity to dream up and carry out projects. They are highly motivated by their desire to innovate or to bring their own approach to doing things. Never satisfied or content, they believe there is always a better way to get a job done.

8. **Am I good at making decisions? Are my decisions generally sound?**

Successful business people tend to be comfortable making their own decisions. They say, "When I decide to do something, I carry it through to the end, overcome any obstacles and face all the issues."

9. **Am I willing to market my product or service?**

Successful business people do not believe the old saying: "Build a better mousetrap and the world will beat a path to your door." They know that proper marketing is critical to business performance. They advise: "You must sell, sell, sell."

"Marketing is the single most important aspect of small business. You must be able to market your product effectively. If your product is not selling as well as you had hoped, and your financial picture is not what you expected, you may want to re-evaluate your sales pitch and work harder to get people to pay attention. You want your customers to recognize you as someone who has done their homework, and who has their heart and soul poured into their work. Marketing requires hard work and dedication because if your marketing plan is poor, it will reflect on the outcome of your business."

—J.O., Stephenville, Newfoundland and Labrador

Reflection

What do you think of this quiz? Remember—at this stage in your life, you're just entertaining possibilities. Now you know what is involved in going into business for yourself.

10. Am I a good organizer? Do I pay attention to details?

Conducting a successful business requires organizational skills and competence. As a small business owner, you *are* your own boss. Since there is no one looking over your shoulder to make sure you are doing your job well, you will need self-discipline. Your ability to pay attention to details can make the difference between success or failure.

11. Am I flexible? Do I adapt to change? Can I handle surprises?

Change is a fact of life. To succeed in business, you must accept this fact and use it to your advantage. Successful business people monitor social trends, adopt new technologies, compare themselves to the competition, and listen and watch with an open mind.

Do You Have What It Takes?

This quiz should help you see the qualities and skills required to succeed in your own business. You are likely to be happy and successful in your own business if you:

- possess an inner drive to be independent
- are able to set and achieve goals
- are flexible and adaptable
- are willing to work hard
- have confidence in your ability to succeed
- possess self-discipline, leadership abilities and organizational skills
- have the confidence to make decisions and take calculated risks

Except for the first item, these characteristics will help you to be successful in whatever work you decide to do.

Reflection

Go back to the field map you created on page 117. What have you learned by doing this activity? Have you discovered occupations that you hadn't thought of before?

Understanding the World of Work

Whether you work for somebody else or end up hiring other people to work for you, it is important to know what rules govern the workplace.

Employment Scenarios

Derek is a flight attendant with a major airline. What rules apply to him?

Emily is a 15-year-old student who works at a clothing store. Her boss has scheduled her to work from 6 p.m. to 11 p.m. on Thursday night. Is she allowed to work that shift?

Nathan is a server at a restaurant. He works six days a week, four to six hours a day. Sometimes he gets frustrated—friends of his work as many hours, but they get two days off each week. Does he have any grounds to demand that his employer change his hours?

Mindy works part-time at a florist shop. Today, she expected to work four hours, but was only needed for two hours. What is the "three-hour rule," and how would it apply to her?

Tim has worked for over a year at a warehouse, packing boxes. He has made plans to vacation during the Labour Day weekend, and would like to take the Tuesday off as well. Is he entitled to be paid for Labour Day?

Rights and Responsibilities

The **Labour Standards Act** is the provincial law that contains Newfoundland and Labrador's basic rules about employing people. Employees and employers both have rights and responsibilities under the Act.

The Labour Standards Act covers such aspects of work as:

- hours of work and paid time off
- wages (including minimum wage) and methods of payment
- pregnancy and parental leave
- termination and layoffs
- the role of the Ministry of Labour

In addition, there are other laws that apply to the workplace. These include federal laws, the **Newfoundland and Labrador Human Rights Code**, and other provincial laws.

The Labour Standards Act sets minimum standards that must be observed in all Newfoundland and Labrador workplaces it governs. Your job may also be governed by a contract or collective agreement between the employees' union and the employer. Such a contract would give additional specific rules on wages and working conditions that are at least equal to or better than the rules in the Act.

Links

In Newfoundland and Labrador, the Labour Relations Agency is responsible for enforcing the Labour Standards Act. The agency has a number of regional offices around the province.

Links to more detailed information concerning Newfoundland and Labrador's Labour Standards Act and the role of the Labour Relations Agency can be found on-line at <www.careers.nelson.com>.

Employment Scenarios: Answers

Here are the answers to the questions posed in the employment scenarios.

Derek. Derek works in an industry under federal jurisdiction. The Canada Labour Code applies to him. It covers a series of federally regulated industries. Find out which ones they are.

Emily. No. Children under the age of 16 may not work more than 3 hours on a school day. They must also not work between the hours of 10 p.m. of one day and 7:00 a.m. of the following day.

Nathan. No. He works 24 to 36 hours a week. The Act says that 40 hours a week is the normal working limit for workers in Newfoundland and Labrador.

Mindy. The 3-hour-rule: If you are called into work, but work less than 3 hours, your employer must either allow you to work at least 3 hours or pay you minimum wage for the unworked portion of the 3 hours.

Tim. No. Although he has been employed for 30 days prior to the holiday, he will not have worked his regularly scheduled day before and after the holiday.

Profile: Rob Ellis

Safety on the job is an issue that affects us all. The Young Workers Awareness Program was set up to educate young people in Ontario about safety issues. One of the forces behind it is the energy of Rob Ellis, whose son was tragically killed on the job.

Every employer is supposed to have safety procedures. But for the ones who don't, or who fail to adequately protect their staff, the results can be disastrous. David Ellis was 18 years old, an honours student and athlete of the year at his school, when he took a three-week contract in February of 1999.

"I heard about the job and arranged for David to get it," says his soft-spoken dad, Rob. "He was fast-tracking through high school, and he wanted money for university."

The job was in a local bakery. It seemed like a safe working environment, so David wasn't surprised when he was given no safety training and little supervision. On his second day on the job, he was given the job of cleaning out a dough mixer while the rest of the staff were on lunch. The machine had no safety guards and had not been locked out, and when David began work it started accidentally. He was crushed by it and died.

—David Ellis, 1980–1999

In memory of his son, Rob decided he had to do something to alert other young people—and their parents—to the dangers they can meet on the job. "I can hear David say it to me, 'Dad, don't get bitter, get better.'" Rob's energy and commitment were instrumental in helping start the Young Worker Awareness Program, and he has since told his and David's story to many high school classes.

"David was given no instructions and he wasn't told about safety procedures," says his father. "His mother and I tried to steer him away from jobs we thought were dangerous, but neither of us thought of a bakery that way. In fact, the machine that killed David is a very dangerous piece of equipment. The same accident happened six months later to a 16-year-old Toronto boy, Ivan Golyshov. He and his mother were recent immigrants—they wouldn't have known the dangers. It was exactly the same machine, an unguarded dough mixer."

Workers need to know what to look for, and what questions to ask. And that's doubly true for young workers. "Often kids don't ask questions—they just do the job," Rob says. "They can be very vulnerable—they need the work for school or college, and they don't think to ask about safety." He points out that young people are often so eager to prove they can do the work that they don't stop to question how things are done.

"I don't want to paint a negative picture," says Rob Ellis. "Ontario is full of opportunities for young people. But I want to emphasize that you should inform yourself, and if you don't think the job is safe, you can walk away from it. Keep your eyes open and ask questions like:

- Will I have supervision or training?
- Will I be buddied with an experienced worker?
- Will I require any safety equipment for the job?
- Will there be on-the-job training, or will I be trained before I start work?
- Has there been turnover on the job? If so, why?"

ACTIVITY

Creating public awareness

1. Research some facts about workplace safety.
2. Survey your class to find out if anyone has any stories about safety (or the lack of safety) in the workplace.
3. Use the information to create a public awareness campaign about safety in the workplace.
   - Be sure to identify your main audience.
   - Choose a medium that is suitable for that audience.
   - Use visuals and language that will engage that audience.

The Top Five Causes of Injury to Young Workers

- slips and falls
- overexertion
- being struck by, or against, an object
- bodily reactions (toxic effects from chemicals)
- burns

Health and Safety

You have the right to work in a safe place!

Newfoundland and Labrador workplaces are regulated under the **Occupational Health and Safety Act** (**OHSA**), with the exception of those regulated by the **Canada Labour Code**. Both laws were created to make all workplaces safe. They define the rights and duties of everyone in the workplace—owner, employer, supervisors and workers.

The **Workplace Health, Safety and Compensation Act** also applies in Newfoundland and Labrador. It was created to promote healthy, safe workplaces, to encourage safe, timely return to work and to provide insured benefits to workers who get injured on the job. It is administered by the Workplace Health, Safety and Compensation Commission.

Each workplace should also have its own safety policy and procedures, and they should be clearly posted.

Your Rights

The Occupational Health and Safety Act stresses three rights for every worker:

To know. Your employer must inform you of any hazards in your workplace, and provide training so you can work safely.

To participate. You have the right to participate in health and safety issues in your workplace.

To refuse unsafe work. You have the right to refuse work that you believe is dangerous to your health or safety, or the health or safety of another worker.

Reflection

What hazards have you seen at the places where you've worked?

Have you ever had an injury on the job? If so, can you discuss it with the class?

Your Responsibilities

To inform yourself. If you don't know, you can't take care.

To work safely. Don't fool around. Use all equipment safely, the way your supervisor shows you. Use required protective equipment at all times, the way your supervisor shows you.

To report any unsafe condition or occurrence. Tell your supervisors—they need to know.

To report any injury. Tell your supervisors. Any injury on the job must be reported to the Workplace Health, Safety and Compensation Commission. And of course—go to your doctor! What might be some of the reasons that young workers don't report unsafe conditions or injuries?

Links

It isn't a legal requirement, but it's a good idea to know basic first aid. The St. John's Ambulance Society offers first aid courses in your community. Contact them and find out how to take one.

Hazardous Materials

One of the key regulations of the Occupational Health and Safety Act (Newfoundland and Labrador) concerns the **Workplace Hazardous Material Information System**, or WHMIS for short. The WHMIS regulations require:

Labelling. Every hazardous material must have a warning label that tells you what class a hazardous product is in and how to work safely with it.

Material safety data sheets. Every hazardous material must have a material safety data sheet (MSDS). These must be kept where workers can find them, so they can read about the hazards of a product, how to use it safely and what to do in an emergency.

Training. Every worker must be trained in how to work safely with the product.

ACTIVITY

What do these symbols stand for?

1. 

2. 

3. 

4. 

5. 

6. 

7. 

8. 

She Saw the Symbol

A young woman working at a health club noticed that the liquid she used to wash down the handball court had a WHMIS symbol. She wondered if this substance was responsible for the headaches and nausea she suffered at this job. When she asked the manager, he located the MSDS, which stated that the liquid should be diluted with water and used only in well-ventilated areas. Rubber gloves and a respirator were required, because the chemical could be absorbed through breathing passages and skin. The effects of the chemical were nausea, headaches, convulsions and death. The club decided to use a less toxic substance.

Links

The Workplace Health, Safety and Compensation Commission maintains a Resource Centre with information on hazardous materials and WHMIS as well as various other safety-related reports. Workers and employers can borrow print materials and videos from the resource centre free of charge.

To learn more about the Commission visit <www.careers.nelson.com>.

ACTIVITY

Research

1. What is the Labour Standards Act? What does it cover?
2. What is a bargaining agent? What is a collective agreement?
3. What is the Workplace Health, Safety and Compensation Commission?
4. Does the Employment Standards Act require employees to join a union?
5. What is an occupational health and safety committee?

Navigating the World of Change

How do you keep on course in the world of work when everything is changing around you so rapidly?

You keep your eye on your ultimate destination—what is most important to you. Ultimately, you need to know where to look for information as the landmarks change around you. And you've got to be able to find new options for yourself if you need them.

DISCOVERY

Predicting change

Make a list of changes that could affect the direction of your career. If you're short of ideas, talk to older people about what changes affected their careers.

Now look at your list and brainstorm ways in which you might be able to predict each change. This won't be possible in each case—some things are unpredictable.

Dealing with Change

Effective and Ineffective Approaches

Do you know some people who thrive on change? Do you know other people who like things more predictable? Some people want constantly new experiences, and others prefer to live in as stable a world as possible. But a certain amount of change is inevitable, and there are some ways we can learn to cope with change more easily. The ability to handle change well is called **adaptability**.

Dealing With Change

Effective Ways	Ineffective Ways
Look at the positives involved.	Focus only on the negatives.
Accept the reality of what is happening.	Be in denial: refuse to accept the reality of what is happening.
Talk about your concerns with family or trusted friends.	Worry excessively and keep all your feelings inside.
Set new goals.	Make no realistic plans for the future.
Take care of yourself, to deal with the stress of change: eat well, sleep well, exercise.	Neglect yourself.
Try to focus on future opportunities.	Keep focusing on the good old days.
Stay informed about the world around you.	Ignore information that might help you prepare for change.

Case Studies

Rohit

Rohit is 14 years old, and has just moved from India to a big city in Canada. His parents felt that there would be better opportunities for the family here. They moved in the middle of January, during a snowstorm, and Rohit had never seen snow before. The first day of school was difficult, because he did not know how to speak English well, and he didn't know his way around the school. He was put in an ESL class with other newcomers, but he did not know anyone in the school.

Michelle
Michelle worked for the same company for 10 years. She recently learned that the company is moving its operations to another region. She is being laid off, with a settlement—but that won't last long. Michelle is a single mom with two small children. She is frightened, because she thinks she has no special skills. She has lived in the same small city all her life. As far as she knows, no one in town is hiring.

Carl
All through high school, Carl was a star basketball player—the best in his school for sure, and one of the best in his league. He had his heart set on playing for the Toronto Raptors, or another NBA team—he knew all the players, all their moves, and everything about the game. However, he has not been able to interest any professional squad in giving him more than a try-out.

Sarah
Sarah was with the same group of friends all through public school and junior high. They were all going on to a particular high school for grade 9, and Sarah assumed she was going with them. But her parents had different ideas. There is another high school in town with a program that they think is better for Sarah, and they arranged for her to go there. Sarah is going to the new school, but she is determined to hate it. She phones her old friends every night, and tells them how horrible it is.

ACTIVITY

What should they do?

All of these people have had to deal with change in their lives.

1. Think of some ways that each person could deal with change.
2. List these strategies in order of how effective you think they could be.
3. Choose one very effective and one less effective strategy and describe why you identified them that way.

ACTIVITY

Identifying changes

1. Make a list of the changes in the case studies.
2. Add other common major changes.
3. Choose one change that you (or someone close to you) has had to deal with. Write a letter giving advice about how to cope.

Trends to Watch

What's a Trend?

We live in a trendy world. What are the trends that most affect your daily life? Are you thinking about music, clothes, leisure activities? Maybe you are thinking about the way people in your peer group talk, or what they talk about most often. Maybe you're thinking about bigger **trends—social trends** (like environmental awareness) or **economic trends** (like the move toward on-line shopping).What do trends have in common? They define a direction for a significant number of people. And, because a trend is widespread, it is likely to affect your life.

Trends—big and small, short-term and long-term—will affect your career. An entrepreneur may find ways of making money by taking advantage of a North American trend like watching Japanese animation. You may lose your job in the textile industry because of a trend toward greater automation. There may be a greater demand for health care workers because of the **demographic trend** of a growing elderly population.

Being aware of trends is a way of increasing the information you need to make good decisions about your future.

ACTIVITY

Trends in your life

1. Working with a small group, list trends that affect you in your daily lives.
2. Give both positive and negative examples of how these trends affect you.
3. Choose one trend, and describe how it could affect how people work.

Predicting Trends

Trends don't come from a vacuum. It is often possible to analyse the history of a trend, and to make predictions about where the trend is leading. Successful business people are often very good at doing this—predicting change and preparing for it.

But, since predictions are about the future, they can fail. And as the pace of change accelerates, it is more difficult to know what current information we should consider when we make predictions. Does this mean we should ignore the future? No—it means we should be cautious about how it is depicted.

"We should all be concerned about the future because we will have to spend the rest of our lives there."

—Charles Franklin Kettering

Failed Predictions

In the 1940s, Thomas Watson, Sr., then chairman of IBM, predicted that there would never be a need for more than five computers in the whole world.

In 1895, Thomas Edison said: "It is apparent to me that the possibilities of the aeroplane, which two or three years ago were thought to hold the solution to the (flying machine) problem, have been exhausted, and that we must turn elsewhere."

In 1899, Charles H. Duell, then the Commissioner of the U.S. Office of Patents, said: "Everything that can be invented has been invented."

In a 1932 article for *Mechanics Illustrated*, Winston Churchill predicted: "We shall escape the absurdity of growing a whole chicken in order to eat the breast or wing, by growing these parts separately, under a suitable medium."

In 1955, President Eisenhower's special assistant, Harold Stassen, predicted that nuclear power would lead to a world where "hunger is unknown... where food never rots and crops never spoil... a world where no one stokes a furnace or curses the smog, where the air is everywhere as fresh as on a mountain top and the breeze from a factory as sweet as from a rose."

Western Union wouldn't buy the patent on Alexander Graham Bell's 1876 invention, saying the public couldn't be trusted to master such complicated equipment.

In 1946, Darryl F. Zanuck, head of 20th Century Fox Studios, stated that television "won't be able to hold on to any market it captures after the first six months. People will soon get tired of staring at a plywood box every night."

ACTIVITY

Why do predictions fail?

With a group, brainstorm possible reasons why some predictions—even if they are made by people with good information—fail.

Trends in Technology

Although it is impossible to predict with certainty where **technological trends** will lead us, there is no doubt that technological advances are radically changing how we live and work. For instance, technology has led to automation, which has led to a reduced need for human labour. On the other hand, there now exist a large number of jobs that hadn't even been thought of thirty years ago—for instance, any occupation related to the World Wide Web.

ACTIVITY

Impact of technology

Use a reference tool, like the NOC, to make a list of occupations that have come into existence as a result of advances in information technology.

Advances in technology also affect *how* we work, no matter what we do. Think of all the different ways we can communicate with each other: mobile telephone, fax, e-mail, video conferencing, etc. People don't have to work in the same physical space in order to be part of a team. People can travel and still be in contact.

In the workplace itself, technology has become important to a business's success. It would be hard to find a multinational company that doesn't have a large information technology department. And technical know-how is no longer limited to a few IT specialists. Fewer and fewer people will be able to compete for jobs if they don't have adequate knowledge of new technologies.

How do you find out what impact emerging technologies are having on the world of work? Information is everywhere—newspapers, magazines, television and radio, educational institutions, career centres, government agencies and books. Not surprisingly, that impact is of wide interest and concern, and is researched and reported on regularly.

Links

Don Tapscott is a well-known Canadian futurist. He was one of the early "cyber gurus," people who wrote and spoke about the "digital revolution." Best-selling books that he has written or co-written include *Paradigm Shift: The New Promise of Information Technology* (1992), *The Digital Economy: Promise and Peril in the Age of Networked Intelligence* (1996), and *Growing Up Digital: The Rise of the Net Generation* (1997). He is also chair of the Alliance for Converging Technologies, a think tank on the impact of new media on business, government and society.

Go to <www.careers.nelson.com> for links to Don Tapscott's work and to other sources related to the impact of technology on society.

ACTIVITY

Report on technology

Report on one way in which changing technology has affected the world of work, or is likely to affect it in the future. Use a variety of research tools.

Economic Trends

"The new electronic interdependence recreates the world in the image of a global village."

—Marshall McLuhan, 1962

Electronic interdependence is much more of a reality now than it was in 1962. High technology and the high-speed transfer of ideas, information and capital have had a huge impact on economics. Distances and boundaries are much less significant than they have ever been before—in many important ways, people half-way around the world are our neighbours. We can easily get goods, services and information from these "neighbours" now. Delivery can be made in record time.

Globalization is a term that defines an economic trend toward international trade and competition. That trend has its roots in technological developments, but is also affected by government policies that are opening the markets of the world.

A large business today can move money and management anywhere in the world. But it is bound by national and international rules. Before World War II, Canada protected its home industries by taxing imports, thereby decreasing competition from international industries. Since then, international trade agreements have loosened barriers between countries. So, for example, it is much easier now for a Canadian-owned company to manufacture a product in a different country where labour costs are lower.

The effects of these trends have sometimes been painful. By the mid-1990s, for example, the average Canadian family had seen its income decline because wages had not kept up with the cost of living. Nevertheless, according to the history text *Canada: Our Century, Our Story*,

> ...Canadians did adapt to the new economy. By 1984, Canada's economy was much more diversified than it had been after World War II. More than 60 percent of working Canadians were employed in the service industries. However, often these jobs provided little career growth and paid poorly—for example, food services, retail, and so on. Many Canadians who had lost their full-time jobs had to take two or three part-time jobs in the service industries to maintain their standard of living.
>
> But as Canadian businesses and entrepreneurs met the challenges of the new economy, new employment opportunities opened up. What was becoming clear was that the new workplace was unfamiliar to the average Canadian. New, well-paying jobs demanded workers who had a broad educational background and who were highly skilled, people who could work as team members, be flexible, and take part in creative decision making.

Links

Globalization is a topic that you will cover in Level II Canadian Economy. Check your school's selection of history and economics books for a more in-depth understanding of this trend and how it has affected Canadians.

ACTIVITY

Globalization and Canadian business

Research the effects of globalization on one sector of Canadian business. Possible choices include: digital telecommunications, high-tech transportation, textile manufacturing, automotive manufacturing and fisheries.

Demographic Trends

Demography is the study of human populations. Demographic trends can help us predict how our society will evolve and, consequently, how the world of work will be affected. Things to consider when studying demographic trends include:

Size of the population: What is the birth rate, and how has it changed? How many people between the ages of 20 and 30 live in Canada? What are our patterns of immigration?

Territorial distribution: Where are the majority of people living in Canada? How has that changed in the last ten years? What percentage of the population lives in urban areas?

Composition of the population: What is the age distribution in the Canadian population? What are the prevalent values of each age group? What is the income range of the urban-dwelling population?

The study of demographic trends can help us predict things about our social and economic lives and, consequently, about how the world of work will change in the future. According to Canadian author David Foot, "demographics explain about two-thirds of everything." In his best-selling book, *Boom, Bust & Echo,* he focuses on the age of the Canadian population, asserting that age is a powerful predictor of human behaviour. If you know, for example, that a large proportion of the Canadian population will be over 60 in 2025, you can predict that there will be work opportunities for people who provide services for older people.

In *Boom, Bust & Echo,* David Foot concentrates on three major segments of the population, organized by dates of birth, which he calls the Baby Boom, the Baby Bust, and the Baby Boom Echo. As you look at the following chart and graph and think about the number of people in each group, remember this simple principle: every year each person gets a year older.

Population Group	Size	Fact
Baby Boom (1947–1966)	10,000,000 people	• This group accounts for about one third of the Canadian population. • By 2007, the first Baby Boomers will be 60 years old.
Baby Bust (1967–1979)	5,500,000 people	• This group, because it is smaller, has significantly less competition than the Baby Boomers.
Baby Boom Echo (1980–1995)	6,900,000 people	• These are the children of the Boomers. • This group will have grown up in the digital era.

Age Pyramid of Population of Newfoundland and Labrador, 2001

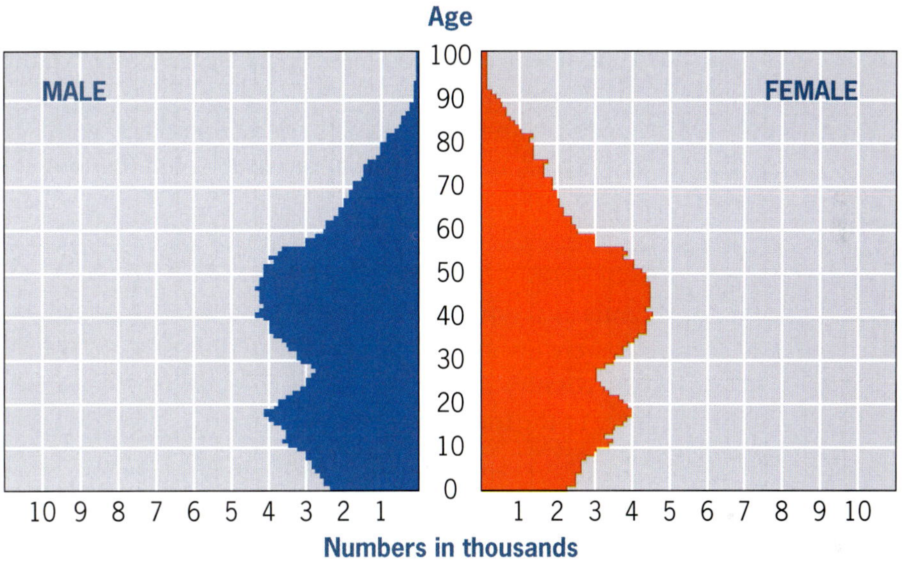

ACTIVITY

Analyse the demographics

Work with a group to analyse the graph and the chart. What conclusions can you draw about occupational opportunities for people in your population group (the Baby Boom Echo)?

Answering the following questions will get you started:

1. a) How old will the first Baby Boomers be when you are 25?
b) Will there be more men or women in this group?
c) What needs will Baby Boomers have then (think of real estate, health care, leisure activities)?

2. a) How would you describe the amount of competition you will have when you enter the world of work?
b) What qualities will a young would-be employee need in that environment?

Links

In every society there are people who study the present in order to predict the future. Names you might want to investigate include: Michael Adams, Colin Campbell, Faith Popcorn, William Bridges, Nuala Beck and John Naisbitt. Go to <www.careers.nelson.com> for an annotated bibliography, and for links to on-line information about these people.

Change in the Workplace

How Will Trends Affect the World of Work?

In Julia's Story (page 104), Julia's mother has just been laid off. Take a poll of the class—what percentage of students has a parent or guardian who has experienced a major career shift in the past five years? Ten years?

In the early 1990s, Canada went through a prolonged recession. Many businesses closed and many people lost their jobs. Have those businesses re-opened, and the people been hired back? Or have other changes happened since?

Many people who have studied the issue think that we are going through a change as profound as the industrial revolution, and that our society is altering fundamentally.

"As recently as the 1960s, almost half of all workers in industrialized countries were involved in making things. By the year 2000, however, no developed country will have more than one-sixth or one-eighth of its work force in the traditional roles of making and moving goods."

—Peter F. Drucker, *Post-Capitalist Society*

If people are no longer in manufacturing jobs, what are they doing?

Predictions About the New Workplace

A traditional career has often been pictured as a "job ladder": you start at the bottom and work your way up. You go to school, you get educated, and you go to work. You stay at one job, and eventually you retire and get a pension.

Some people still have careers like that, but they are no longer the norm. American author William Bridges says that we're entering a "dejobbed" society. The idea of "jobs," with fixed hours and fixed descriptions, is fading away. Bridges points out that the *work* isn't going away—it's how the work is being done that is changing. Less and less is work being made into parcels called "jobs," with nine-to-five hours, benefits, secure employment and a steady management structure.

Instead, the world of work is increasingly organized on a project-by-project basis. Teams of people with different skills come together to accomplish a specific task. When it's done, the team breaks up, and the people go on to other tasks.

The way the movie industry works is an example. When a project is accepted, the producers assemble a team—from stars to carpenters to administrators. Everyone is hired on contract. A "wrap party" is traditional, to acknowledge that everyone is saying good-bye at the end of the project.

Predictions About the New Workplace

The Traditional Workplace	The New Workplace
job that you keep for life	6 to 8 major changes in a career
predictable salary with benefits and pension	temporary and contract work
hierarchical structure	project-based structure
larger organizations with thousands of employees	smaller organizations with specialty focuses
9 to 5 schedule, with predictable routine	flexible schedule
special skills required	transferable skills required
services like answering phones and typing provided by support staff	each person handles most of own services—voice mail, e-mail, word processing
community-based economy	economy responsive to global pressures
education first, then work	life-long learning
work for someone else	work as an independent contractor, consultant or entrepreneur
most jobs in manufacturing and mass production	most jobs in information technology and the service industry

But as William Bridges says, the work isn't going away. There's still work to do, more than ever, with more variety than ever.

The new flattened-out, dejobbed world that's coming is less secure. But there is also more opportunity. More than ever, the emphasis is on building and steering your own career.

ACTIVITY

Analysing the new workplace

Look through the table comparing the new and traditional workplaces.

1. Identify some attractive things about the new workplace.
2. Identify some drawbacks.
3. Consider the Employability Skills on page 66. Which of these skills will be most needed in the new workplace? Why?
4. Choose two features of the new workplace. Explain how social and economic trends might contribute to these features.

Skills for the New Workplace

Janis Foord Kirk is a Canadian journalist and career specialist who has identified ten Survivability® skills:

Technical Literacy. You use new technology competently.

Attitude. You have a positive outlook, are flexible, show tolerance and empathy, are goal-oriented and able to make good decisions.

Self-Promotion. You are confident and assertive about your abilities—your work may not always speak for itself.

Communication. You are able to make yourself understood, and to listen actively.

Learning. You keep learning in order to be a valuable participant in the workplace.

Information Gathering. You are skilled at researching, making connections and using information strategically.

Consultative Problem-Solving. You recognize problems and are able to solve them.

Creativity. You think creatively to overcome obstacles.

Entrepreneurial Initiative. You take an entrepreneurial perspective on your work.

Self-Management. You manage yourself—stress, time, finances—and keep a balance in your life.

Links

These skills are described in detail in Janis Foord Kirk's book *SURVIVABILITY: Career Strategies for the New World of Work*. Survivability® is the registered trademark of Kirkfoord Communications Inc. Go to <www.careers.nelson.com> for guided links to online information about Janis Foord Kirk's work.

ACTIVITY

A quick skills analysis

1. How would you rate yourself in each of the above skills, using a scale of 1 (low) to 5 (high)?

2. How do your experiences in school, extracurricular activities, community involvement and family life help you develop these skills?

3. What personality traits do these skills favour? Can you think of people who will have a problem in the new workplace?

Change in Fields of Work

Where the Jobs Are

by Jeff Buckstein
(reproduced from *The Globe and Mail*, November 8, 1999)

High-tech jobs top everybody's list. It's impossible to compete with the opportunities in the software development industry.

"That's really where it's at, and students who have the right skills in those areas are just being gobbled up like crazy—both by Canadian and American companies," says Connie Campbell, co-founder of Career Fit, Inc.

Other popular high-tech areas include: electrical engineering (with microchip wires), computer engineering, biotechnology, biopharmaceuticals and e-commerce applications.

But high-tech positions aren't the only ones in demand. Other popular employment areas include: business administration applications, including human resources, marketing and finance, and health care practitioners with a specialization in geriatrics to deal with an aging population.

Also expected to open up are civil service positions in both the federal and various provincial governments to fill many positions vacated through retirement, such as in the field of education.

Then there is the growing phenomenon of self-employment. According to a recent Statistics Canada survey, more than 2.5 million Canadians are self-employed.

"I think there's going to be continued growth in entrepreneurial ventures of all types," predicts Ann Burdette, manager of consulting services at KPMG.

She adds that, contrary to popular belief, many individuals setting up their own businesses are choosing to get out of a corporate environment themselves rather than being pushed out.

Links

The Internet, along with newspapers, magazines and news broadcasts are important resources. Your library will have a selection of these; however, more and more news agencies are making current information available on the Internet. Go to <www.careers.nelson.com> for guided links to related sites.

ACTIVITY

What did you learn?

1. Based on the article on page 149, make a list of the following:
   - fields of work that are predicted to employ more people in the future
   - sources that the newspaper cites for making these predictions
2. If you had to write an article like this, what other sources of information might you use?
3. Answer three of the questions in the box below.

Questioning Predictions

When you read predictions about the future of work, ask yourself these questions:

1. Does the present situation represent the future situation?
2. What predictions are reliable?
3. Where can I support or refute these predictions?
4. Is a particular article biased to make an argument for a lobby group?
5. How will consumer behaviour affect opportunities?
6. What public policies will impinge on this career?
7. How many workers are already in this field?
8. How many new workers will be needed in the future?
9. How will technology change the industry?
10. What is the next most likely position to move into?
11. Is this occupation mobile across the country?
12. From which training programs do employers prefer to hire?

Researching Labour Market Information

When looking for **labour market information**, start with government agencies like Statistics Canada and the Human Resources and Skills Development Council. But don't forget the resources you used to navigate the world of work in Section 1.

For example, the Canadian Technology Human Resources Board conducted an on-line survey about trends in the technology sector. It received approximately 1300 responses.

According to survey results, flexibility and mobility are two key characteristics of the technology–engineering field. The study found that career advancement frequently involves changing employers. Employers are looking for technologists who can do a variety of tasks: 32 percent of those in the survey reported having more than one area of specialization.

There was also no correlation between the length of time spent with one firm and the number of jobs workers are being assigned. Factors other than seniority and experience, such as training and non-technical skills (communication and leadership), are most important to gaining advancement. Workers indicated verbal and written communication skills as the top job priority.

ACTIVITY

Your own research

Using your resource tools, research the future employment prospects in a field of work that interests you, and write your information as a news article.

ACTIVITY

What's being replaced?

Given some of the social and economic trends you've looked at, what are some occupations that will be less necessary in the future? Back up your predictions with information and analysis.

Will Everything Change?

If you read too many predictions, you can get the impression that soon everything will have changed. Well, that's not true. What things won't change? What things will always be important for people?

Predictors so often talk about "the market"—labour market, money market, job market, world market. But is it right to talk about a market for everything, as if everything was buying and selling?

Think of Mother Teresa, or Doctors Without Borders. Would you describe them as "marketing humanitarian services"?

SECTION 3

Navigating the World of Learning

What are your plans for after you finish high school? Which of these **options** are you considering?

- university
- apprenticeship
- distance education
- on-the-job training
- travel
- college of applied arts and technology
- private colleges
- work
- continuing education
- something else

It's important that you know what your options are. You should research different options so you have a better sense of what is possible.

In this section you will look briefly at all your options. The activities will help you learn a little about each one. Then you can spend more time on the ones that are important to you. No one option is better than any other. The question is: "Which options are best for you?"

DISCOVERY

What is required?

Think of the fields of work that most interest you, and of the occupations that you'd most like to investigate. Jot down what you think the education and training requirements are for those occupations. If you have ideas about where you could get that education and training, jot those down as well. What credentials will you need for that education? How much will it cost?

Universities and Colleges

What's the Difference?

About 32 percent of high school graduates in Newfoundland and Labrador go on to pursue post-secondary studies at **university** or **community college** right out of high school. The percentage varies from region to region and from school to school within the province.

Educational Trend: Adults Returning

More and more adults are taking college and university programs. Many of those who did not go to college or university when they finished high school, and many who did, are going back to school to retrain or to upgrade their skills.

In most high schools, the university and college options get emphasized more than others. In part, this is because of the long and complex application process. College and university representatives often visit high schools, and senior students may go on campus visits. So you will hear many announcements about this.

What are some differences between university and college? What type of educational experience do you get from each? How much does each cost? Where are the colleges and universities located?

University and College: A Comparison

	University	College
Type of educational experience	A theoretical and academic educational experience. There can be a generalist or specialist approach.	A practical, hands-on approach to education. Training is specialized for particular occupations.
What do you get?	Degree	Diploma or certificate
How long does it take?	Three or four years for an undergraduate program, considerably longer for a master's or Ph.D.	One year for a certificate; two or three years for a diploma. Generally speaking, "technician" is a two-year program and "technologist" is a three-year program.
How many are there in Atlantic Canada?	There are 18 universities in Atlantic Canada.	There are 10 colleges in Atlantic Canada.

ACTIVITY

A comparison

To compare college and university, use the various publications that these institutions create for high school students (e.g., "view books", course calendars). Your guidance or student services office should have these. For this activity, use one college and one university publication.

1. Select one of your preferred fields of work.
2. Using the information books, find as many programs as you can that prepare students to work in that field. Do this for both the university and the college.
3. Select two college and two university programs. For each, find the following:
    - the admission requirements (high school courses and marks)
    - courses you would take in first year (use the institution's calendar to help you with this)
    - tuition fees for one year of study
    - the degree, diploma or certificate you would receive for successfully completing the program
4. Based upon this quick search, which program appeals to you most? Why?

Information Resources for Universities and Colleges

Guidance/Student Services: Ask your guidance counsellor about Spectrum (Ontario, Eastern Canada, Western Canada), computer/Internet programs such as Career Explorer, School Finder, and The Education Planner (which gives you an interest inventory, then connects your results directly to college and university programs that are related to your interests). Go to <www.careers.nelson.com> for direct links to related websites.

Universities: View books, calendars, Department of Education, campus visits.

Colleges: View books, calendars, campus visits, employment statistics for college graduates.

Media: *Maclean's* magazine publishes an annual survey of Canada's universities.

Internet: The Department of Education has links to universities and colleges. Most schools also have their own websites, with online application services.

You should also talk to people who have been to the colleges or universities you are interested in.

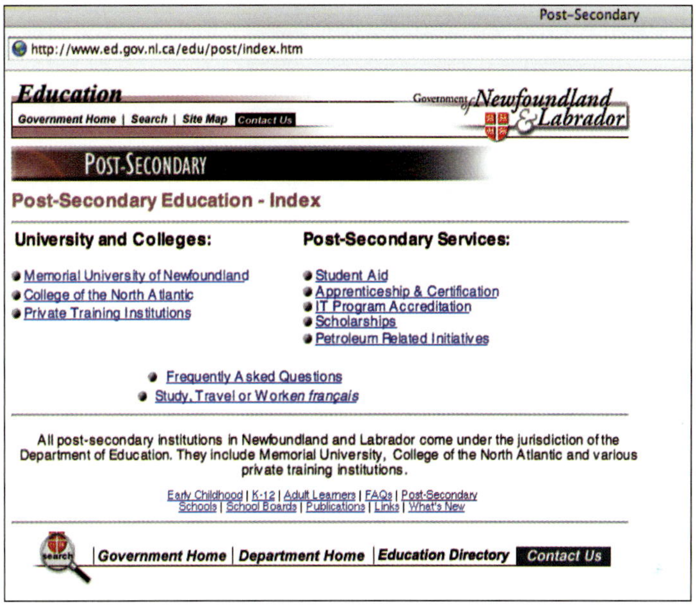

Educational Trend: Switching

Many people start at a college, and move on to a university program, sometimes before they complete their college program. The opposite is also true with university students moving to a college program. Many are looking for a combination of theoretical background and specific work-related skills.

Something to Think About

Many post-secondary students drop out. Once you've narrowed your choices, find out the dropout rate in any program that interests you. Why do students drop out? Find out, and be prepared.

Apprenticeship, Distance Education and Other Post-Secondary Options

Apprenticeship

Apprentices are individuals who work with certified artisans and earn wages while they are training. **Apprenticeship** programs vary in length, with the average being four years. To become an apprentice in Newfoundland and Labrador, you must first find an employer who is willing to hire you in that capacity and then register with the Industrial Training Section of the Department of Education. High school graduation is generally a prerequisite. Trade areas include, but are not limited to, construction, service, motive power and industry.

DISCOVERY

Your choice

Would you rather: go on to higher education, travel and think things over, or enter the working world and train for an occupation?

Links

Your guidance/student services office should have print material on apprenticeship. You can search the Internet for information also: start at the Department of Education's website. (Go to <www.careers.nelson.com> for a direct link to this site.) Or search using key words like "apprenticeship," "Canada" and "Newfoundland and Labrador."

ACTIVITY

Apprenticeship

Research answers to the following questions:

1. What is an apprenticeship?
2. How can you become an apprentice?
3. How long does it take to train as an apprentice?
4. What are the advantages?
5. What trades are designated for apprenticeship in Newfoundland and Labrador?
6. How much will you earn at the end of the apprenticeship?

Women in Trades and Technology

It used to be that most skilled trades—like plumber, mechanic, carpenter and tool-and-die maker—were done by men. That has been changing. Groups like IWITTS (National Institute for Women in Trades, Technology and Science), WISE (Women Interested in Successful Employment) and Techsploration encourage women to go into the trades and technology fields, and encourage employers to hire them. In particular, Techsploration connects girls to female role models working or training in trades and technology careers. Go to <www.careers.nelson.com> for links to more information about IWITTS, WISE and Techsploration.

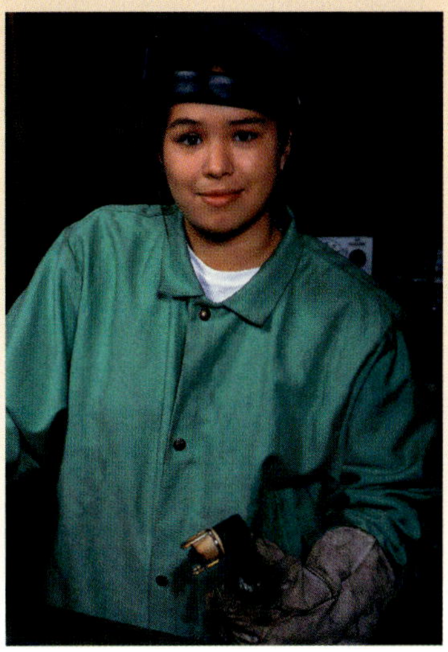

Private Colleges

Private colleges are also known as private training schools. They offer specialized training for specific occupations. Many of the programs teach computer-related and other technological skills. These colleges are privately owned, but are often approved and regulated by the government of Newfoundland and Labrador.

Private colleges generally have higher tuition costs than public colleges and universities. Many of the specialized training programs can be completed in less time than in community colleges. As well, some private schools offer job-searching assistance upon graduation.

Private schools are constantly developing new courses and programs to comply with specific job demands. As industry and demands change, so, too, do the courses and training offered. A list of private schools in Newfoundland and Labrador is available on-line: <www.careers.nelson.com>.

ACTIVITY

Private colleges

Research information on one private college. If possible, find a college that offers programs related to one of your preferred fields of work. Look for the same information you found in the university/college activity:

- admission requirements (high school courses and marks)
- courses you would take in first year (you might need the calendar)
- tuition fees for one year of study
- the degree, diploma or certificate you would receive

Other Colleges

There are various other specialized, government-supported colleges throughout Canada:

- agricultural colleges
- colleges of health sciences
- Nova Scotia College of Art and Design
- Royal Military College

Links

You can search the Internet to find information about most post-secondary options. One good place to start is the Department of Education's site. Another is the School Finder website. Another good site with links is maintained by the Newfoundland and Labrador Association of Career Colleges. Go to <www.careers.nelson.com> for direct links to these sites.

Distance Education

Distance education offers some students the chance to learn independently without attending an actual school. For some programs, you need a computer and Internet service. Others are still conducted by mail. Distance education can work for someone who is self-motivated.

In Newfoundland and Labrador, distance education courses are offered through Memorial University and the College of the North Atlantic. Many rural high schools also benefit from e-learning opportunities through the Centre for Distance Learning and Innovation.

However, you need to be able to motivate yourself, and to work independently. Many students find they need actual contact with a teacher, and you can't get this over the Internet.

Links

The Department of Education's website provides valuable information related to distance learning and supports. Go to <www.careers.nelson.com> for a direct link to this site.

ACTIVITY

Distance education

Individually, or in small groups, locate one distance education program.

1. How did you find it?
2. What would you be doing if you took the program?
3. How would you learn?
4. How would you be marked?

Continuing Education

Continuing education or **continuing studies** programs are offered by many colleges, universities and school boards to help people who cannot attend school full-time, usually because they are working, or only want to take one course at a time. Many distance education programs come under the general heading of continuing education.

Most of us know these other programs as "night school." Their great advantage is flexibility, but they also offer more structure than distance education programs.

ACTIVITY

Night school

What night school programs are offered in your area? If you live in a rural area, how far would you have to go to attend a night school class?

Travel

Travel is definitely educational, and a form of training. There are many opportunities to travel, either by yourself or as part of an organization.

Travel can be costly, but there are ways to travel on a budget. It is very useful if you can work at the same time. For example, Canadians between the ages of 17 and 27 can apply for a "working holiday makers" visa to the United Kingdom. "The purpose of the working holiday maker scheme is to allow young Commonwealth citizens, who do not have commitments which require them to earn a regular wage, to come to the UK for an extended holiday, which they may help fund by working in the UK up to a maximum period of two years."

For further information, you can contact the British High Commission in Ottawa, or visit their website.

Each country has its own rules governing whether you can legally work there when you are travelling, but it is often possible to pick up casual work to help extend your travelling budget.

ACTIVITY

Travel

You can do this activity individually or in small groups:

1. Research student exchanges. Start with the *Exchanges Canada* website, sponsored by Heritage Canada. Answer the following questions:
   - What is the name of the student exchange organization?
   - What does the student exchange organization do?
   - What aspects of the exchange are most interesting to you?
2. Research CUSO:
   - What does CUSO stand for?
   - What does this organization do?
   - What opportunities might it offer you?
   - How would you find out more?

Go to <www.careers.nelson.com> for links to help you with your research.

Focus on Your Best Options

Now that you have completed an overview of **options**, you can focus on what interests you most. Of course, you are still looking for opportunites that suit you, rather than making definite decisions. The first step is to use good information resources to find as many possibilites as you can. Don't start narrowing your options until you've really explored them.

Links

How much will your post-secondary education or training cost? How will you pay for it? The Department of Education's website provides information on financial assistance, including how to apply, who qualifies and how much money is available.

There are also financial assistance programs for individuals considering apprenticeship programs. Go to <www.careers.nelson.com> for links to this information.

ACTIVITY

Your options

You are still exploring opportunities rather than making definite plans. (Unit 4 will focus on the decision-making process.) Using your new research skills, do the following:

Find education/training programs that fit one of your preferred work fields:

1. Pick an educational or training path that interests you.
2. Within that path, find five programs that relate to your preferred field of work.
3. For each program, find the following information:
   - schools that offer the program
   - high school courses you need to take to qualify for *three* of the different schools
   - marks you need to get to qualify for each program in the *three* schools
   - courses you would take during the first year of the program in each of the *three* schools
4. Organize your information in a way that others could easily understand.

For those looking at apprenticeship:

1. Pick a trade that interests you.
2. Telephone or visit the nearest apprenticeship office. What would you have to do to become an apprentice in your chosen trade?
3. How much would you be paid during each term of the apprenticeship?
4. Talk with an employer who hires apprentices (preferably in your chosen trade). What qualities are being looked for in an apprentice?
5. Organize and present the information, as above.

For those going to work, but not to an apprenticeship:

1. Pick an occupation that interests you.
2. Talk with an employer in that field. What qualities are looked for in an employee?
3. Find three continuing or distance education courses in your field:
   - Where can you take them?
   - When?
   - How much do they cost?
   - Are there any prerequisites for the courses?
   - If yes, what are they?
4. Find three courses that would prepare you for starting your own business:
   - Where can you take them?
   - When?
   - How much do they cost?
   - Are there any prerequisites for the courses?
   - If yes, what are they?
5. Organize and present the information, as above.

For those who are planning to travel after high school:

Complete one of the activities listed above—what you might do when you get back.

My Career-Related Learning Has Started

Learning Is Ongoing

Students: "Why are we doing this?"
Teacher: "This course is designed to prepare you for the world of work."

All the learning you do, in school and out, can be connected in some way to occupations and fields of work. For example:

The math skills Ahmed is learning are directly related to accounting, statistics, sciences, banking, trades and technology. Ahmed is also learning transferable skills in his math course, such as thinking logically, following procedures and solving problems. Ahmed's math skills will be useful whenever he is responsible for a budget, or has to follow detailed procedures.

If Ahmed investigates his other courses in this same way, he will find similar connections. And he will be able to answer for himself the question: "Why are we doing this?"

ACTIVITY

School courses and the world of work

What is the connection between your future and the courses you are taking right now? (Remember, your career is more than just your work.)

Part A

1. Investigate the career connections for each of the courses you are taking this year. Ask yourself, teachers and/or other students the following questions:
   - How do the skills we get from this course relate to work we might do in the future?
   - What occupations are related to this knowledge and these skills?
   - How could the knowledge from this course relate to other aspects of my life?
2. Use the answers to create a chart like the one below for each course you are taking:

Subject		
Knowledge & Skills Related to Work	**Knowledge & Skills Related to Life**	**Related Occupation**

If you are involved in a co-operative education program, include this fact on the chart.

Part B

Now go back to the fields of work that you selected in the first section of this unit. For each one, list the subjects that are related to that field. List, also, reasons why they are related. Keep this information in your portfolio.

When you are working on your Three-Year Plan, selecting your courses for next year, keep this information in mind. (Relevance to future work is an important reason for taking a course, but not the only one.)

ACTIVITY

Extra-curricular activities and the world of work

This activity is like the previous one, except now you focus on the knowledge and skills you get outside class:

- school activities (*e.g.*, sports, music, clubs)
- community activities (*e.g.*, lessons, youth groups, clubs, sports, part-time work, volunteer work)
- hobbies
- activities at home (*e.g.*, chores)

1. Make a list of the things you do that fit into one or more of these categories.
2. For each one, list the knowledge and skills you have gained. Get family members and friends to help you with this. Using a chart, map, or some other method, show the connections between the activities and the knowledge and skills.
3. Think of fields of work and occupations that might be related to the skills and knowledge you have identified and add those to your map, chart, etc. Keep this in your Employability Skills Portfolio.

Key Terms

fields of work
occupation
community contribution
job shadow
co-operative education
self-employment
Labour Standards Act
Occupational Health and Safety Act
Canada Labour Code
adaptability
trends
labour market information
university
community college
apprenticeship
private colleges
distance education
continuing education/continuing studies
options

Use a concept map or another graphic organizer to summarize the key ideas in this unit. Build on the key terms and add words, phrases and/or images that will help remind you of those key ideas.

Reflection

Find the list of occupations (and the guess about the number of occupations in Canada) that you made in the Discovery activity on page 103. How many occupations are there actually? Write down as many occupations as you can think of in two minutes. How much has your understanding of your options increased since beginning this unit?

Questions

Knowledge/Understanding

1. List at least fifteen sources of information about occupations. Choose the three that are most useful to you right now and explain why each is useful.
2. Identify a trend in one of the following areas that you predict will have the most impact on your career options: societal, economic, demographic, technological. Write a paragraph to support that prediction.
3. Create a two-column table that lists:
   a) your post-secondary learning options and
   b) one source of information about each option.

Thinking/Inquiry

4. Write five specific questions that you still have about your work and learning options and make a plan for getting the answers.
5. Go back to your answer to question 1. Create a list of criteria that you could use to evaluate an information source (*e.g.*, written for my age group, readily available).

Communication

6. Write a pamphlet that would help grade 9 students start thinking about the many different work and learning options ahead of them.

Application

7. Go to <www.careers.nelson.com>. Visit one of the linked websites specified for this activity and review it for other students in this class.

Taking Stock: Your Portfolio

1. Review the contents.
2. Reconsider your initial responses.
3. Summarize the most important information.

UNIT 4

How Do I Get Where I Want to Go?

How can I make good decisions? How can I make good plans? What tools are available to help me?

The specific answers are different for each person, but there are some general guidelines that can help anyone.

How do I put it all together to get where I want to go?

SECTION

"Listen and learn and find your dream. When you have found it, don't give up."

—*Alwyn Morris, Canadian Olympic canoeist and kayaker*

How Do I Get Where I Want to Go?

In this unit you will:

- apply what you know about yourself and your opportunities to make informed decisions and plans
- set work, learning, personal and community goals
- review your Three-Year Plan
- research the open and hidden job markets
- identify your network and market yourself
- create job application tools, *e.g.*, résumés, cover letters
- interview and be interviewed
- plan a summer or part-time work search

Each step you take in the ongoing journey of career planning holds the possibility of a new direction, new experiences, new people and new challenges.

Do you find all this newness a little scary? That's not unusual. But imagine following a life trail that was always the same. Would you want to choose a career now and stick with it until retirement? What happens if your interests, needs or dreams change? Imagine being stuck forever with the results of one decision.

Look at the work being done in these photographs. Which appeals to you most right now? Can you imagine doing one of the other kinds of work later in your life? Why? And how would you make that change?

Life is about learning and changing, so you might as well make it work for you.

DISCOVERY

Where are you headed?

1. Write down three fields of work that you do *not* want to enter.
2. Now list reasons why you don't want to work in those areas—at least three or four reasons each.
3. Name one personal strength you have that would not be fully utilized in each of the occupational fields you don't like. Does that one strength point in a positive direction?

Nadia's Story

It is difficult to choose a direction in life. Generally, it's easier to think about where you *don't* want to go. So how do you find a goal you *do* want to steer toward?

Nadia slammed the door of her room and lay down on her bed. Arguing with her mother made her head hurt. Her mother could be so bossy, and she just never let up. Nadia looked at the clock. She hoped her dad wasn't going to be late picking her up for their regular Thursday night together.

The argument with her mother had been about school, like always. They didn't argue much about parties, or boys, or friends. For some reason, Nadia felt really confident in all of these areas, and her mom trusted that confidence. No, it was always about school.

"Your father's here," her mom yelled up the stairs.

Nadia sighed with relief as she got up from her bed. "Bye, Mom," she said as she slipped out the door.

She and her dad did the usual thing—went to his apartment and made dinner. Even though her dad cooked all day for a living, he still had energy for cooking at night, and they had great meals. Nadia loved helping, and the two of them worked together easily.

"What's for dinner?" she asked.

"Something spicy," he answered. "Starting with chicken."

Nadia liked staying with her dad, but his apartment was a mess. At least the kitchen wasn't too chaotic. Nadia was neater than her dad—but in most other ways, she was like him. Her dad was sometimes too easy-going, but he understood people, and she shared this with him, too.

She started to tell him about the fight. "So, it was about math. I said, 'Hello! Mother? Are you listening? I don't like math. I'm not good at math.'" Her mother was getting a master's degree in business part time at night, and she seemed to think that everyone else should do the same. "Everyone else" meant Nadia. But Nadia thought that, for her, 12 years of school would be enough for now.

Her dad grated ginger over the de-skinned chicken breasts. "Uh-huh?"

"I joined the school drama society like she wanted me to," Nadia went on. "She should be happy!"

Nadia cut up vegetables while her father finished the sauce and poured it on the chicken. Finally, everything was in the oven. As they sat down and relaxed, her dad said, "Why do you think she feels that way?"

"She's always going on about 'choice.' It's one of her favourite words. You know, 'life's about choices.' But she doesn't want to give me any!"

Nadia's father nodded. "When I was your age, I was always fighting with my dad. He'd gone to McGill University and insisted I go there too. I was determined not to."

"So what happened?" Nadia asked with interest. She hadn't heard this story before.

"I failed grade 12, and had to do it again. It drove him crazy. I didn't know what I was doing, but I was sure I wouldn't do what he wanted. When I did go to university, I only lasted one year."

Who cares about university, Nadia thought, but her dad was continuing, "University wasn't right for me. But my point is—I was making choices, even when I thought I wasn't. If I had only been able to think clearly about what I did want to do..." He sighed. "If there's one thing I learned from your mother, it was this: 'Play from your strengths.' You've got to do the things you're good at."

He cleared his throat, and Nadia waited for him to go on. "Believe it or not, your mother is interested in what's best for you too. We both know her well enough to know that's true."

Sure, thought Nadia. *She's just not interested in what I want.*

Her dad must have known what she was thinking, because he smiled at her. It made her feel good, and she smiled back. "I know she can be difficult to talk to sometimes," he acknowledged. "But she's steering you on the right track. Making choices—we're doing it all the time, even when we don't realize it. Are you with me?"

"Maybe," Nadia said. "But I don't know what direction I want to take."

"Whatever it is you want to do," he said, "you're going to need school to get there. No easy way out of that one. But it's all about choosing what you want. That's all your mother wants you to do... Well, it looks like dinner's ready."

Nadia helped her father dish up the food. She was glad they'd had the talk. She was glad she had her mom too. She just needed to choose her own way.

ACTIVITY

About Nadia

1. What is the message that both of Nadia's parents are trying to give her?
2. What other piece of advice does her father give her?
3. Examine the way Nadia and her parents think. What ideas would you challenge? What is the basis for your challenges?
4. It is not unusual for teens and parents to disagree about educational and career decisions. When you and your parents disagree about school, how do you handle the situation?

Making Good Decisions

Many people, like Nadia, find it difficult to make important decisions about their lives. Or, if they do make decisions easily, they may not be willing to rethink those decisions if the results are disappointing.

Making good decisions in a changing world is what career development is all about. In this section, you will expand on the decision-making model presented in Unit 1, and use it as you set some concrete goals.

DISCOVERY

How do you set goals?

Jot down as many words as you can think of that relate to the idea of goal setting for your career and education. It will help you to think back to an important goal you have set in the past. Think of:

- why you set goals
- what you have to think about
- what you have to know
- how you might go about it
- who can help you

Balanced Decision Making

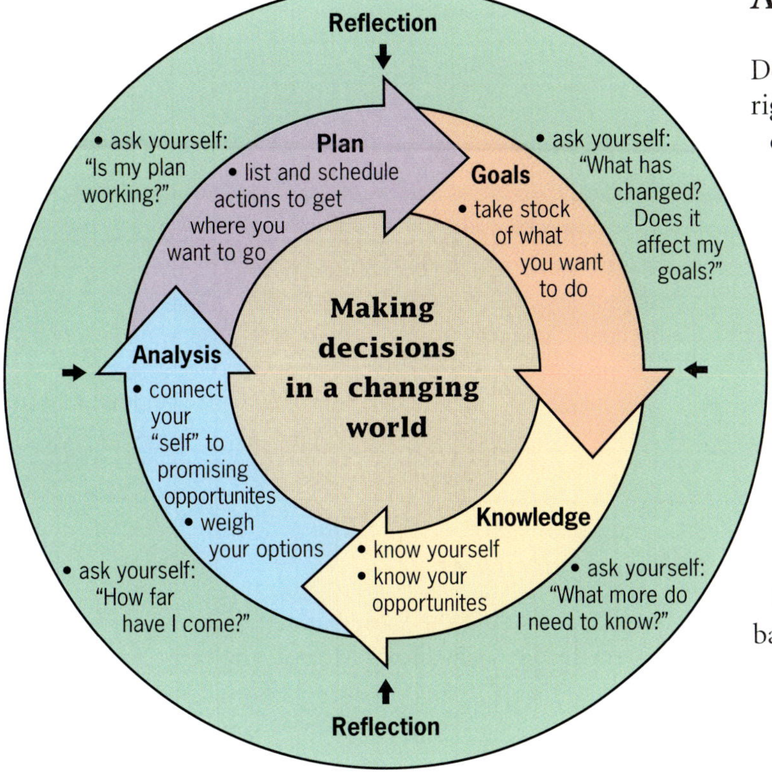

A Decision-Making Model

Decisions cannot always be made in a rigid, linear way. The world and you are changing: new information affects your goals, which affects your plans, which affects the results of your plans, which affects your goals, and so on…

Seeing the decision-making process as a series of steps—even if you know that in reality the steps are not so regular—can help you move forward. The chart below provides more detail. The examples in the last column combine reason with intuition. Ultimately, you should look for the balance that works best for you.

Balanced Decision Making

	Using Logical Thinking	Using Intuition	Examples
Goals	**Focus on goals as targets:** Identify clearly the decision to be made. Identify a number of possible choices.	**Be flexible—prepare to change your goals and decisions:** New options appear. Old options disappear.	The decision to drop a course may be about dealing with frustration, not about the value of the course.
Knowledge	**Acquire knowledge about yourself and the world:** Collect relevant information about each of your options.	**It's OK to be uncertain:** There are no guarantees. You may not have all the information you need. And the information you have will likely change.	The courses offered by your high school, and by post-secondary schools, may change every year, so any planning beyond next year cannot be definite.

continued

	Using Logical Thinking	Using Intuition	Examples
Analysis	**Analyse the situation:** Look at the pros and cons of each option. Evaluate each option and choose the best one. **Note:** Your best option is your new goal!	**Use your intuition. Listen to your gut feelings:** Ask yourself whether each option "feels right." Figure out why or why not.	Logic tells you that a particular choice is the best, but a nagging feeling tells you that it isn't. Keep re-assessing your options and stay flexible.
Plan	**Organize a plan of action:** Plan a series of short and medium-term goals. Take action.	**Use your imagination:** Discover different ways to do things.	Use visualization, the way athletes do, to create a clear picture of your goal.
Reflection	**Evaluate your decision:** Analyse the results of your plan and adjust your goals and your plan if necessary.	**Pay attention to your state of mind:** Remember that your goals are for you. How happy are you?	You choose courses to prepare yourself for a particular college or university program, then you decide that that program is not what you want after all.

ACTIVITY

Making balanced career decisions

Reproduce the chart below, providing the information indicated in the second column. Refer back to the chart above. Most of the information you need exists in your portfolio.

Making Balanced Career Decisions

Stages in the Decision-Making Cycle	My Summary
Goals	• most important things in the picture of "Who Can I Become?" • occupations I want to think about as options for my future
Knowledge	• brief summary of what aspects of myself are most likely to influence my goals • brief summary of most important information about opportunities (occupational and educational) that I want to pursue
Analysis	• summary of how those opportunities suit me • analysis of the pros and cons of options available to me
Plan	• 3 or 4 things I can start doing now to meet my goals
Reflection	• questions I should be asking myself on a regular basis

Redefining Goals

Different Kinds of Goals

Up until now you have expressed very general goals, such as:

- "I want to work with people."
- "I want to have a flexible schedule."
- "I want to work with computer graphics."

To *achieve* your goals, however, you will have to start thinking in more concrete terms. This should be easier now that you have gathered and analysed information about yourself, and related that information back to your broad goals for the future.

To start refining your goals, it helps to think of them in categories:

Personal Goals—concerning yourself, your family, your friends and other people who are important to you
Work Goals—occupations and jobs
Learning Goals—in a school setting or outside, for yourself, or how to achieve other goals
Community Goals—contributions you make and benefits you receive

It is also helpful to think of goals in the categories "short-term," "medium-term" and "long-term."

- **Short-term goals**—These are things you want to accomplish next week or next month, such as: "do the reading on Wednesday, so I can write my English paper on the weekend, and not stay up all night Sunday to get it in on time."
- **Medium-term goals**—These are further in the future, maybe three months to a year, such as: "raise my mark in science by 10 percent on the next report card: paying attention in class, doing my homework, getting my assignments in on time, and studying at least three nights in a row before each test."
- **Long-term goals**—You set these goals for the next ten years, such as: "go to college and get a certificate in media arts, because I want to be a graphics designer" or "get a university degree in history, plus teacher training, because I'd like to teach social studies in high school."

Four Keys to Practical Goals

Measurable	Achievable	Concrete	Scheduled
So you can see your progress:	So you can take each step with confidence:	So it is clear what you will do:	So it is clear when you will do each task:
"I will raise my mark by 5 percent by next test."	"I will eat salad instead of fries at lunch every day."	"I will sign up for intramural basketball in September."	"I will do the outline by Thursday, and the final draft by Monday."

Remember: You can set all the goals in the world, but you have to really *want* to achieve them or they won't get done. Your teacher sets the due date, but you decide to get the work in on time.

ACTIVITY

Analysing goal statements

Rewrite the following goal statements to ensure that they are measurable, achievable, concrete and scheduled (MACS).

1. I'm going to be a great cartoonist someday.
2. I want to be around plants, but I don't want to be a farmer. Maybe flowers…
3. My uncle's a funeral director. I wonder if there are courses for that.
4. If I could open my own day care, I'd love working with toddlers.
5. Those places where they race dirt bikes—I could build one of those tracks.

ACTIVITY

Be a goal-setting consultant

Working in pairs, each of you can act as a consultant for the other as you do the following:

1. Write *a long-term work goal,* one that you want to achieve by the time you are 25.
2. Write *a medium-term learning goal* that will help you achieve your long-term goal. It should be one that you want to achieve over the next three months to a year.
3. Write *a short-term learning goal* that will help you achieve your medium-term goal. It should be something that you want to accomplish within the next week or month.
4. In each case, incorporate the four characteristics of a good goal.
5. Acting as the consultant, check your partner's goals to make sure that they include all four characteristics. Offer suggestions for improvement, if needed.

Reflection

Going back to the Balanced Decision-Making model on page 171, notice that there is a "Goals" stage. Does it cover everything you've been doing while you've been setting goals? If not, what other stages are important to goal-setting? Explain your answer.

Be a "Goals Getter"

Want It
The more you want something, the more motivated you will be.
Need It
Knowing how you will benefit will increase your motivation.
Time It
Set time limits, so your goal won't take forever.
Check It
Keep track of your progress.
Step It
Take "baby steps." (As you become successful with short-term goals, and become more confident, you can take bigger steps.)
See It
Write, draw, or collect pictures of what you want. (Look at the images every day, remind yourself why you are doing what you are doing.)
Do It
Dream big in the long term, but set realistic goals for the short term.

Setting My Own Goals

Try It!

You've been learning and using a balanced decision-making model. You've learned more about goals, and how to set them. You've tried some goal setting with a partner. Now you can apply these skills to set medium to long-term:

- work goals
- learning goals
- personal goals
- community goals

Remember to relate these goals to your own characteristics and needs, and to existing opportunities. Also, be sure that your goal statements include the four keys to practical goals on page 174.

ACTIVITY

Setting work goals

Your objective is to select at least two occupational fields that might be suitable for you. You are choosing a range of possibilities. Learning the process is the important thing in this activity. Follow these steps:

1. **Identify the decision you have to make, but be aware that the nature of the decision could change.**
   In this activity, the decision is to choose the two occupational fields that relate best with your interests, skills and personal characteristics.
2. **Identify possible options, keeping in mind that new options are created all the time and some old options disappear.**
   Select four occupational fields that you looked at in Unit 3. (By the end of this activity, you will have narrowed these down to two.)
3. **Collect information about each of the options, but keep in mind that the information may change.**
   You should have all or most of this information from your previous work.
4. **Evaluate each option, comparing it to what you think is important, but use your intuitive "gut reaction" also, about whether an option "feels right."**
   In this case, "what you think is important" is the set of interests, skills and personal characteristics that you identified in Unit 2. They are your "measuring sticks" for evaluating each possible field. Make a chart that shows which of these fit each of the four occupational fields.
5. **Choose two of these options, but keep in mind that things change. Take some time to discuss these two occupational fields with your parents or your teacher.**
   Your task here is to choose the *two* fields that seem to suit you best. These choices may change. Explain why you selected the two that you did.

ACTIVITY

Setting learning goals

Your objective is to set your learning goals, up to when you enter the work world. Your goals should prepare you for *both* of the occupational fields you selected in the previous activity. Again, learning the process is the important thing in this activity. Follow these steps:

1. **Identify the decision you have to make, but be aware that the nature of the decision could change.**
   In this activity, the decision is to choose learning goals that relate to the two occupational fields that you chose in the previous activity.

2. **Identify possible options, keeping in mind that new options are created all the time, and some old options disappear.**
   In Unit 3, you explored educational and training possibilities. For this activity, select five possible post-secondary education/training programs.

3. **Collect information about each of the options, but keep in mind that the information may change.**
   From your work in Unit 3, you know how to find this information. You may have some of it already. You will be looking for information that is given in the next step. *(e.g., An MBA is one or two years. Medical school is four years, then there's being an intern.)*

4. **Evaluate each program by comparing it to what you think is important, but use your intuition also about whether an option "feels right."**
   In this case, "what you think is important" is your set of interests, strengths, needs and learning preferences. You also need to obtain the qualifications and skills to enter these fields. Use these to evaluate each of the five programs. Make a chart that shows which of these fit each of the two occupational fields.

5. **Choose one of these options, but keep in mind that things change.**
   Choose the learning goals that will prepare you to enter both of the occupational fields. These are choices that suit you best now. These choices may change. Explain why you selected these goals.

ACTIVITY

Setting personal and community goals

Your objective is to set one personal improvement goal and one community contribution goal that you want to achieve before you graduate from high school. Follow these steps for each:

1. **Identify the decision you have to make, but be aware that the nature of the decision could change.**
   In this activity, the decision is to choose one personal improvement goal and one community contribution goal that seem to fit best with your interests, skills and personal characteristics.

2. **Identify possible options, keeping in mind that new options are created all the time, and some old options disappear.**
   For each category, select five possible options.

3. **Collect information about each of the options, but keep in mind that the information may change.**
   Seek information from parents, other adults and friends, about opportunities and activities that exist in your community.
   (e.g., Mrs. Laki next door says that I could volunteer at the Out Of The Cold program this winter.)

4. **Evaluate each option by comparing it to what you think is important, but use your intuition also, about whether an option "feels right."**
   What is important to you? What will you use as your "measuring stick" for each goal? Make a chart comparing your options to what is important to you. *(e.g., I think it's important to help the homeless.)*

5. **Choose one of these options, but keep in mind that things change.**
   Choose two goals, one in each category, that seem to suit you best now. These choices may change. Explain why you selected the goals that you did. *(e.g., I'll take a life-saving course, and I'll volunteer at the Out Of The Cold program. Then, if a homeless person is hurt, I might be able to help.)*

Making Good Plans

You are head of social activities at your school, and are in charge of a dance that's happening in six weeks. What do you do? You get a dance committee together, and you make a plan, right?

Having a successful dance in six weeks is your goal. You can't organize the dance without a plan. A **plan** is a way of making your goal a reality.

DISCOVERY

How will you plan the event?

Work as a group to plan a large-scale activity: a dance, an outing, a trip. Keep a record of your planning process. What tasks are necessary? What information do you need? Who will be involved?

Creating a Plan of Action

Starting Out

Career planning is about being more aware of the decisions you're making.

You have already made decisions about the courses you take. This is part of your Three-Year Plan (see page 189). You've made decisions that helped you develop the skills you now have.

Some people think that if you plan something, it won't be free and spontaneous. Actually, the reverse is true. Good planning means that you do what needs to be done. Then, when your goals are achieved, you have the freedom to be spontaneous, and you don't have to worry.

Here are some planning questions that will help you:

1. What goal do I want to achieve?
2. What tasks need to be done?
3. What steps do I need to take?
4. What do I need to learn in order to take those steps?
5. Who could help me do what needs to be done?
6. What possible obstacles or barriers could get in the way?
7. What are the timelines? In what order do things need to be done, and by what date?
8. Do I need to change the list of tasks because of my answers to questions 3, 4 and 5?

If you are planning with a group, you need to add:

9. Who is responsible for doing each task?
10. How will we communicate with each another?

After you've answered these questions, review and reconsider the plan constantly as you follow it. You have to be flexible with plans—as you are with goals, decisions and portfolios—and ready to make any changes that are needed.

Barriers

A **barrier** is something that gets in your way. For example, not answering any one of the above questions would be a barrier to planning your event. People also have barriers: different people, different barriers.

Take Paul, for example. He's shy, and hates being shy. He has trouble speaking up in class. If he has a problem, he can't ask for help. He also has trouble making friends.

Paul's shyness is a barrier to doing things he wants to do—like feeling comfortable in groups, or going new places. Paul wants to be a teacher some day, but how is he going to manage that when he's so shy?

Dina has physical barriers. She needs a wheelchair. Every time she has a goal, she has to include accessibility in her plans. "When I think about going to a restaurant, I have to make sure I can get in," she says. "That means I have to phone in advance." Dina would like to be a travel counsellor, but she knows that job might require travelling. She says that her wheelchair may be an obstacle to achieving that career goal.

Other people have knowledge barriers. Saad says, "I'd really like to be my own boss someday." He'd like to create a great new software company. Saad has computer skills, but he lacks business skills.

ACTIVITY

Breaking down barriers

1. Brainstorm ways that Paul, Dina and Saad could overcome the barriers they face.
2. Make a list of some of your barriers.
3. How do you handle them?

Tips for Breaking Barriers

Think creatively
If going at a problem in one way brings you up against a barrier, go at it a different way. Brainstorming with a group, for instance, can help you look beyond first solutions and build upon the creativity of others.

Ask for help
This is a fairly simple solution that many people won't use. You probably know people who will not ask their teachers for help when they are having difficulty. Make a list of people in your school that you could go to for advice.

Links

The Aladdin Factor, by Jack Canfield and Mark Victor Hansen (Berkeley Books, 1995), can help you ask for what you want and need. Go to <www.careers.nelson.com> for links to resources that can help you overcome other barriers.

ACTIVITY

Looking for barriers

Go back to your personal, occupational, learning and community goal statements, from the activities in Section 1 of this unit.

For each goal, list at least five possible obstacles. Keep this list with your goal statements in your portfolio.

ACTIVITY

Dealing with barriers

This is like brainstorming, except you do it by yourself. It pushes you to go beyond your usual way of thinking.

1. Select one of your more challenging learning goals.
2. Identify one barrier that could cause difficulty in reaching your goal. Ideally, this is a barrier that is facing you right now in your life.
3. Sit by yourself, where you will not be interrupted.
4. Describe the barrier in writing at the top of a sheet of paper.
5. Now write down 15 ways to overcome the barrier. The first solutions will probably come to you easily. If 15 solutions come easily, do more. If thinking up solutions becomes difficult, don't give up until you have 15. This activity makes you really push yourself to think differently. Often it is the last few solutions that are the most valuable.

Taking Action

After you have answered all the questions on page 181, you need to make your detailed plan—the more detailed the better.

Action is the key word—you have to *do* something. Some people make wonderful plans, but don't follow them! Then they wonder why things didn't work out the way they wanted. Sometimes they even decide that planning doesn't work.

"The plan won't work unless you do!"
"If you fail to plan, you'll plan to fail!"

ACTIVITY

Planning strategies

Use this activity to help you draw up an action plan. This involves:

- setting realistic long-term goals (pick one of your goals from the summary activities in the last section)
- identifying short-term goals (which are part of your plan to reach your long-term goal)

Record one long-term goal, and then a medium term and short-term goal that lead to it.

Long-Term Goal	**Medium-Term Goal**	**Short-Term Goal**
Goal: My goal is to:	**Goal:** My goal is to:	**Goal:** My goal is to:
Steps: To reach my goal, I plan to:	**Steps:** To reach my goal, I plan to:	**Steps:** To reach my goal, I plan to:
Obstacles: I must watch out for:	**Obstacles:** I must watch out for:	**Obstacles:** I must watch out for:
Knowledge: This is what I need to learn:	**Knowledge:** This is what I need to learn:	**Knowledge:** This is what I need to learn:
Helpers: These are the people who can help me:	**Helpers:** These are the people who can help me:	**Helpers:** These are the people who can help me:
Timeline: I plan to achieve this goal by:	**Timeline:** I plan to achieve this goal by:	**Timeline:** I plan to achieve this goal by:
Reward: My reward for achieving this goal will be:	**Reward:** My reward for achieving this goal will be:	**Reward:** My reward for achieving this goal will be:

A Parable: The Sinking Ship

During the Second World War, a ship was crossing the ocean at night, carrying oil. Its cargo was needed desperately. The weather was dark and cold, and the sea was running rough. A cold wind blew over the decks.

An explosion—the ship had been torpedoed! Every crew member felt the same fear, caught between fire and the icy black sea. Sailors came racing up the ladders from the lower decks and began to head for the lifeboats to get as far from the stricken tanker as possible. They could smell oil leaking from the ruptured hull. Soon the ship would sink or burn.

"Follow me! I have a plan to save the ship, and ourselves too!" cried the captain, but others shouted back, "Are you crazy? She's going to blow up any minute!"

Some sailors did follow the captain, and he led them below. He knew that a tanker full of oil is hard to sink, because oil is lighter than water. The tanks that hadn't been ruptured would keep the ship afloat. If they worked together, and quickly, perhaps they could prevent a fire, and save the ship.

And so it happened. No one died, or had to drift in an open boat on the cold sea. By morning, the damaged ship was underway again, and eventually it reached port.

Reflection

What is the value of planning as illustrated in the parable? Can you think of a story in your own life that illustrates the same point? When has positive leadership had an impact on you?

Case Studies

Joe
Joe is doing very well at his part-time job. Unfortunately, his co-worker, a full-timer, tends to leave much of his own work for Joe to do. Joe makes less money per hour than the full-timer, and doesn't think this is fair. What should he do?

Carolyn
Carolyn is hardworking, and does well in school. Her favourite subject is music. It comes easily to her, but she still practises for hours each day because she loves it so much. Her parents think this is a waste of time, because they want her to become a doctor, like her mother. What should she do?

Dominic
Dominic is a great hockey player—everyone says so. If he keeps playing so well, he has a chance of moving up in the divisions. Unfortunately, hockey interferes with school, and his marks have been suffering. What should he do?

Tiffany
Tiffany is in Level I, and has just moved to a new school, in a new town, in the middle of November. All of the other kids have made friends and settled into their groups. Tiffany is feeling like an outsider. What should she do?

Chantelle
Chantelle is an average student in all her academic subjects, but she really does well in her automotive technology course. Sometimes she feels awkward, however, because she is the only girl in the class. Although her teacher and classmates are friendly and encouraging, she still feels uncomfortable. She is thinking of not taking the senior automotive technology course next year. What should she do?

Links

There are resources that can help you work through goal-setting and planning scenarios. The *Career Wise* CD-ROM is one such resource. Go to <www.careers.nelson.com> for links to others.

ACTIVITY

Be a consultant

State a goal for each case study, and write a short action plan for each person, outlining steps. Keep in mind the planning questions on page 181.

Planning My Education

Don't Avoid It!

Every year, from Grade 9 to graduation, at least one teacher or counsellor will remind you of the requirements you need to get your Senior High Graduation Diploma. You will be tempted to tune them out. Don't! Unfortunately, every year in Newfoundland and Labrador, there are students who don't graduate from high school because they failed to meet the necessary **graduation requirements**. Make sure you know exactly what you have to do, and do it. The next activity takes you through the requirements, and your plan to obtain them.

ACTIVITY

Graduation requirements

1. Find the graduation requirements. They are usually in your school's course calendar.
2. Make a list of the requirements. Use the following questions as a guide:
   - What is a required credit? How many do you need to graduate? List your required credits, and when you will have each completed (month and year).
   - What is an optional credit? How many do you need to graduate? List your optional credits, and when you will have them completed.
   - What is the requirement for community contribution? How many hours are required? When will you do this?
3. Here are some additional questions. Find the answers and write them down. You do need to know them.
   - What are the types of courses offered in Grade 9 and Level I? How are they different from each other?
   - What types of courses are offered in Level II and Level III? How are they different from each other?
   - List five places in your community where you could volunteer and help complete your mandatory 30 hours of community contribution.
   - What are Public Examinations? Which courses require the completion of a Public Exam?
   - How are the Senior High Graduation Diploma and the School Achievement Certificate different?
   - What are the different types of graduation designations?
4. Write a list of questions that you still have about earning a Senior High Graduation Diploma.

Keep this information in your portfolio and use it in your planning.

Reflection

Discuss why graduation requirements exist. Give reasons for each of them.

Links

Newfoundland and Labrador Senior High School graduation requirements are set by the Department of Education. You can get copies of policy documents for free, or you can go to the Department's website and view them on-line.

The Department of Education has also published a booklet, *On Course: Handbook for Grade 9 Parents and Students* that is designed to help students understand what is required of them. It too is available on-line. Go to <www.careers.nelson.com> for direct links to these resources.

Your Three-Year Plan

In Grade 9, you and your parents were introduced to the Senior High School Program. At that time, the course offerings at your local high school were probably discussed, as well as requirements for placement in these courses. You were also presented with the three-year course planning guide entitled *On Course: Handbook for Grade 9 Parents and Students.* This guide, produced by the Department of Education, outlines all the senior high graduation requirements and includes a planner that allows you to keep track of your credits earned over the course of your three years. This handbook also includes information regarding admission requirements to Memorial University, the College of the North Atlantic and other local private training institutions.

ACTIVITY

Review your Three-Year Plan

Review the credits required to earn your graduation diploma. Are there any course areas you have not included in your Three-Year Plan? If so, be sure to make the necessary changes to your plan.

Links

Your teacher-advisor and guidance counsellor are there to help you make informed choices at key transition points in your schooling. They have access to many resources that can help you.

Using Good Tools and Strategies

Maybe you want a part-time job so you can gain work experience, or you need a summer job to start saving for college, or you intend to work full-time once you graduate from high school. Whatever your occupational, learning or personal goals are, you need to know how to put a work search plan into action. In this section, you will learn how to find out about jobs, how to apply for them and how to go through the hiring process.

DISCOVERY

Are you hopeful or discouraged about finding a job?

How do you feel about these statements?

> *"Employers need to find creative, self-motivated people to work for them just as badly as I need to find a job and make a living. This fact gives me power."*
>
> *"I am afraid that there is no place in the working world where I will feel at home."*
>
> *"I can't get a job because I don't have any experience, and I can't get experience because I don't have a job."*

Develop a creative response to one or more of these.

The Job Market

Open and Hidden

Perhaps you're thinking about getting a part-time or summer job, and wondering where to start. Maybe you would like to know how easy or difficult it is to get work in general. This section is about techniques for locating job openings, and then getting the work you want.

How do you find jobs? You have to look through both the **open job market** and the **hidden job market**. Here's how they work.

Open Job Market (15 percent of all available jobs)	Hidden Job Market (85 percent of all available jobs)
Jobs are advertised in: • newspapers • Internet job banks, such as the National Job Bank and the Electronic Labour Exchange • company websites • Human Resource Career Centres • youth employment centres • trade publications, (magazines published by specific industries, such as the retail industry) • professional association magazines such as the Canadian Nurses' Association.	**Jobs are not advertised anywhere.**
How jobs get filled: • Employers take applications or résumés, and interview applicants.	**How jobs get filled:** • Employers hire people who have been recommended to them. • People hear about the jobs through "word of mouth."

Four Stages of a Job Opening

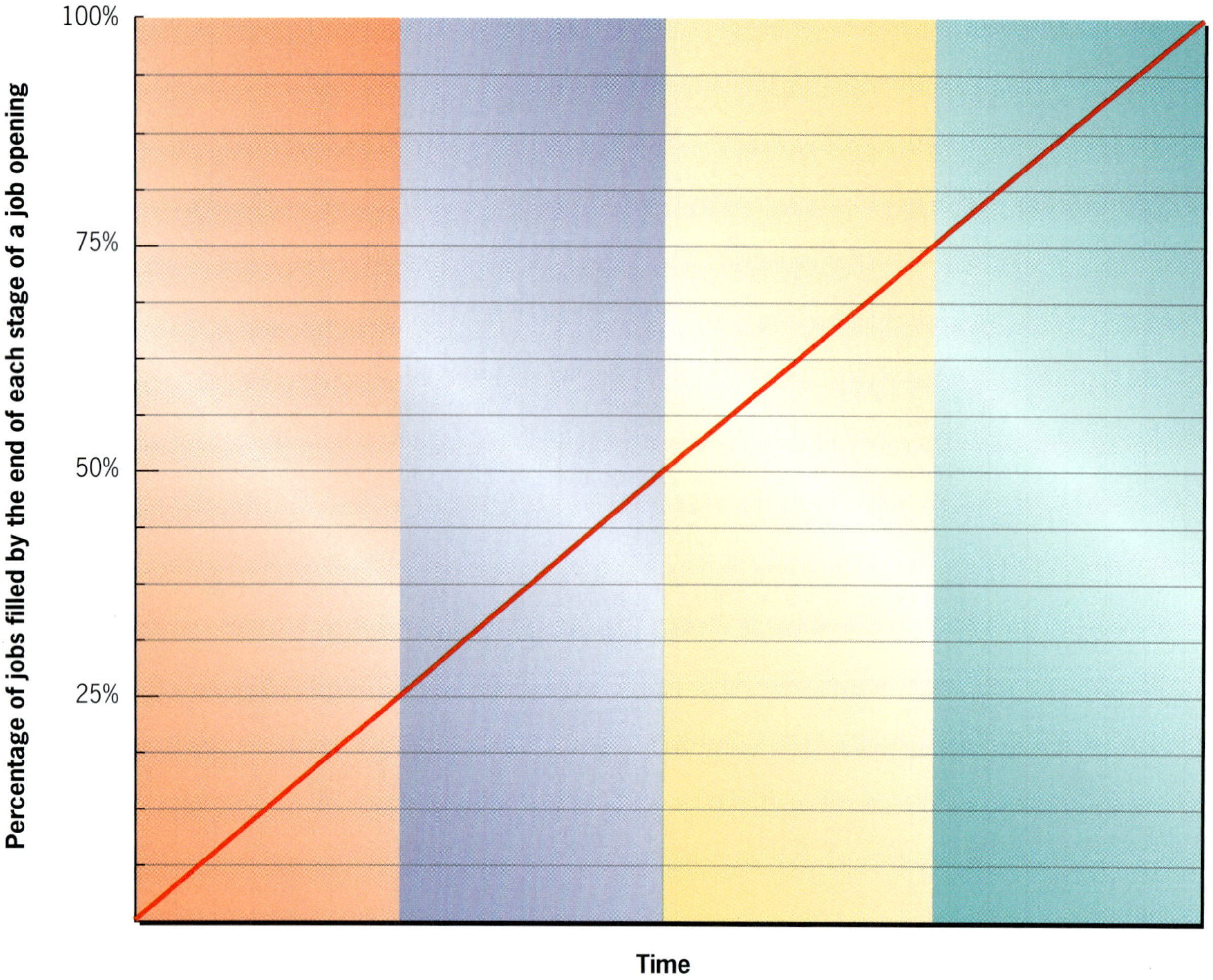

First Stage
There's no opening. But good managers are always looking for good people.

Second Stage
Managers are beginning to think they need somebody, but they haven't done anything about it.

Third Stage
A job opening exists. The word is put out in the company: "Does anybody know someone?" Applications are accepted—yours, if you know about it.

Fourth Stage
Most job openings don't get this far. An ad is placed, and hundreds apply. Now you're competing against them all.

Most hirings take place by stage three, on the basis of a personal referral.

ACTIVITY

Survey

Conduct an in-class survey to find out how many people have had paying jobs, what those jobs were, and how they found them.

Finding Summer and Part-Time Work

The Job Market for Young People

Of the market that you would be entering for part-time and summer jobs, only 15 percent is open. When you conducted your in-class survey (page 192), how many people got jobs by answering ads and how many got jobs by knowing someone? This information should help you plan your own immediate work search.

ACTIVITY

Find a job

Apply your goal-setting and planning skills to your own job search. Whether you would like part-time work during the school year—even if it's next year—or whether you hope to find a summer job, you can start the search now.

1. Set your short-term, medium-term and long-term job search goals.
2. Create a plan. Don't forget to include research as part of your plan.
3. Make a list of tools that you will need (*e.g.*, a résumé—see page 202).

Links

There are organizations that try to help people your age find work (*e.g.*, HRSDC's Student Summer Work Experience Program, and the Department of Human Resources, Labour and Employment's Student Employment Program). *Youth Link*, a publication of the HRSDC, is a comprehensive list of useful contacts. You can also go to <www.careers.nelson.com> to start a database of useful websites.

Networking

Jeremy's Story

Jeremy wanted part-time work at the new mall where his friend Achama had just gotten a job at the video store. When he saw Achama before English class, he congratulated her on her new job and asked, "Are there any more jobs at the video store?"

Achama shook her head. "No, but my friend Jake told me there's a new restaurant opening at the mall and there are going to be some jobs there."

"Jake? Does he go to school here?"

"No, you don't know him," Achama answered. "But I'm sure he wouldn't mind if I gave you his number. He'd be glad to help."

Jeremy's spirits lifted. "That would be great," he said. "I'll give him a call. Thanks."

Have you ever had a conversation like this? Then you were **networking**—connecting with someone for help or advice. If you work at building your **network**, it can be one of your most important tools for finding work and achieving your dreams.

Why Networks Work

Do you know the expression "It isn't what you know, it's who you know"? Maybe it's not fair, but most employers would rather hire a person recommended to them than take a chance on a stranger.

So, *who* you know gets you to the door. It's still *what* you know that gets you through the door—your education, skills and experience have to fit the job.

But getting to that door often requires a network. The bigger your network, the more people you know, the more doors you'll find open to you. Why? Because each person in your network has unique knowledge and experience that might help you. Not only that, but all the people in your network have networks of their own. By tapping into one person's knowledge, you may also be tapping into the knowledge of many other people.

ACTIVITY

Network know-how

Create a map of people who might help you learn about occupational fields or find work. To keep it relatively simple, focus either on one occupational field that interests you or on one kind of part-time or summer work.

- Put your name in the centre of a sheet of paper. You will probably need a large sheet.
- Around it, write the names of the people you know who could give you leads to other people (family, friends, neighbours, friends' families).
- Talk with these people, and ask if they can give you leads to other people who might help you. It is like the ripples created when you throw a pebble in a pond. You start the process, and contact waves spread out.
- Contact these people to let them know what you are looking for, whether it is information or actual work. Ask if they have any leads, and if they know anyone else you might talk to.

Your own contact card

When you are networking, you may want to have a contact card on which to list your name, contact information, and what your focus and/or experience is. Office supply companies print cards for a reasonable price, or you can create your own using computer software and blank cards, which you can purchase at business supply stores.

Frances Slaney

Telephone: 709-555-1975

Experienced in:
Customer Service
Event Planning
Cash and Sales

134 Elizabeth Avenue, St. John's, NL A1A 3Z3

Applying for a Job

Some Practical Advice

When you see a job that interests you, read the advertisement thoroughly and take note of the details:

- job responsibilities
- job hours
- required skills
- required education
- required experience
- whether an application is necessary
- closing deadline if you have to send in a résumé

If it's a job you've heard about from someone, ask that person to tell you as much as possible about it.

Research the employer. Find out more about the business. For example, if it's a store that's hiring, visit the store. What can you learn about the merchandise and the customers?

If you need to send a résumé, make sure you know *exactly* who to send it to. Phone for the correct name (spelling!) and title of the person.

If there's not enough information in the ad, don't be afraid to call—people who are hiring are used to getting requests for information.

Network—if you know people who can give you the inside track on the job, phone them.

See how well your qualifications match the job requirements. If the match isn't perfect, that doesn't mean you shouldn't apply. A job ad is a "wish list" in which the employer describes the ideal job applicant. Chances are that no candidate will be a perfect match.

A Sample Work Application

APPLICATION FOR EMPLOYMENT

POSITION APPLIED FOR Sales clerk

WAGES EXPECTED $7.50/hour

DATE AVAILABLE immediately

LAST NAME Jones FIRST Keith MIDDLE Sydney

STREET ADDRESS 51 Cornwall Heights

St. John's, NL A1E 3G7

TELEPHONE—HOME (709) 555-7125 TELEPHONE—WORK —

IF YOU HAVE WORKED FOR OUR COMPANY BEFORE, STATE WHEN, AT WHICH LOCATION AND THE REASON FOR LEAVING N/A

NAME EMPLOYED UNDER (IF NOW DIFFERENT) N/A

PLEASE INDICATE THE HOURS YOU ARE AVAILABLE TO WORK EACH DAY

DAY	EARLIEST TIME	LATEST TIME
SUNDAY	10:00 am	6:00 pm
MONDAY	4:00 pm	10:00 pm
TUESDAY	4:00 pm	10:00 pm
WEDNESDAY	4:00 pm	10:00 pm
THURSDAY	4:00 pm	10:00 pm
FRIDAY	4:00 pm	10:00 pm
SATURDAY	9:00 am	10:00 pm

ARE YOU LEGALLY ELIGIBLE TO WORK IN CANADA? YES ☒ NO ☐

EDUCATION AND TRAINING

SCHOOL	GRADE/LEVEL COMPLETED	COURSES STUDIED	CERTIFICATE, DIPLOMA, DEGREE OR LICENSE RECEIVED
SECONDARY SCHOOL	12	Business	Senior High Graduation Diploma in progress
COLLEGE/UNIVERSITY	—	—	—
OTHER	—	—	—

WORK EXPERIENCE

LIST YOUR PREVIOUS EXPERIENCE, BEGINNING WITH YOUR MOST RECENT EMPLOYER

EMPLOYER Pete's Pizza		STARTING POSITION Server	STARTING WAGES/SALARY $7.00/HR
STREET ADDRESS CITY 630 Kenmount Avenue. St. John's TELEPHONE (709) 555-9911	POSTAL CODE A1B 3P9	LAST POSITION same	LAST WAGES/SALARY $7.25/HR
SUPERVISOR Jimmy James	TITLE Manager	DUTIES/RESPONSIBILITIES taking tickets	
REASONS FOR LEAVING Restaurant closed		DATES OF EMPLOYMENT FROM Aug 2004	TO Jan 2006

EMPLOYER Sun Valley Supermarket		STARTING POSITION Stock person	STARTING WAGES/SALARY $6.50/HR
STREET ADDRESS 850 Topsail Road TELEPHONE (709) 555-2100	CITY St. John's POSTAL CODE A1E 2E3	LAST POSITION cashier	LAST WAGES/SALARY $6.85/HR
SUPERVISOR Dave Nelson	TITLE Head cashier	DUTIES/RESPONSIBILITIES ringing up groceries	
REASONS FOR LEAVING Too far from home - moved		DATES OF EMPLOYMENT FROM Jan 2004	TO Aug 2004

If currently employed, may we contact your employer? YES ☒ NO ☐

Address: ______________________

List two (2) people (no relatives) you have worked with and whom we may contact for reference if necessary.

Name	Lisa Miller			
Occupation	Asst. Manager, Bella Villa Restaurant			
Phone Number	Street	1100 Water Street		
555-1121	City	St. John's	Province	NL

Name	Matthew Brock			
Occupation	Teacher			
Phone Number	Street	475 Canada Drive		
555-6017	City	St. John's	Province	NL

ADDITIONAL INFORMATION

Have you ever been convicted of a criminal offense for which a pardon has not been granted?

YES (NO)

If yes, please give details.

____

____

List any hobbies, activities or professional associations.

movies, music, baseball, hockey, computers, video games

____

Please enter any other data you feel would add to your qualifications for the position you seek with our company. Include work-related skills.

I have been in customer service for 2 years and have shopped at your store for 1 year.

____

____

ALL OF THE INFORMATION THAT I HAVE PROVIDED IN THIS APPLICATION IS TRUE AND COMPLETE. IF EMPLOYED, I AM AWARE THAT ANY FALSE INFORMATION COULD RESULT IN MY IMMEDIATE DISCHARGE.

SIGNATURE Keith Jones

DATE January 21, 2006

Filling Out the Application Form

A job application form can tell an employer many facts about you that are not asked directly on the form: How have you been at keeping jobs? What have you achieved?

- ***Follow instructions.*** If you can, take the form home to fill it out. This will allow you to take your time and really think about your answers. Write your answers down on a rough copy first, and then transfer them to the form. Or ask for two forms, and use one for your rough copy.

- ***Be careful and thorough.*** Follow directions carefully. Make sure you print, write or type, depending on which is asked for. Always use a pen for printing or writing. Black ink is preferred by employers, because it is much clearer on photocopies.

- ***Never leave a blank space.*** Use "N/A" (not applicable) to answer questions that do not apply to you.

- ***Provide your full name.*** Always give your names in the order they are asked for.

- ***Be specific.*** Specify the kind of position you are looking for. "Anything" doesn't look good.

- ***Be neat.*** Write or print carefully, so you don't cross anything out.

- ***Be clear.*** Make sure that what you say about yourself is clear.

- ***Double check.*** Everything: spelling, grammar and correct use of capital letters.

- ***Include all necessary information.*** Here are some things you'll need:
  - Social Insurance Number (SIN)
  - health card
  - references (name, position, company, address, phone)
  - dates available
  - days/hours available (for some kinds of work)
  - doctor's name/phone number
  - emergency contact

ACTIVITY

You are applying

Imagine that you are applying for one of these jobs (or use an actual local job advertisement that interests you). Get a blank application form from your teacher and fill it out (or simply record your information on a separate sheet of paper, using the sample form as a model).

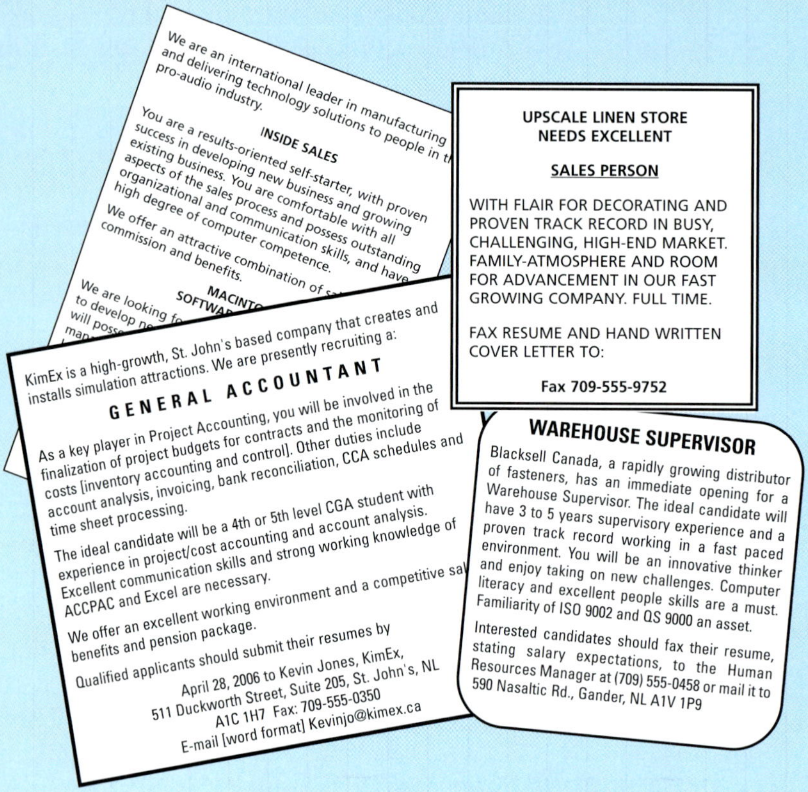

References

References help the employer make a final hiring decision. So select your references carefully! Here are some possible people you can go to for references:

- teachers
- principals
- coaches
- volunteer supervisors
- previous employers

Keep at least three references current—make sure you get their permission. Keep the information ready to write on your job application. Telephone numbers are important, because most employers contact references by phone.

ACTIVITY

Your references

Make a list of people you can use as references and keep it in your Employability Skills Portfolio.

Telephoning

Sometimes a job advertisement will provide a phone number and a contact name, and direct you to call if you're interested in the job. You need to plan your contact, using the same skills you use for networking.

Say hello. Explain why you're calling, and whom you wish to speak with: "I am calling about the sales position, and I would like to speak to your director of sales, please," or "I saw on your Internet site that your company offers great opportunities in sales. Could you please give me the e-mail address of the person I should contact?"

If you use e-mail, leave a message on voice mail or send a fax, you should follow up with a phone call to confirm that your message was received.

Be assertive when trying to contact the right person, and continue to communicate an interest in the job. And always remember to thank anyone who helps you.

Smile

Believe it or not, it helps if you smile when you pick up the phone to make an important business call. Try it both ways. Are you convinced there's a difference?

ACTIVITY

Telephone contact

Work with a partner to practise making telephone contact with a prospective employer. Again, use one of the job advertisements in the last activity (or one of your choice) to set the scene. Use the communication skills you learned in Unit 2.

The Résumé

A Portrait of You

Your major job search tool is a clear picture of *you*, so pay close attention to the following particulars when you write your **résumé**.

Résumé Do's and Don'ts

Yes or No?	The Real Story
One good résumé is enough for every situation.	You have to develop different résumés, and target them to each type of work within a specific organization.
If your résumé shows you're willing to work hard, you'll impress the employer.	You need to show the employer that you can help make the business successful. For example, if you're applying for a retail job, let the employer know you can give great service.
List your skills clearly.	Fine—but you need to focus on the needs of the company, and show how your skills can help the company.
Put in everything you've done that sounds good.	Put in only what would interest the employer you're trying to reach. Keep your résumé to one or two pages. Don't pad it!
The name of the game is to make yourself sound as good as possible. Talk everything up.	Not really. Employers want the plain, unvarnished facts. Don't exaggerate, and don't pretend you've done things you haven't.
It's the information that counts.	Correct—but appearance counts too. Most employers won't look at a résumé that's handwritten or sloppy, has misspellings, is printed on coloured paper, or has strange-looking fonts.
Employers read résumés carefully.	Unfortunately, no. Most employers scan a résumé in 10 to 20 seconds.

Employers Speak Out on Résumés

"Any résumé that looks like it's part of a mass mailing goes into the garbage. And if there's one spelling mistake or bad punctuation, out it goes."

—Marc Bowles, Senior Geologist/Office Manager, Komex International Ltd., an environment and water resources engineering company

"I want brief, to-the-point résumés that highlight work experience and education. Tailor your résumé to show me why you should work for my company."

—Joanne Tully, Employee Services Manager, Holiday Inn, Peterborough Waterfront

"When I see neatness in a résumé, I get the feeling that the job candidate will keep his or her work area and tools clean. That's important in my business."

—Clark Johnston, President, Clark's Quality Woodwork, a company that manufactures cabinets and furniture

Résumé Types

There are two types of résumés: **chronological** and **functional**. They provide the same information, but in different formats to highlight certain skills, experiences or education. Each type has its advantages and disadvantages.

Chronological Résumé	Functional Résumé
Advantage You can demonstrate, at a glance, a summary of your education and experience. Some career specialists believe that employers prefer this format.	**Advantage** You can highlight your special skills and any awards and achievements that come from work, volunteer or school experiences.
Disadvantage You don't have a place to indicate your skills and qualifications up front.	**Disadvantage** You have to back up your list of skills and qualifications with education, work or volunteer experiences. You can't just list skills you believe you have without demonstrating how you got them.
Structure • starts off with a job objective or a personal profile • groups education, work and volunteer experiences and lists items in reverse chronological order • may include a section on awards and accomplishments • provides information on interests • provides references	**Structure** • starts off with a job objective • list of skills and/or achievements that support the objective • groups education, work and volunteer experiences and lists items in reverse chronological order • provides information on interests • provides references

Dana's Résumés

Dana wants to apply for two separate summer jobs. The first is as a clerk in a video store. The second is as a counsellor at a city day camp.

She knows that she can't use the same résumé to apply for both, because the work is so different. It takes some help from her parents and her English teacher, but Dana creates two résumés, each one targeted to the specific job, each in a different format.

Dana's Chronological Résumé, Targeted to a Summer Camp Job

Dana Pareau
2256 Main Street
Anywhere, NL A9Q 2P2
555-3331
dana@internetaddress

Personal Profile	I am an enthusiastic, energetic person who enjoys sports and coaching children. I've also had two years' experience on my school's basketball team.
Employment History	
2002-2005	Newspaper carrier • Collated 3 to 5 sections of the newspaper for delivery • Served 75 homes daily • Collected cash and provided receipts for 75 customers
Volunteer Experience	
2004-present	Sports Program, Community Centre • 45 hours as assistant coach for junior soccer team • 10 hours helping at Sports Registration Day
Education	Completing Level II Monroe High School
Awards	Received 2004 Top Newspaper Delivery Certificate
Interests	Exploring the Internet, playing basketball, reading

References available upon request.

Dana's Functional Résumé, Targeted to a Retail Job

Dana Pareau
2256 Main Street
Anywhere, NL A9Q 2P2
555-3331
dana@internetaddress

Job Objective To use my strong interpersonal skills in a sales clerk position

Highlights of Qualifications

- Reliable daily newspaper delivery to 75 customers
- Internet and computer skills
- Excellent school attendance record

Accomplishments and Awards

- Received 2004 Top Newspaper Delivery Certificate
- Sold 300 tickets for class play and handled all cash transactions

Employment History

2002-2005 Newspaper carrier

- Collated 3 to 5 sections of the newspaper for delivery
- Served 75 homes daily
- Collected cash and provided receipts for 75 customers

Volunteer Experience

2004-present Sports Program, Community Centre

- Assistant coach for junior soccer team
- Attendant at Sports Registration Day

Education Completing Level II
Monroe High School

Interests Exploring the Internet, basketball, reading

References available upon request.

ACTIVITY

Dana's résumés

1. Compare the two résumés.

2. Show how Dana targeted each résumé.
- What was she trying to show each employer?
- How did she show each employer that she was right for that job?

3. Look at Dana's chronological résumé.
- What does the Personal Profile section tell the employer?
- What detailed information did she include under Volunteer Experience so the summer camp employer would have a better idea of her qualifications?

4. Now look at the Dana's functional résumé.
- Why wasn't it a good idea to include a Personal Profile section in the functional résumé?
- How did Dana support her list of qualifications with her work experience?

5. Which type of résumé do you prefer? Why?

ACTIVITY

Write your résumé

Match your career interests with your skills and experience, and write a sample résumé, either chronological or functional, targeted to a specific job that you think you might like to get. Work in small groups to share ways of doing this, and share your résumés with each other, offering helpful feedback.

Links

It is becoming more and more common for companies to list job openings on their websites. Often it is possible to apply for work on-line by filling out electronic application forms and completing pre-formatted résumés.

There are also a number of websites that are virtual job banks. For example, the *Globe and Mail* provides an extensive database of job opportunities that can be accessed on-line.

Visit <www.careers.nelson.com> for links to some of these sites.

The Cover Letter

Making a First Impression

If you're sending a résumé to a prospective employer, you need to send a **cover letter** too. A cover letter explains more about you and why you fit the job. It is the first thing the employer looks at, so you want it to make a good impression. Therefore, it should be:

- ***Short:*** It should have three or four brief paragraphs, and fit on one page.
- ***Personal:*** Use the exact name/title of the person responsible for hiring, if you can. You can often phone and get this information. Make sure to ask for the right spelling—it's a turnoff to be called Dyanne when your name is Diane. If you don't know the name, you can address it to Human Resources.
- ***Focused:*** Match relevant details from your experiences to the responsibilities and qualifications of the job as stated in the ad you're responding to.
- ***Researched:*** Refer to the organization's goals and needs. Tailor your letter specifically to the position/company.
- ***Interesting:*** Demonstrate your enthusiasm.
- ***A request for action:*** Make clear your interest in the position, and request an interview.
- ***Perfect:*** Read and re-read for punctuation, grammar and spelling errors.
- ***Appealing to the eye:*** Use the same quality paper as for your résumé.

Dana's Cover Letter to the Video Store Manager

Make sure you put in **your complete address** and all the ways you can be contacted	Dana Pareau 2256 Main Street Anywhere, NL A9Q 2P2 555-3331 dana@internetaddress
Date	June 3, 2006
Address the letter to the right person and make sure the **name, title and address** are accurate	Ms Jeannette Lincoln, Manager Winners Videos Anywhere, NL A9Q 3Z8
Salutation	Dear Ms Lincoln:
First paragraph • state why you are writing • state the position applied for • make a general comment about the company	I am responding to the ad in the *Tribune* for a full-time video sales clerk at the Stanwell Shopping Centre. I have often rented movies from Winners Videos at the Heron Mall and always been impressed by the quality of service I found there.
Second paragraph • state your academic qualifications, if needed • match your skills with those required for the job • highlight experience relevant to the job	As a long-time newspaper deliverer, I know how important it is to be reliable and on time, and to handle cash carefully. In addition, I am an avid movie-goer and knowledgeable about many different types of movies. I believe that I have excellent qualifications for your position.

Third paragraph

- request action
- say you will follow up (and try to do so)

I have attached my résumé for your consideration. If I haven't heard from you by June 15, I will call to follow up. In the meantime, if you have any questions, please don't hesitate to give me a call.

Closing

Yours sincerely,

Dana Pareau

- If you write a very good cover letter, the employer will be more likely to read your résumé.
- If your résumé is very good, you are more likely to get an interview.
- If your interview is very good, you are more likely to get a job offer.

Nothing is guaranteed, because there are many people looking for work, but you have a better chance if you develop job-search skills and create excellent tools.

Beyond the Résumé

The Trouble with Résumés

Résumés are the standard method of presenting information about yourself to a potential employer. While they allow you to highlight some of your education and work experience, they don't always provide adequate space to describe some of your more specific skills and talents. Employers are often looking for specific characteristics and skills that cannot always be provided on a résumé.

Your life experiences can be just as valuable as any paid jobs you've held. But standard résumés don't have a "life skills" section. So, how can you show employers that you have the skills they are looking for?

Mark's Story

Mark, a hiring manager for an import/export business, was looking for a financial administrator. The newspaper ad pulled in 200 résumés. Mark reduced the pile to 10 candidates, and called them in for interviews.

Nine of them were disappointing. "You have expectations that the applicant will take the time to learn about you and your company," he says. "But that was far from the case."

Eight of the applicants had no idea what Mark's company imported and exported. One applicant had read the company brochure while waiting in the reception area. Only one applicant had the "right stuff."

"In addition to her knowledge of international trade," Mark said, "she knew what our company did, and how our markets operated."

Guess who got the job?

Tina's Story

Tina got married after high school, and had two children right away. Her husband had a good job, so she didn't need to work outside the home. But her husband was recently in a car accident, and can't go back to work for a while. So now Tina has to get a paying job.

But Tina only has her high school diploma, and very little work experience. She's been a babysitter, and has worked as a sales clerk at a clothing store. She intends to take night courses and become a practical nurse, but she needs to find work right now.

"My résumé looks terrible," she says. "It sounds like I can't do anything. But I've been taking care of a family and a sick husband. I have great organizational, management and caring skills."

Tina hasn't found a job yet, or even gotten one interview. She wishes she had a way to tell an employer about the skills she has developed through her life experiences.

You Can Do It!

We all possess skills and talents that employers seek. Learning how to read the needs of employers and how to market ourselves to meet these needs are critical for successfully gaining employment. Learning how to market our unique experiences can also mean the difference between success and failure. In Newfoundland and Labrador, the restructuring of the fishing industry and the growth in the oil and natural gas industries have led people to re-evaluate their skills and experiences to make themselves marketable.

Essential Skills

Sometimes you can overlook the many basic skills you possess. For example, are you comfortable talking on the telephone? Are you able to write a letter or a note to someone? Can you read important notices and memos? Perhaps you're good at fixing things or using the computer.

Human Resources and Skills Development Canada (HRSDC) has identified nine **essential skills** that provide a foundation for learning all other skills. They enable individuals to evolve with their job and adapt effectively to workplace changes. These nine skills have been identified as:

- Reading Text
- Document Use
- Numeracy
- Writing
- Oral Communication
- Working with Others
- Thinking Skills
- Computer Use
- Continuous Learning

While specialized training and experience are important, possessing these nine essential skills will show an employer that you would be an asset in any position.

Links

In 2003, HRSDC launched the Essential Skills and Workplace Literacy Initiative. Its goal is to equip workers with the skills necessary to thrive in an ever-changing work environment. Go to <www.careers.nelson.com> for a direct link to this site.

ACTIVITY

Using essential skills

Choose an occupation that interests you. Using the essential skills above, identify the skills required for your occupation of interest. Describe how you would use each one in that occupation.

What Are Employers Looking For?

Read the following ads. Think about how you would approach each one as you read them.

We are a family-run convenience store. We are seeking a long-term employee to handle customers. Day and evening availability is required. Cash experience preferred. Great opportunity for someone seeking a challenge! Please mail résumés to:

P.O. Box 5555, St. John's, NL A1A 2P3

Marketing Assistant

Marketing assistant needed for busy head office. The successful candidate must be enthusiastic, well-organized and be able to work in a fast-paced environment. Daily tasks include updating websites, answering customer queries, and assisting marketing managers. Strong computer skills are a must! E-mail résumé to

humanresources@delkey.com

CAMP COUNSELLOR WANTED!

Minimum 2 years' experience required. Must be outgoing and enjoy working with children. CPR training also required. Great wages! Accommodations are provided.

709-555-5454

ACTIVITY

What skills are required?

For each of the ads above, create a table like the one below.

Specialized Skills Required	Essential Skills Required
1.	1.
2.	2.
3.	3.
4.	4.
5.	5.

Marketing Yourself

Now that you have identified what employers are looking for, what can you do to highlight your skills to make them aware of what you have to offer?

One tool that you can use to market yourself is an **Employability Skills Portfolio**, as mentioned on page 66. It can guide you through your career development journey, as well as help you set and achieve your goals. This portfolio allows you to store important information about your career development, such as your transcripts, awards and list of references, in one place so that you can easily access them when asked about your achievements. It also allows you to reflect on and assess your areas of strength and limitations so that you can work toward continued improvement and development of your skills. You have already started a portfolio as a part of this course. Staying focused on your journey and compiling information will help you plan and achieve your goals.

While a résumé can summarize and outline your education and achievements, an Employability Skills Portfolio can work as a visual representation of your abilities, as it highlights your academic, personal management and teamwork skills to employers. You can present it for review either before or during an interview. While the contents may not get discussed during the interview, it does provide the employer with additional information on which to base his or her decision.

Your Employability Skills Portfolio will continue to develop along with you. You will continue to add newly acquired skills to its contents and remove items that are no longer current. Just remember that your portfolio represents you and all you have to offer.

ACTIVITY

Your Employability Skills Portfolio

Use the Internet to identify the common features of an effective Employability Skills Portfolio. What material should you include? How should it be organized?

Look over your current Employability Skills Portfolio. Is there anything else you could add to it to make it more effective? Is there anything in your Course Content Portfolio that would be useful?

The Interview

A Two-Way Exchange

If you are called for a **job interview**, congratulations! This is your chance to personally show an employer what makes you the best candidate for the job. It's also your chance to find out more about the job, to see if it suits you.

Interviews make most people nervous. Not many people are really comfortable talking with strangers in any situation. In a formal job interview, where the stakes are high, it can be even more uncomfortable. Practice can help. Work through the following interview-related activities with a partner.

ACTIVITY

You're the boss

You're the manager—you need to hire the right people for the job. In each of these cases, assume all candidates have the certificate, licence or degree necessary. Work with a partner, and list up to 10 qualities or characteristics you would look for when hiring people for the job.

1. You are hiring for a large computer company. You need a receptionist/secretary for the front desk.
2. You are hiring for a fast-food restaurant. You need cashiers.
3. You own a taxi company and you've purchased new cars. You need drivers.
4. You are the managing partner of a large legal firm. You need caretakers in your corporate offices.
5. You are the manager of a construction company. You are hiring someone to supervise a crew of 50 on a building project.
6. You own a chain of photography shops and you need to hire a manager for one of the shops.
7. You are the director of a summer camp and you need to hire counsellors.

Reflection

Of the qualities you've listed in the previous activity, which ones do you think you possess? Could you strengthen them? How would you convince an employer that you had those qualities?

Are there qualities you lack? Are there ways to develop them? Or are some people just more suited for some jobs than others?

Before the Interview

Be prepared!

1. Research the company and the job. Try to find literature on the company, such as an annual report. Visit the website, if there is one. Network to find out what you can.
2. Know what employability skills and experience you have to offer.
3. Write down questions you might be asked.
4. Prepare some questions for the interviewer.
5. Prepare a portfolio to take with you, including:
   - extra copies of your résumé
   - a list of references and letters of reference
   - school transcripts, certificates, etc.
   - a pen and a notepad to write on
6. Plan, and write down, what you'll wear.
7. Make sure you know when and where the interview is, and leave plenty of time to get there.

ACTIVITY

Preparing yourself

You and a partner are working toward an interview role-play. You will role-play two interviews: in one you will be the employer and in the other you will be the job-seeker.

1. With your partner, choose one of the scenarios in You're the Boss (page 214) for each of your interviews (or invent a scenario that better suits your interests and abilities).
2. Find an actual company that could fit that scenario (*e.g.*, use a real summer camp for scenario 7).
3. Complete steps 1 to 6 as outlined in Before the Interview, above.
4. Discuss with your partner how you've prepared for the interview. Help each other be as prepared as possible.

During the Interview

Here's how an interview might go:

1. It starts with rapport-building questions. Everyone's uncomfortable, and these are questions to relax the tension:

   - Did you have difficulty finding the office?
   - Can I get you some water?
   - Can you believe this weather?

2. General questions with open-ended answers will follow, like:

   - What interests you about this job?
   - How did you hear about it?

3. Specific questions about your past job performance will come next, such as:

   - Give me an example of your people skills.
   - Can you tell me about a time when you dealt with a crisis?
   - You say on your résumé that you are good at problem-solving. Can you give me an example?
   - Can you describe how you deal with time pressures?

   This may be a good time to pull out your Employability Skills Portfolio.

4. If you're having difficulty answering, the interviewer will sit through the silence, smiling at you. Remember that everyone is nervous in an interview, so allow for that. Don't be too hard on yourself, and carry on regardless. How you respond gives a sense of how you might respond to pressure on the job.

5. Don't say more than you're asked to say.

6. You may also be asked a question such as, "Tell me about a weakness you have." We all have weaknesses and, in our minds, they loom as huge flaws. But an employer won't see the flaw the way you do. Be honest about something you believe you can improve. Don't talk about your fears that you won't be able to do the job.

7. Employers will want to know about the skills you list on your résumé. They may want examples from you about how you dealt with a problem. If you can show how you once dealt with a particular problem, the employer will have an idea of how you would do so again.

   Suppose the interviewer asks what you would do if other employees weren't doing their share of the work. The right answer might be something like this: "That's a good question. Let me answer it by telling you about a situation I dealt with at school on a group project (or at my last job) when one of our members wasn't doing her share."

8. The interviewer will often ask, "Do you have any questions you want to ask me?" Show you've researched the position and the company. Ask about future plans. Even if they don't consider you for this job, they may for a future opening, if you make a good impression. And remember that you are interviewing the company also, to make sure this is the right job for you.

9. The employer will want time to evaluate the interview. You can't expect an answer right away. But you can ask when you might hear about the hiring decision.

Links

There are many external resources designed to help people with work-search skills and strategies, like interviewing. Search your library for books on the subject "job hunting" or go to <www.careers.nelson.com> for links to useful information about interviewing.

Questions You Can Ask the Interviewer

One of the difficult points in an interview is when you are asked if you have any questions to ask. Here is a list of suggestions:

- How would you describe a typical day in this position?
- What personal characteristics are necessary to do this job well?
- What qualities are you seeking in the person to fill this position?
- What are the main objectives and responsibilities of this position?
- Who would I directly report to?
- How much evening or weekend work is expected?
- Will there be any on-the-job training?
- When can I expect to hear from you?

ACTIVITY

The questions

Resume the role-play preparations that you began in the previous activity.

1. Create a list of questions you will ask your partner, the job-seeker.

2. Create a list of questions you will ask your partner, the employer.

Interview Do's and Don'ts

The scene is a job fair where companies have booths. Each booth has a hiring manager who is willing to interview people interested in working for the company. Read the two interviews that follow.

Mike's Interview

Rachel: Hi, I'm Rachel Smith, Personnel Manager at O.T.I.S.

Mike: Hi, I'm Mike McNeil.

Rachel: Please sit down. You look like you've been running.

Mike: I almost didn't get here in time.

Rachel: Did you bring a résumé?

Mike: I didn't know I needed one.

Rachel: It was mentioned in the ad for the job fair, Mike.

Mike: Oh.

Rachel: Well, perhaps you can tell me what you know about O.T.I.S.

Mike: Well, not too much. I know your company is involved with computers.

Rachel: Tell me a little about yourself, Mike.

Mike: Well, what can I say? I need a job so my mom will get off my case, and I would like to make some money for going out with my friends. So how much do you pay for this job?

Rachel: Perhaps it would be more appropriate for us to discuss what kind of jobs we're interested in filling.

Mike: Sure, whatever. Do you mind if I smoke in here?

Rachel: Actually, this is a smoke-free building.

Mike: O.K.

Rachel: We are looking for someone to work in marketing, to make calls to various companies to let them know about our services.

Mike: I could do that.

Rachel: Why don't you describe for me the skills you think you have that would be useful in marketing?

Mike: Well, I'm a great talker. My friends tell me I never stop.

Rachel: I see. Have you any experience in marketing?

Mike: No.

Rachel: Do you have any work experience?

Mike: Not really. I worked for a couple of weeks at the burger restaurant across town, but the boss was a real pain. He expected me to work on weekends.

Rachel: Are you telling me that you are unavailable for work, then, on Saturdays?

Mike: What, are you open on weekends? I can't see coming in on a Saturday night, but I could work say 1:00 until 4:00 in the afternoon, I guess.

Rachel: Well, this has been an interesting interview, Mike. Do you have any questions that you would like to ask me?

Mike: Nope. Can't think of any.

Rachel: Well, we are still interviewing for this position, Mike, but thanks for coming in.

Mike: Yeah, no problem. See you.

John's Interview

Rachel: Hi, I'm Rachel Smith, Personnel Manager at O.T.I.S.

John: Good afternoon. My name is John Lee. I'm very interested in your company.

Rachel: You know about us?

John: After I saw your ad for the job fair, I did some research. I know that On-Line Technical Information Systems is a fairly new company, and that you offer technical advice and services to companies who use the Internet for business. Your company appeals to me because I am very interested in becoming part of a new growth area like the Internet.

Rachel: You enjoy the Internet?

John: I spend time surfing. Recently, I've been learning HTML from on-line instruction web sites.

Rachel: Did you bring a résumé?

John: Yes.

Rachel: *(Reads résumé.)* This looks impressive, John. I see that you have completed a two-year marketing program at college, and you have some experience in the field. Tell me more.

John: My college marketing program included a co-op work term, and I had the opportunity to work for Company X, where I learned practical research and sales skills, as well as customer service.

Rachel: Well you certainly have good credentials. Tell me, John, do you work well under pressure, to meet deadlines?

John: I'll give you an example from my last job. We had to prepare catalogue material for the sales department, and the copy had to be ready by a strict deadline. The morning of the deadline, I found out that a key piece of the information was missing. I had to call people in other offices to get the information, then I had to make sure that the information got fitted into the rest of the copy. It was a bit of a scramble, but I was able to complete everything, so we made our deadline.

Rachel: That is good to hear, John. Tell me, if I spoke to your previous boss, what would he say are your strengths and weaknesses?

John: Well, I think he would say that my strengths are teamwork and communication. My weakness is that I find it difficult saying no to people. I am always trying to help everyone else, and sometimes I should focus on my own tasks first, then help others out when I am finished.

Rachel: Do you have any questions you would like to ask me?

John: Could you tell me what qualities you are looking for in someone to fill this position?

Rachel: We need someone with initiative, who is familiar with marketing, and willing to work hard. I am glad we had this chance to meet today, John.

John: It's been a pleasure. Will I be hearing from you soon?

Rachel: I'm interested in talking to your references. Do you have a list?

John: (Hands her the list.) I hope we talk again, Rachel. Good-bye.

Rachel: Thank-you and good-bye, John.

ACTIVITY

Analysis

1. Compare the interviews above. List what Mike does wrong and what John does right.
2. Now list things to remember when you play the job-seeker in your practice interview.

Three Questions

The interviewer has three main questions in mind:

- Can you do the job?
- Will you do the job well?
- Will the people in the company or organization want to work with you?

Who you are is often as important as what you can do.

After the Interview

1. ***Review how you did.*** What went well? What could be improved for next time? Don't be too hard on yourself. Almost everyone thinks of things they could have said or done differently.
2. ***Send a brief thank-you note.*** Within a day of the interview, write to thank the interviewer for taking the time to speak to you, and to re-affirm your interest in the job.
3. ***Follow up.*** If you haven't heard by the time agreed upon, you should call. If you didn't get the job, politely ask why, and really listen to the reasons. What you learn can help your next work search.

ACTIVITY

Practise interviewing

Work with a partner to perfect two good job interviews. Practise and learn from each other before presenting your interviews in class.

UNIT 4 • SUMMARY

Key Terms

goals
knowledge
analysis
plan
reflection
personal goals
work goals
learning goals
community goals
job market
barrier
network
reference
résumé
cover letter
essential skills
Employability Skills Portfolio
job interview

Use a concept map or another graphic organizer to summarize the key ideas in this unit. Build on the key terms and add words, phrases and/or images that will help remind you of those key ideas.

Reflection

Reread your responses to Where Are You Headed? (page 167). How did the strength that you identified affect how you set your work, learning and community goals? What evidence do you have to support your claim to having that strength?

Questions

Knowledge/Understanding

1. Represent the decision-making model in a format that is useful to you. For each stage, include an example drawn from your own personal experience. Keep this in your portfolio.

2. Create a checklist of work-search tools and strategies. For each item, provide the name of one reference that you would use again if you had to revise a tool or strategy. Check the contents of your portfolio against this checklist and add anything that's missing.

Thinking/Inquiry

3. Write five specific questions that you still have about career planning and create an action plan for getting the answers.

4. Talk to your teacher-advisor, a coach or a parent about his or her work, education or community involvement. Find out about the person's career path. Analyse how closely your subject's planning process matches the model described in this textbook. What can you conclude about

a) the effectiveness of the person's plan, and

b) the usefulness of the model in this book?

Communication

5. Make a one-page flyer that illustrates the four principles of goal setting. You are your own audience—choose a format that will be memorable for you.

Application

6. Go back to your plan for finding part-time or summer work (page 193). Revise the list of tools you made based on what you learned in this unit. Create a job-search kit that includes your goals, your plan and your tools. Keep it in your portfolio.

7. Go to <www.careers.nelson.com>. Explore the Department of Education's site and analyse its usefulness.

Taking Stock: Your Portfolio

1. Review the contents.

2. Reconsider your initial responses.

3. Summarize the most important information.

UNIT 5

How Far Have I Come?

Will I know when I've finally arrived? How do I know if I've made the right decisions?

Career development isn't a one-time process. The more attention you give it, the better it gets. It's a journey, not a destination.

Are there signs I should be looking for?

SECTION

"Everybody has inside him or her a piece of the good news. The good news is that you don't know how great you can be! What you can accomplish! And what your potential is!"

—*Anne Frank, The Diary of Anne Frank*

How Far Have I Come?

In this unit you will:

- reflect on the career development process, and on where you are in that process
- examine your attitudes toward future planning and change
- incorporate the notion of lifelong learning into your career development plan

What am I going to be? What am I going to do? How do I know what I want?

You'll probably think about questions like these for the rest of your life. It isn't as if you get them solved and then forget about them. They are difficult questions for anyone to answer.

Look at these pictures. Each of them represents one of the roles that you play in your career. If you want to find out how far you've come in the career development process, you have to make sure you consider all of the aspects of your career. Think about each of the roles represented. How successfully are you playing each role? How closely does what you are actually doing fit with what you would like to be doing?

This unit will help you ask questions that will keep your career development plan on track.

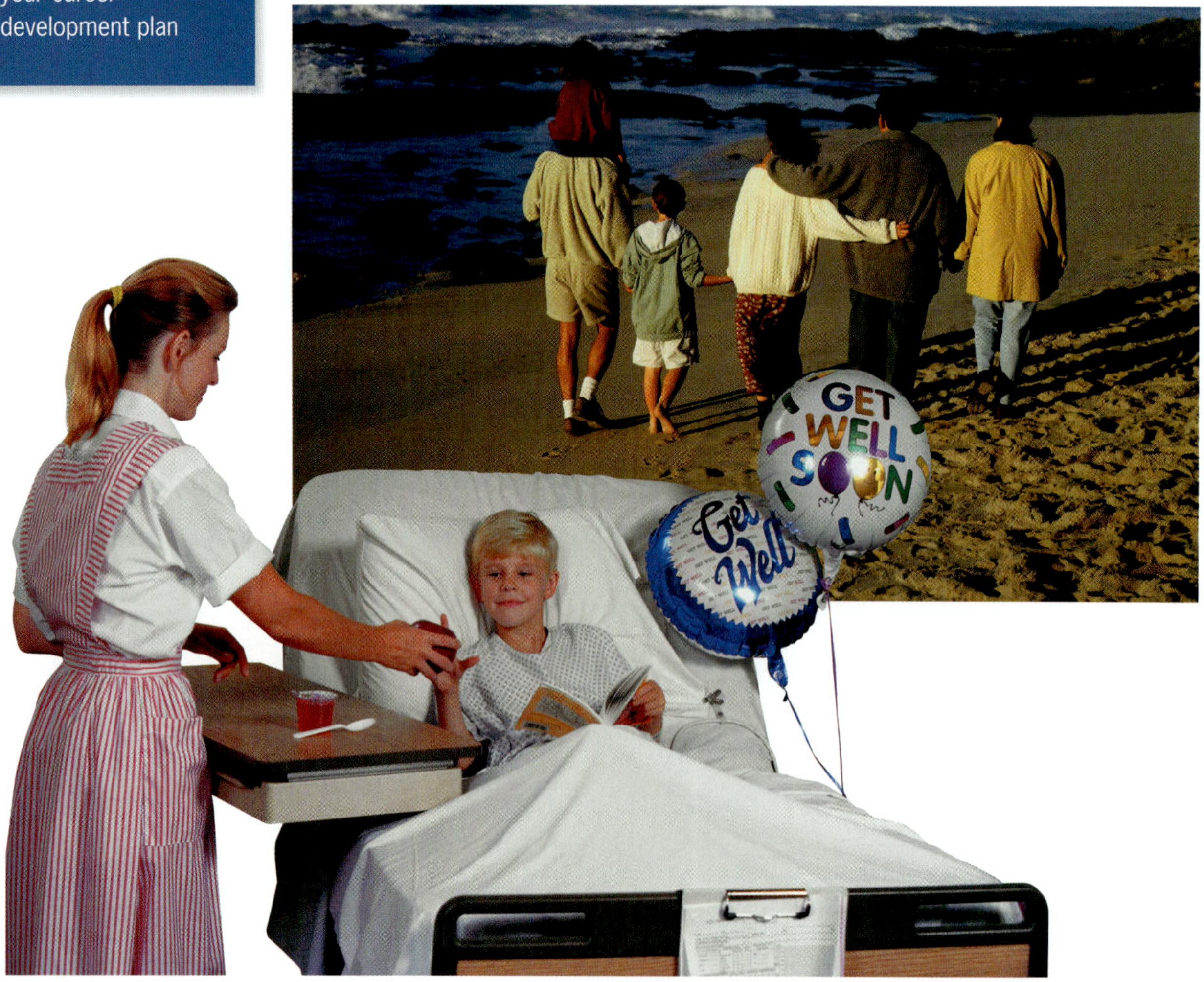

DISCOVERY

Take stock

Career development is a lifelong journey. Take a few moments to jot down the highlights of your journey and what you have learned about yourself and the world of work.

Jason's Story

You won't be able to get where you're going without making mistakes, recognizing them and bouncing back. Be resilient and adaptable. Keep re-assessing, and stay on track.

N*ow what?* Jason asked himself.

His canoe coasted to a stop on the muddy bottom of the tiny creek. The other two canoes were coming up behind. In each canoe there was a counsellor and two nine-year-old campers.

Marco, one of the campers in Jason's canoe, turned around to look at him. "What do we do now?"

"I'm thinking," said Jason. "Time to look at the map." After a minute he added, "This creek's supposed to go all the way to Little Loon Lake, but it looks like a swamp to me."

Well, this was a stupid decision, he thought to himself. He had been responsible for planning the route. He had hoped to paddle through this creek to their campsite on the next lake by nightfall. He had gambled, and now there was no more creek. He was responsible to two other counsellors and six nine-year-olds.

I guess this is what the map meant by "seasonal creek," he thought. *But now I've got to get us out of here.*

Marco was still looking at him. "What're we going to do, Jason?"

Jason grimaced. "If we can't get through one way, we'll try another. Hold the canoe steady, please."

He climbed over the side, and was up to his knees in gooey muck. A swampy smell filled his nostrils. Telling the other counsellors to wait with the campers, he slogged forward. It was difficult wading, but eventually he saw where the shallow water opened out, and it became deep enough again to float canoes.

He worked his way back to where the others were waiting. "Well gang, are we ready for a hike?"

By the time the campers had wrestled their way through into Little Loon Lake, everybody was covered in mud. It was so dark they had to use their flashlights to set up the tents.

"Well, at least it isn't raining," Jason joked. He showed Marco how to pump water through the filter. He lit the cook stove, and started rooting through the food bag. He was ravenous, and he knew the others were too.

Oh no! At first Jason couldn't believe what he was seeing. *This is even more terrible than losing our way earlier,* he thought.

He called the other two counsellors over and got them to search through the food bag also. Then they went through all of the baggage.

"Well, I guess we brought the wrong food bag," said Jason ruefully, rubbing the back of his neck.

"Okay you guys—I've got good news, and bad news. First the bad news—there's only one thing for dinner. Now the good news—there's lot of it! Who wants some fried granola?"

"Oh, great," said Marco. "We get the Holiday Special—a mud bath and no dinner!"

When he'd finished laughing, Jason realized this was his chance to make a point. "Well," he said, "This trip is supposed to be about leadership. Right? And leadership is about learning from your mistakes, right? So what can we learn from this?"

Marco thought, and then said, "Always put two people in charge of packing the food?"

"That's a good idea," agreed Jason. "But I think there's a more general lesson. Maybe it's about choices."

Maybe no one was in the mood for a life lesson. "We're here now. Choices were made that brought us here—choices made by ourselves, by our parents, by the people running the camp. But whatever those choices were, we're here now, and we can make other choices right now. Am I right?"

There were groans, but no one had any serious objections.

"Next time, someone will make better choices when planning the trip. In the meantime, we're out here for two more days. We won't starve. So let's choose to make the best of it. Let's show resilience. You know what that is? Resilience means being resourceful when you run into an obstacle. Okay?"

Silence. "Sounds like a plan, Jason," cracked Marco.

"Okay," said Jason, feeling his tension relax. "So after the fried granola we can roast marshmallows—we didn't forget them."

The marshmallows were a big hit, considering what dinner was like, and afterwards they put everything safely out of the reach of bears and raccoons before going to bed.

After that, the canoe trip got better. The weather was perfect, there was plenty of granola, and they did find a patch of blueberries.

On the last morning, after breaking camp, they paddled right up to a cow moose and her calf. Up to their bellies in the lake, the two animals raised their heads out of the water, lily pads trailing from their dripping mouths, and watched the awed campers paddle slowly by.

Jason shared a seat with Marco on the bus back to camp. "So what do you think, Marco?" he asked.

"That was a neat canoe trip. I thought it was going to bomb out when we didn't have any food, but it was fun."

"You're right," Jason said. "It worked out okay. Do you know what we've learned?"

Marco looked at him. "This another one of your talks?"

"Yup," Jason smiled. "I'm the leader, so it's my role. Choice and resilience—that's what we learned. You make the best choices you can, but you can never predict what's going to happen. You have to be resilient—and keep going on the path you chose."

He had made up the lesson as he went along, just dealing with problems. But it sounded pretty good anyway.

The bus bounced them all safely back into camp.

ACTIVITY

About Jason

1. Describe the "resilience" lesson in your own words.
2. What is your attitude when something goes wrong? How do you deal with it?
3. Pick an example from your own life in which things did not go (or are not going) as you planned. Describe how resilience applies to that situation.

Attitude Counts!

The attitude you bring to any decision, including career choice, has a big influence on its success or failure. Being open to change makes it possible for you to learn; and the more you learn, the better your decisions will be.

DISCOVERY

Learning from experience

"You learn to win by losing." Have you ever learned how to succeed from an experience in which you did not succeed? Find an example in your own life. What did you learn? How has it helped you since then?

Key Attitudes

Resilience, Adaptability and Self-confidence

Resilience and **adaptability** are important for success in any endeavour. But what do these qualities depend on? They depend on **self-confidence**.

If you are confident in yourself and your abilities, you will be able to overcome apparent failure, adapt to circumstances and find a new way of going forward. If you are less confident, you may assume that you'll just fail again, and give up. You may be afraid to try something new.

What you expect to happen usually affects both your attitude and your actions. If Jason had expected the canoe trip to be ruined, it probably would have been.

If you expect to be bored, you probably will be. If you expect to fail, you probably will.

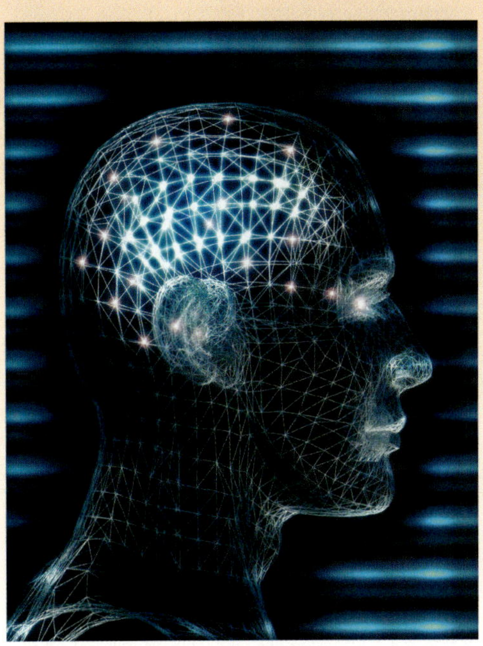

Current brain research suggests that habitual ways of thinking and doing things become hardwired into the brain, and then become difficult to change. According to U.S. psychologist Jane Healey, "Habits of the mind become structures of the brain."

Self-confidence is built on experience. Confidence is not achieved by blindly saying, "I'm the greatest." Instead, it comes from measuring yourself against the world, and having that measurement confirmed.

You develop self-confidence by growing your own strengths and abilities; by dealing with family and friends; by solving issues in your education; by challenging your inner resources.

Stories can help. Here are two stories about achieving self-confidence.

Profile: Pamela Wallin

Many people credit adversity they overcame when they were young with making them strong. Journalist, broadcaster and Canadian Consul General to New York City Pamela Wallin tells such a story.

When I was 13, I left my hometown of Wadena, Saskatchewan, to live with my 83-year-old grandmother in Moose Jaw. Wanting to earn spending money, I got a job as a baker's assistant at the Moose Jaw Co-op.

I was low person on the bakery's totem pole, which meant getting up at 3 a.m. on the days I was to open the bakery. First I turned on the ovens. Then I had to scrub all the pots and pans from the night before. Predictably, I got all the dirty jobs, a little like slave labour.

The head baker was an especially gruff man, fond of yelling at us younger workers. "Hurry up!" he would bellow as I was scrubbing a muffin pan caked with burned-on batter. "We haven't got all day." Nothing I did, it seemed, was good enough for him.

Once, when I dropped a dozen loaves I was taking from the oven, he reduced me to tears with his shouting. But I didn't quit. I took my lumps, and I learned an important lesson in the process: No matter how well you think you do your job, there is room for criticism.

That lesson has served me well. During my 20-year career in front of the public, I've had my share of criticism, some deserved, some not, at least from my point of view. But my first job taught me that it comes with the territory. If you want to get ahead, you have to take the bad with the good. A working life isn't always smooth sailing.

ACTIVITY

Understanding Pamela Wallin's experience

1. Explain how this is a story about resilience.
2. What would you have done in Pamela Wallin's situation?
3. Can you think of events like this in your own life? What happened? What did you do?

Profile: Scott Adams

Scott Adams is the creator of Dilbert, *a cartoon read by more than 150 million people every day. He has been a bank teller, a computer programmer, and a product manager. As Adams relates, helpful criticism and encouragement are often what it takes to encourage people to do their best work.*

You don't have to be a "person of influence" to be influential. In fact, the most influential people in my life are probably not even aware of the things they've taught me.

When I was trying to become a syndicated cartoonist, I sent my portfolio to one cartoon editor after another—and received one rejection after another. One editor even called to suggest I take art classes. Then Sarah Gillespie, an editor at United Media and one of the real experts in the field, called to offer me a contract. At first, I didn't believe her. I asked if I'd have to change my style, get a partner—or learn to draw. But she believed that I was already good enough to be a nationally syndicated cartoonist.

Her confidence in me totally changed my frame of reference: it altered how I thought about my own abilities. This may sound bizarre, but from the minute I got off the phone with her, I could draw better. You can see a marked improvement in the quality of cartoon I drew after that conversation.

And it doesn't take much to make that kind of difference in someone else's life. Once, at a tennis tournament, I was paired with a woman who had just learned how to play. Every time she missed a shot, she immediately turned to me, expecting that I would be disappointed or frustrated. Instead, I talked to her about our strategy for the next point. By doing so, I sent a very clear signal: the past doesn't matter. I didn't encourage her with empty praise—that approach rarely works. But I knew that if she dwelled on a mistake, she was more likely to repeat it, and that if she focused on how we were going to win the next point, she was more likely to help us do just that. Over several days, her abilities improved dramatically—and we ended up winning the tournament.

Realize that in some way you influence everyone you come in contact with. Then pay careful attention to what pushes people's mental buttons. If you can push those buttons for the better, do it.

ACTIVITY

Understanding Scott Adams' experience

1. How do you respond to the concept that increasing your self-confidence is often able to make you perform better?
2. What events in your own life can you think of where encouragement from someone else increased your self-confidence, and made you better at something?
3. Describe a situation in which discouragement or criticism has damaged your self-confidence.

Learning Throughout Life

Learn or Lose

Guidance counsellors, career specialists, teachers and employers will all tell you how important **lifelong learning** is for a successful career. Most successful people will tell you the same thing.

Thomas Alva Edison was more successful than any other inventor in U.S. history, registering 1,093 patents. Among his many inventions that have affected our lives today, probably the most well-known are the phonograph, the motion picture camera and improvements to the telephone. The most important, perhaps, was the incandescent electric light bulb, which brought light into homes all over the world. It took Edison thousands and thousands of experiments before he found the right combination for the filament (the little wire inside the light bulb). During that time, he was criticized for his lack of results. His reply (along with the fact that he was ultimately successful) is a good reminder of the need for lifelong learning.

> "Results? Why, man, I have gotten lots of results! If I find 10,000 ways something won't work, I haven't failed. I am not discouraged, because every wrong attempt discarded is another step forward. Just because something doesn't do what you planned it to do doesn't mean it's useless... Reverses should prove an incentive to great accomplishment.... There are no rules here, we're just trying to accomplish something."
>
> —Thomas Edison

Consider this legend about the Scottish king Robert the Bruce:

At one low point in his long campaign to free Scotland from English rule, Robert was hiding in a cave after a defeat in battle. Stuck there for days, he watched a spider trying to anchor the first strand for its web. It was trying to spin a web between the two sides of the narrow cave, swinging out again and again in its attempt to reach the other side. Bruce watched the spider try again and again over three days to bridge the gap, until finally it succeeded. The spider's persistence inspired the king to keep fighting for independence, and finally he succeeded as well. It was Bruce who first said, "If at first you don't succeed, try, try again."

Perseverance is important. But success does not come from doing the same thing over and over again. It comes from learning from experience.

ACTIVITY

Illustrating lifelong learning

1. Think back over what you have learned so far in this course. Jot down anything that you can put under the heading "Things I will keep learning more about throughout my life."
2. Write a fable, a story, or a scenario that shows the pitfalls of thinking you have nothing left to learn.

Reflection

Career development is based on good decision making. And good decision making is very difficult without **reflection**. You often have to step back from what you are doing to see if it is actually getting you where you want to go.

The word "reflection" has appeared in two contexts in this course—as one of the stages in the decision-making process, and as a category of question (in the Reflection boxes).

DISCOVERY

What is reflection?

Work with a partner to write a definition of "reflection." Your definition can take any form you like.

Reflecting on Career Development

The High Five

There is always more than one way of looking at an issue. That's certainly true of career development. Many people and organizations have come up with ways of expressing what is key to the career development process. One model is **The High Five**, a list of principles that sums up in a new way much of what appears in this book.

The High Five principles are as follows:

1. **Change is constant.** Adaptability is one of the most important skills you'll carry into the new century.
2. **Learning is ongoing.** The end of school doesn't mean the end of learning. Opportunities to learn are all around, and you will need to take advantage of them.
3. **Focus on the journey.** Life is not a destination. It's an exciting trip with many directions and goals that may change.
4. **Follow your heart.** Let your dreams shape your goals so that you go after what you really want.
5. **Access your allies.** Your friends, family and teachers can be valuable resources and supporters in helping you achieve your goals. Be sure to be an ally for others, too.

1 *Change Is Constant*

2 *Learning Is Ongoing*

3 *Focus On the Journey*

4 *Follow Your Heart*

5 *Access Your Allies*

ACTIVITY

Creating your own High Five

Work with a group to create your own High Five.

1. What are your five keys to successful career development?
2. Create a poster that gets your message across.

Reflection

The decision-making model presented in Unit 4 (page 171) describes briefly what it means to reflect upon your decisions and plans. Reflection means laying out all the pieces of the process to see if they still make sense. It means adjusting any piece that needs adjusting.

You may find that your goals were set based on information that is no longer current. You may be nearing your goals and realizing that they don't match your interests and skills anymore.

In any case, both external and internal changes will affect decisions you've made about your career.

Questions you should ask yourself include:

- What am I doing and why am I doing it?
- What new information is available?
- Am I missing any information that I should have?
- How can I use new information? (What does it mean to me?)
- What have I been doing that really works? Why does it?
- Do I need to adjust my plan or my goals? If so, how?

ACTIVITY

Understanding your questions

1. Make a chart of the elements of the High Five decision-making model, and relate each of the above questions to the appropriate element by writing them in the corresponding rows.
2. Add questions that are more specifically relevant to you.

Answering the Questions

When you reflect upon your own career goals and plans, you will probably find that not everything is working out as you had expected. Does that mean that decision making, goal setting and planning are a waste of your time? Of course not!

You are not in control of everything that happens in your life. There will always be surprises. That's why you have been focusing on *balanced* decision making.

Think of all your decisions, goals and plans as "best estimates." Review them constantly.

ACTIVITY

Understanding your answers

1. Analyse your career development plan by answering the questions you charted in the previous activity. This will give you a good idea of where you are now in the process.
2. Identify things that need adjustment. (Your goals? Your plan? The information you are using?) Write a statement of what you plan to do next.

Key Terms

resilience
adaptability
self-confidence
lifelong learning
reflection
High Five

Use a concept map or another graphic organizer to summarize the key ideas in this unit. Build on the key terms and add words, phrases and/or images that will help remind you of those key ideas.

Reflection

Look back at what you wrote in Take Stock (page 225). What are the next steps in your journey? What skills and attitudes will help you get there?

Questions

Knowledge/Understanding

1. **a)** What is meant by lifelong learning?
b) How does this tie into the High Five Model of career development?

Thinking/Inquiry

2. Create a profile of someone who has overcome adversity to achieve his or her goals. This can be done by interviewing someone you know or by researching a well-known person such as Terry Fox.

Communication

3. Respond to one of the statements below. Your response can be an essay, a poster, a collage, a piece of music, or an oral presentation.
- When planning a career, you should aim for a field where there is going to be lots of demand.
- When planning a career, you should follow what you love to do.
- A job's a job. As long as you make enough to pay the rent, you can do whatever you want in your free time.

Application

4. Many of your portfolio pieces could have been created electronically. If you have a number of electronic files, make sure they are organized in a way that is useful to you now and that will make sense to you in the future. Organizing folders according to divisions in your portfolio is one possibility. Make sure you include useful website bookmarks and that they are organized logically.

Taking Stock: Your Portfolio

1. Review the contents.
2. Reconsider your initial responses.
3. Summarize the most important information.

UNIT 6

What Can I Expect From Here?

How will my life change? What new things will I experience? How will I know if I'm successful?

Both life and work experiences will provide you with skills and knowledge help you to continue to grow and develop as both a worker and as a productive and contributing member of society.

What do I have to offer to the world?

SECTION

"If I'd had some set idea of a finish line, don't you think I would have crossed it by now?"

—*Bill Gates, CEO Microsoft*

What Can I Expect From Here?

In this unit you will:

- examine personal areas of life change
- explore the impact of lifestyle and life roles
- identify strategies for dealing with diversity
- discuss the importance of contributing to your community and society
- identify personal achievements
- evaluate hopes and dreams

Imagine you have a crystal ball. How do you see yourself in 10 years? Are you married and raising children? Or maybe you're travelling around the world, living in exotic places. Have you achieved success in your chosen field of work?

Don't be surprised if you don't recognize anyone or anything around you. As you continue your career development journey, you will have many opportunities to meet new people and try new things.

Look at the people in the photos. Do any of these photos depict what you saw in your crystal ball? What steps would you have to take to adapt to their lifestyles?

You already know that you have to play an active role in your career development. This unit will help prepare you to deal with your evolving life circumstances.

DISCOVERY

Coping with change

1. List 5 major life changes you think you will experience in the next 10 years.
2. Which changes are you most looking forward to? Which ones may cause you anxiety?

Jessica's Story

As you grow up, you may think about getting a part-time job and earning your own money. Having independence and freedom from your parents and being able to buy your own clothes and CDs are just some of the benefits of having a job. But the world of work brings both new responsibilities and challenges, as Jessica quickly discovered.

"I got it. I got the job at the restaurant!" Jessica shouted excitedly to her mom.

"Way to go honey! Your dad will be so excited."

Jessica had dreamt of the day she would be able to start working. She had wanted a part-time job ever since some of her friends had started working at one of the local restaurants in town. They had all started buying new clothes, taking weekend trips to St. John's, and doing things she couldn't always afford. Her parents would always say, "Do you think money grows on trees?" Jessica felt such a great surge of pride and excitement. Now she wouldn't have to ask her parents anymore for money to buy the things she wanted.

"So, when do you start?" her mom asked.

"Friday after school," Jessica replied. "I should get a couple of shifts every weekend. They will probably take me on full-time in the summer if everything goes well."

Her mother nodded. "That's great, sweetheart. This will be such a great experience for you. It will be an opportunity to meet new people and to see what working is all about."

Jessica had already tuned her mom out. All she could think about was waiting on all the cute boys who would be dropping by after basketball practice and that new skirt she had seen at the mall with the sweater to match. She would look great wearing that to the school dance. She couldn't wait to get her first cheque!

Friday came and Jessica left for work a little early. She wanted to make a good first impression on her employer. When she entered the restaurant, things were quite busy. She immediately spotted her new boss talking to several customers. He waved her over.

"Hi, Jessica. Great to see you're here early. We're getting quite busy. Head on to the back and grab an apron. I'll be along shortly."

Why do I need an apron? Jessica thought to herself.

As Jessica entered the kitchen, she noticed that several of her friends were also working. There were others there she didn't know. For the first time she felt a little scared and nervous.

"Hey, Jess!" Nathan called. "Welcome aboard. Come over and I'll introduce you around." Jessica smiled and walked over to the grill area.

"This is Jeff. He's our lead cook. This is Saskia. She just moved here. She's new too. Over there are Ryan, Mac and Dimitri. So what do you think?"

Jessica was feeling a little overwhelmed now. "So far, so good," Jessica replied.

"Once you get the hang of it, it's a piece cake!" Nathan smiled. "You're in the kitchen tonight. We'll be taking you through how this all works. If you have any questions, just ask. We'll also have to get you set up for payroll. Did you remember your Social Insurance Number?"

"Yeah, I think," Jessica answered, slightly bewildered.

Jessica learned the ropes in the kitchen, but she couldn't wait to graduate to the dining room. It seemed like her co-workers were always complaining about something and she found Dimitri and Saskia a little hard to understand. They were always so friendly with her, but their English just wasn't that great. Her boss had told her to be patient. She was doing well and she would get a chance in the dining room when she was ready.

Jessica was looking forward to her first paycheque. After two weekends of hard work, she felt that she had earned a great treat. That skirt and sweater would finally be hers! On Thursday, Jessica headed to the restaurant with her mom and dad to pick up her cheque.

Jessica came out with an excited smile. "Here it is," she exclaimed, holding the envelope high. Jessica ripped it open and took out the cheque inside. Jessica's smile quickly faded.

"What's wrong?" her mom asked.

"They didn't give me all my money!" Jessica answered angrily.

"What do you mean?" her dad questioned.

"They've taken money from my cheque. I worked so hard and put up with working in the kitchen and then they didn't give me my $7.00 an hour!"

Jessica's father smiled. "It's called 'deductions,' sweetheart. It's the money the employer has to take out for the government. You know, taxes."

"But I'm only a teenager," Jessica responded.

"But you're a working teenager now and a contributing member of society. Welcome to the world of work."

ACTIVITY

About Jessica

1. What was Jessica's motivation for getting a part-time job?
2. What lessons did Jessica learn about the world of work?
3. How do you think Jessica's view of working will change after her first paycheque experience?

SECTION 1

I Will Grow and Change

You are constantly developing and growing as an individual. Although you play an active role in your development, certain life stages and transitions are inevitable. Like right now, for instance, you are experiencing adolescence. This is a time when you want to become unique and differentiate yourself from your parents. Your friends become more of a priority in your life, and you are constantly challenged by the expectations and limitations set on you. Your body is also physically changing and developing as you mature and become an adult. As you get older, you will continue to take on new life roles and experience new lifestyles. Adapting to personal changes can be difficult. It is therefore important that you develop skills and strategies to face these challenges.

DISCOVERY

Your life

Take a few minutes to think about your life. Ask yourself the following questions:

- What life roles do I currently hold?
- What are my priorities in life?
- How do I cope with stress?
- How will my personal life look in five years?

Personal Development

How Will External Factors Affect Your Personal Development?

Personal development is ongoing. With age comes a new circle of friends, new relationships, a new outlook on life, and renewed motivation. As you learn more about the world, you will discover new interests and new opportunities. Your life will continue to experience change as you mature. The choices you make will guide your development, but sometimes things that are beyond your control will influence the path you take.

For example, you may be required to move to a new city or town to seek employment or to further your education. Throughout your career, you may be required to take additional training as a result of new technologies or company reorganization. As we saw in Unit 3, changes in the economy, as well as shifting demographics, will cause changes in the workplace in the coming years. New demands will be placed on businesses to meet the changing needs of the population. With each of these changes you will be required to adapt as well. You may have to find new accommodations, make new friends and/or seek new employment.

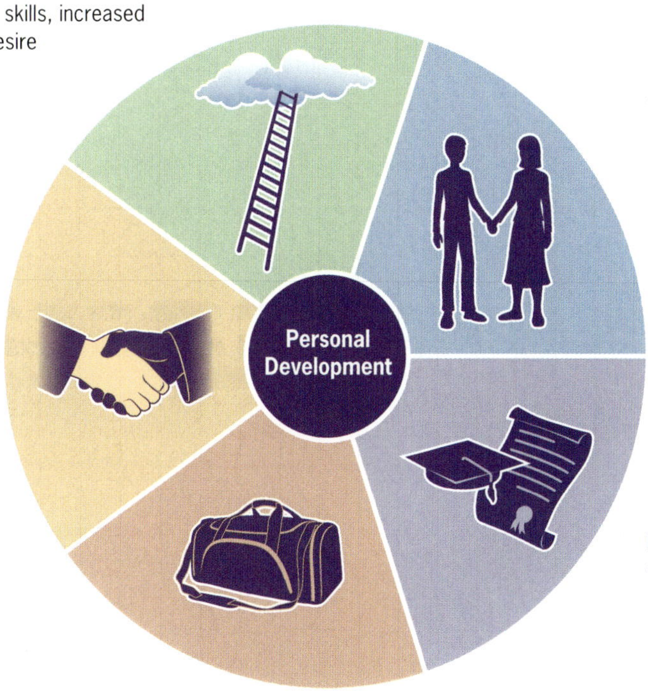

Personal Life Changes

Right now you are experiencing one of the most demanding and stressful developmental periods of your life. You probably feel some pressure to please your parents and, at the same time, fit in with your peers. You likely face choices that challenge your thoughts and beliefs on a regular basis. For example, you may have to decide whether to do your schoolwork or go to a party. Choosing to participate in extra-curricular activities or getting a part-time job are also examples of decisions you might face. The choices you make reflect your personal priorities right now, but these priorities will change as you grow and mature.

ACTIVITY

How will you change?

1. Think about the five areas of personal development listed on page 245. How will each one change over the course of your career development? List any external factors that may have an influence on you. As you do this, think about the following:
    - In what kind of relationships do you see yourself?
    - What training and education will you acquire?
    - What are some of your social activities?
    - How are you contributing to your community?
    - What are you doing to improve yourself physically and spiritually?
2. Think about how you will deal with each type of change. List as many coping methods as you can think of next to each area of change.

Reflection

As a teenager, your life continues to change. How have you changed since first entering high school? What changes are you currently experiencing? How will these changes have an impact on your career development and your life?

Lifestyle and Life Roles

Making Wise Lifestyle Choices

As a teenager, the lifestyle you lead today is quite different from the one you will lead as a young adult in your early twenties. As an adult in your thirties, your lifestyle will be different yet again. The **lifestyle** you choose represents your particular way of living. It's how an individual lives his or her life.

Looking Ahead

In early adulthood, much of your time may be spent socializing with friends, keeping late hours and developing new relationships. You may also have the opportunity to move around or travel. As you get older, this lifestyle may switch to one more focused on having children, spending time with family, creating a home and establishing a routine that provides structure and balance.

Every individual is unique and has a unique way of living his or her life. Perhaps you will choose to become self-employed, operating your own business on your own schedule, or you may choose to travel the world, seeking employment as you go. Or maybe you will choose a more traditional route that will allow you to buy your first car and your first home. While some of these lifestyles may not seem appealing to you right now, your choices will evolve and develop as you mature. Lifestyle choices change depending on your standard of living and income as well as your personal goals and priorities.

ACTIVITY

Your family's lifestyle

Think about your life at home. Create a visual representation of your family members' lifestyles. Include any words or images that represent how the different members of your family live their lives.

The Many Roles I Play

Life Roles

As your lifestyle evolves, so too will your life roles. Your **life roles** are the roles and positions you hold throughout your life. For example, right now you may be a brother or sister, a niece or nephew, or a cousin. You may also be a friend, a tutor or team captain. As you mature, you may become a spouse, a parent or both. Each life role, including the life role of a worker, brings with it a new set of responsibilities and expectations, as Jessica learned in the opening story. These new responsibilities can cause significant changes in your life and lifestyle.

Your values and beliefs play an important part in your lifestyle choices and your life roles. For example, if family is your first priority and you become a parent, your lifestyle will change as a result. More of your time and energy will be spent on caring for your loved ones. However, if you value work above all else, your priorities and, consequently, your lifestyle, will be quite different.

Balancing Life Roles

Your future happiness will depend on how you achieve balance between your personal and work roles and responsibilities. It can be quite easy at times to lose sight of your personal needs. Spending more time at work means you have less time to spend with family and friends. This may become a problem if you are a spouse and/or have children. As well, it can cause you to lose contact with friends and lose the support network you once had. It is important to recognize that as your work and life roles change, you will have to make changes to your lifestyle in order to accommodate and maintain the things that are important to you. You should also regularly make time to do the things you like to do, such as going to movies or going out for a meal. If your day-to-day life revolves solely around work, you may become overwhelmed and frustrated.

ACTIVITY

What roles do you play?

Make a list of all the life roles you currently play. For each life role, indicate some of the responsibilities associated with it. Consider how these responsibilities affect your lifestyle and well-being. The chart below provides one example.

Life Role	**Responsibility**	**Impact on Lifestyle/ Well-Being**
e.g. friend	*e.g. listen and support during a time of crisis, share in the good times.*	*e.g. need to make time to be with others and socialize, while balancing work and home responsibilities; as a result, I will also have friends who will do the same for me.*

Reflection

Sometimes we choose our life roles and sometimes they just happen. Think about your life roles as outlined in the activity above. Which of these did you really choose? Which would you change if you could?

Responding to Change

How Will You Cope?

Change is inevitable. Whether it comes suddenly and unexpectedly, or naturally as you age and mature, you will have to respond to such change. You will need to be resilient. Developing effective strategies to deal with situations as they arise will help you adapt to change.

We all have choices and options. Sometimes when we encounter stressful situations it can be difficult to see the choices we have. It's important to talk to people you trust and can count on to give you good advice and support. Talking to friends and family and listening to their suggestions can often give you new insight to see things you couldn't see on your own.

Dealing with Stress

Stress can affect your thinking and physical health. Making choices in a time of stress can have long-term implications, both positively and negatively. Sometimes, for example, people turn to food or other sources of comfort to reduce stress. These choices can actually create further stress and can lead to health problems. Maintaining a good program of diet and exercise as well as getting plenty of rest and having a positive attitude will help you to manage stress and deal with change. Consider the following cases.

Donna's Story

Donna left her home on the Northern Peninsula to attend university in St. John's. She had planned on completing a degree in Business Administration and then moving to Corner Brook to find work. Halfway through the program, Donna's father was diagnosed with a serious illness. With no other family around, Donna decided to return home to help out with her father's care. At first she was devastated by the whole situation. After taking some time to gather her thoughts, Donna began to consider all of her options and decided to enrol in distance education courses. She knew she wanted to fulfill family responsibilities, but also knew that it was important to her and her dad that she continue to work toward her own dreams as well. Within 18 months, Donna was able to return to full-time studies. She completed her degree and moved to Corner Brook. It took her a year longer than she had originally planned, but her father was doing well, and Donna found a job that she loves.

Peter's Story

Peter had always worked for the same company. When he was laid off from the local plant, he was forced to seek seasonal employment away from his home and family. He worked 12 to 15 hours a day and had little time off. Peter often thought about his old life and missed his family. His job was in a remote location up north and there were very few leisure or recreational opportunities. Peter loved cooking and often spent his time trying out new recipes. He found that this helped him relax from the stress of his job. When Peter returned home in the fall, money became an issue and the family struggled. Peter really wrestled with the decision to return up north next season. He found being away from his family stressful. On the suggestion of a friend, Peter decided to pursue his love of cooking and become a chef. Peter was hired by a local restaurant as a chef's apprentice and his wife got a job at the grocery store to help make ends meet.

ACTIVITY

How did they cope?

Examine the two cases above. Draw a chart comparing the two, using the following as headings:

- nature of change
- lifestyle implications
- coping strategies
- alternative coping strategies

My Actions Affect Others

You have the power to change the lives of others. The people closest to you, such as your friends and family, often feel the effects of your decisions. Did you know that what you do can also change the lives of people you don't even know? There are many ways that your actions can have an impact on people in your community. It's up to you to make sure that your impact is a positive one.

DISCOVERY

How do you contribute?

Brainstorm all the ways you contribute. Include your behaviours at home, at school and at your part-time job if you have one. Copy the chart below in your notebook. Complete it with your personal answers.

Where I Contribute	How I Contribute	Other Ways I Could Contribute

Respecting Others

Accepting Differences

No two people are the same. Everyone has different ways of thinking and acting, so naturally there will be times when you don't agree with others. But you need to learn to get along with the people around you and to accept diversity in order to function effectively in society. Right now you probably have friends who believe things that you do not and who participate in activities that you would never consider. That's okay. You may also have friends from diverse backgrounds and cultures.

Each of us possesses unique characteristics, some that distinguish us as individuals and others that identify us as belonging to a particular group. Given our **diversity** and Canada's multicultural heritage, it is important to be aware that we will not always share common belief systems and traditions with those around us. We are truly a diverse society. While many people embrace diversity as an opportunity to experience new things and expand their cultural knowledge, others feel uneasy and shy away from those who are different.

Diversity can sometimes contribute to **stereotyping** and **bias**. Stereotyping places people and groups into strict categories. These narrow beliefs can lead to judgments, misunderstandings and occasionally harassment. Bias can unfairly influence an individual, issue or situation.

Reflection

Examine your community in terms of the various people, religions and culturally diverse groups it represents. Identify the positive aspects and the challenges in your community due to this diversity.

Everyone deserves respect and tolerance. While you may not always agree with people of varying opinions or backgrounds, you do have the responsibility to respect their choices and beliefs. You will be confronted with diversity at home, in social situations and within the work environment. When dealing with such situations, effective communication and being open-minded are crucial. Applying effective negotiating and problem-solving strategies that demonstrate respect for others will help to resolve any stressful situation much more effectively than conflict. As was discussed in Unit 2, learning to give and accept constructive criticism can help you to become a more effective communicator in any situation.

ACTIVITY

Dealing with conflict

With a partner, identify three possible situations where dealing with diversity and differing beliefs may create a challenge. These could be at school, at work or at home. Create role plays that demonstrate effective problem-solving or conflict resolution techniques for each situation.

Being Socially Responsible

Doing Your Part

As an individual, you have rights and responsibilities within society. Similarly, in the world of work, both employers and employees have responsibilities. You do not live in isolation—your behaviour often has an impact on the people around you. It is important to take into consideration your **social responsibilities** and the ways you can give back to your community, as well as to society as a whole. Doing your part to make things better can bring you many rewards, as well as a deep sense of personal satisfaction. Contributing does not necessarily require grand gestures. A simple act, like throwing your empty cans and bottles in the recycling bin, can make a difference.

ACTIVITY

What can you do?

"Every little bit counts" is a common slogan used during fundraising campaigns by many charitable organizations. What does this slogan really mean? How can you do your "little bit" to help your community?

Making a Difference

Contributing to Your Community

There are probably numerous activities that you are involved in right now that contribute positively to your community. Maybe your school does a food drive to help the local food bank, or your music group does a Christmas production at a local seniors' home. Whatever you do to help your community become a better place is a worthwhile contribution.

Community contributions can take many forms. Some people help shelve books at the library, while others spend afternoons reading to children in the hospital. Some people give back to their community by volunteering with local service organizations such as the Lions Club International, YWCA and YMCA, Shriners, Kinsmen Club and Knights of Columbus. These service organizations work hard to provide programs and support for people in need within the local community. They often seek volunteers to participate in fundraising activities that help support their programs. Similarly, national organizations such as the Canadian Cancer Society, Canadian Hard of Hearing Association, Canadian Red Cross and Children's Wish Foundation are always looking for community volunteers to assist in their fundraising efforts.

Giving back to your community in a volunteer capacity can be very rewarding. It is personally satisfying to know that your efforts are having a positive impact on someone else's life. There are thousands of individuals who dedicate numerous hours to helping those within the community and throughout the world.

Prospective employers view community contributions and volunteering as valuable work experience. It demonstrates character and motivation in an individual. It also helps you gain valuable skills and meet new people.

Newfoundlanders and Labradorians: Always Ready to Lend a Hand

Here in Newfoundland and Labrador, we are well known for our kindness and our generosity. When individuals are in crisis, Newfoundlanders and Labradorians pull together and give what they can. This was very evident during the tragedy of September 11, 2001, when all U.S. airports were shut down and thousands of passengers from around the world were forced to land in this province. Newfoundlanders and Labradorians welcomed these stranded strangers into their homes and treated them like they were part of the family, offering both food and shelter until the airports reopened.

Reflection

Think about the ways you have contributed to your community. What else could you do to make a difference? How can you encourage your friends and family to contribute?

Links

To learn more about the Red Cross in Newfoundland and Labrador and how you can help out, go to <www.careers.nelson.com>.

Overview of the Voluntary Sector in Newfoundland and Labrador: Quick Facts

- There are over 4,000 voluntary community-based organizations in Newfoundland and Labrador.
- Twenty-four percent of voluntary community-based organizations in Newfoundland and Labrador are registered charities.
- Fifty-nine percent of voluntary community-based organizations in the province have less than 10 paid employees.
- Only one percent has more than 50 employees.
- Twenty-nine percent have no paid employees.

Volunteering

- Thirty-one percent of people age 15 and older residing in Newfoundland and Labrador volunteered their time and/or skills to help other individuals or organizations fulfill a task.
- The average number of volunteer hours per year is 206.
- Newfoundland and Labrador leads the nation with the highest median participation rate by volunteers, at 96 hours per year (i.e., 50 percent volunteer more than 96 hours, and 50 percent volunteer less than that number). This is almost 20 percent higher than the median of 78.5 hours per year for all provinces.

Financial Donations

- In 2003, 81,750 Newfoundlanders and Labradorians claimed a charitable donation on their tax returns.
- Newfoundland and Labrador is third in median donations at $310, behind Prince Edward Island at $330 and Nunavut at $410.

Links

The information above was taken from enVision, a division of the Community Services Council Newfoundland and Labrador (CSC). To learn more and for a direct link to the CSC, visit <www.careers.nelson.com>.

ACTIVITY

Exploring volunteer work

1. Research two or three organizations in your community that have volunteers. Find out what the organizations' goals are and whom they help.
2. Interview someone you know who is a community volunteer. Why does he or she volunteer? What are the rewards?

Links

Go to <www.careers.nelson.com> for links to various service organizations.

Success and Achievement

Can you remember a time when there was something you truly wanted? Something you were willing to do anything to get? Everyone has desires and goals. There are things you hope to accomplish and achieve. Right now, you may want to be picked for a sports team, or you may be hoping to get a good report card. Or maybe you just want to get all of your credits so you'll be eligible to graduate. Whatever your goals, hard work and determination will help you reach them. All your achievements and successes help contribute to the person you are and the person you will become.

DISCOVERY

How successful are you?

Take a moment to think about some of your achievements and accomplishments. What goals have you already achieved? What awards or prizes have you won? Look back through your Course Content Portfolio and Employability Skills Portfolio. What have you learned about yourself that will help you experience success in the future?

Aspirations, Motivation and Success

The Will to Succeed

Think back to the crystal ball at the beginning of this unit. Why did you see your future the way you did? What was your **motivation** for your lifestyle and career choice? The life you saw for yourself is what you are working toward achieving.

Throughout your career development process, you will have many **aspirations**. Each time you reach a personal goal, a new opportunity will arise. **Success** will inspire you to set new goals and to achieve new things.

Your aspirations are influenced by your values. What is important to you? Money? Fame? Power? Service to others? If you value financial success and stability, for example, you will probably measure your success by the amount of money you earn. Likewise, if you value helping others, you will measure your success by the societal contributions you make. Again, your values may change over time as you take on new life roles and hold new responsibilities.

ACTIVITY

What is success?

Success means different things to different people.

1. Interview three individuals to determine their definitions of successful people. Create a profile of a successful person based on their descriptions.
2. What does success mean to you? Create a profile based on your definition. How does this profile differ from the first one you created?

Profile: Geoff Eaton

This is the story of a local man who was motivated by his personal crisis to create an organization that offers support and inspiration to others facing similar challenges.

In 1998, Geoff Eaton was diagnosed with acute myelogenous leukemia (AML) and began the biggest challenge of his life, dealing with cancer at the age of 22. Throughout his treatment, relapse, two stem-cell transplants and a host of other hurdles, Geoff was made painfully aware of the lack of resources for young people dealing with cancer in Canada. So he decided to change that. In June of 2000, Geoff established RealTime Cancer (RTC) for the purposes of education, awareness and support, centred by a core belief in the value of a positive attitude. Geoff started with e-mails to family and friends, and ultimately grew to include students as he presented at schools.

Geoff began sharing his story with young people through high school presentations in Newfoundland and Labrador, and through his weblog, educating young people about cancer and offering information about prevention, messages of inspiration and how to face any challenge with a positive attitude.

Since 2000, RTC has evolved into what is now a national charity with cancer community partnerships across the country. RTC hosts an on-line peer support community, the RTC portal; delivers a public education program, the RTC Challenge; and in the summer of 2005, RTC hosted a retreat for young survivors, Retreat Yourself.

Links

To learn more about Geoff Eaton and for a link to the RealTime Cancer website, visit <www.careers.nelson.com>.

ACTIVITY

Changing priorities

Consider how a personal life crisis would impact your career development process. Ask yourself the following questions:

1. How would my aspirations and motivation change?
2. How would I define success?

Making the Most of Your Experiences

Personal Achievements

When you hear the word "achievement," what springs to mind? Winning awards? Earning recognition from peers? Doing something good for someone or for yourself? You have no doubt experienced many personal achievements already. For example, if you've made the school hockey or volleyball team or tutored a fellow student, you have experienced an achievement of which you can be proud.

Your accomplishments not only highlight your skills, they also provide you with valuable experience. For example, you may like doodling in your notebook but don't recognize your artistic talent until you place first in a school drawing contest. That's why it's so important to make the most of every opportunity to showcase your talents and to try new things.

As you move through high school, you will have many opportunities for academic and extra-curricular achievements. You may achieve academic success and graduate with honours or complete advanced placement courses that prepare you for post-secondary programs. Your academic achievements can in turn earn you scholarships and awards. Likewise, you may earn medals or trophies for extra-curricular activities, or develop skills that help to boost your self-confidence and make you feel good about yourself. Such awards and achievements can also be quite motivating.

Professional Achievements

In the world of work, opportunities for achievements and advancement, such as promotions, a pay raise or recognition may result from your hard work and dedication. Whatever the case, achievement is not only about the recognition received, but also about how you feel about yourself. You don't need to be presented with a fancy award to feel pride in your work. Every stop along your career development journey will bring opportunities for success and achievements. Don't let these opportunities pass you by!

ACTIVITY

What your achievements say about you

Think about three things you have accomplished that have been important to you. Why was each one meaningful? What do your accomplishments tell others about you? Write a letter to a prospective employer explaining how your achievements—and what you have learned from them—would make you a valuable asset as valuable employee.

Reflection

Sometimes we undervalue our achievements and what they mean to us. Think about the last time your parents or a friend said they were proud of you. What was the situation? How did you feel?

How to Get Where You're Going

Hopes and Dreams

A wise person once said that if you choose a job you love, it won't feel like work. Making decisions about jobs and your career can be overwhelming—especially right now. There are so many options and the world of work is always changing. Skills and trades that are in demand today may not be when you graduate. There may be new opportunities on the horizon. Staying on top of current economic and technological trends, both locally and globally, will help you to stay focused on your dreams and to make good decisions.

Sometimes you may feel as if you are never going to achieve your goals. Do not give up! You will continue to learn about yourself, the world around you and what you need to be successful throughout your career-development journey. A positive attitude, along with a lot of determination and motivation, will go a long way in helping you to achieve any goal you set.

You have already started on your career development journey. You have learned many things about the world of work throughout this course and have no doubt learned many things about yourself. Now is the time to use this knowledge to dream big. Reach for the stars. The sky is the limit!

ACTIVITY

Making your dreams a reality

1. Take a few moments to reflect on who you are. What were your hopes and dreams when you were younger? How are these different from the things you wish for today? What is the one thing you truly want?
2. Using what you have learned throughout this course, prepare an action plan for achieving your dream. What steps do you need to take? What obstacles might you encounter? How will you overcome them? Keep this plan so you can refer back to it in the future.

Key Terms

lifestyle
life role
diversity
stereotyping
bias
social responsibility
motivation
aspiration
success

Use a concept map or another graphic organizer to summarize the key ideas in this unit. Build on the key terms and add words, phrases and/or images that will help remind you of those key ideas.

Reflection

Go back to Coping with Change on page 241 and re-examine the list of life changes that you were anxious about. Has your anxiety about these changes diminished? Can you apply the coping methods you learned in this unit to reduce your worry?

Questions

Knowledge/Understanding

1. Identify the five areas of personal development. Create a timeline indicating possible changes that may occur in each area throughout your life.
2. Explain how diversity can impact a work environment. List potential positive and negative effects.

Thinking/Inquiry

3. Talk to your teacher, coach or parent about his or her first experience with community contribution. Find out how that person got involved and how he or she continues to contribute despite changing lifestyles and life roles.
4. Make a list of five things you would like to achieve. What will keep you motivated to achieve these goals?

Communication

5. Choose a local charitable organization. Imagine you have been asked to recruit volunteers. Create a poster, slide show, pamphlet or any other visual representation that will encourage individuals to volunteer with this organization.

Application

6. As a group, plan an activity that will allow you to contribute in some way to your community. Develop an action plan that assigns tasks to each class member and identify what your goals are.

Taking Stock: Your Portfolio

1. Review the contents.
2. Reconsider your initial responses.
3. Summarize the most important information.

Glossary

Adaptability. The ability to respond positively to change by adjusting goals and plans and being open to opportunities.

Active listening. Using specific, active strategies (like paraphrasing) to ensure comprehension of what is said and to encourage the speaker.

Analysis. A careful and thorough process of understanding that often involves breaking a problem or situation down into simpler parts.

Apprenticeship. A form of education that includes both classroom and on-the-job training, and that leads to certification in a specific trade.

Aspiration. A will to succeed; a cherished desire.

Attitude. A way of thinking, acting or feeling; how one looks at life.

Balanced decision making. A decision-making model that encourages a balance of logical thinking and intuition.

Barrier. Anything that gets in the way of your goals and plans.

Bias. Prejudice that leads to an unfair influence upon an individual, issue or situation.

Canada Labour Code. A law that gives the official list of standards, rights, rules and duties regulating health and safety in all workplaces, for all Canadians—applying to owners, employers, supervisors and workers.

Career. The sum of one's life experiences. Every person has a career, which includes all of the individual's work, learning, recreational, community and family roles.

Career goals. A broad set of goals that includes all aspects of one's career.

Chronological résumé. See **Résumé.**

Community contribution. A volunteer activity that positively impacts both the community and the individual contributor.

Communication skills. The ability to speak, listen and write carefully, with due attention to the message and the audience.

Community college. A post-secondary school that offers diplomas and certificates for completion of specialized, practical courses that use a "hands-on" approach to training for specific jobs.

Community goal. How a person intends to contribute to his or her community; may include the notion of what benefits will be received in return.

Conflict resolution. Strategies used to resolve conflict among people peacefully (*e.g.*, negotiation, mediation, avoidance and accommodation).

Consensus. General agreement.

Constructive criticism. A type of criticism in which the purpose is to benefit the recipient. Comments may be both positive and negative in nature and should be given in a helpful and friendly manner.

Continuing education/continuing studies. Programs offered by many colleges, universities and school boards for those who cannot attend school full-time, or only want to take one course at a time, usually at night.

Co-operative education. An educational program in which students earn academic credits while participating in the workplace.

Course Content Portfolio. The collection of your work throughout this course that mirrors the career development process (which is essentially a decision-making process).

Cover letter. A letter an applicant writes in response to a job opening. It outlines interest in and qualifications for the position; accompanies a résumé.

Credential. Document, reference, or experience that recommends and qualifies a person for a job.

Demographic trend. A pattern evident in the human population (*e.g.*, a growing elderly population).

Demography. The study of human population; includes statistics such as size, age and distribution of populations.

Distance education. Continuing education programs that are conducted by correspondence or over the Internet.

Diversity. The unique characteristics that distinguish us as individuals and that identify us as belonging to a group or groups.

Economic trend. A financial pattern, habit or change that affects society in general (*e.g.*, on-line shopping).

Employability skills. The core competencies required in all work settings. The Conference Board of Canada's *Employability Skills Profile* identifies three critical skills: fundamental, personal management and teamwork.

Employability Skills Portfolio. A portfolio used to collect, organize and present items that demonstrate the acquisition of knowledge, skills, behaviours and achievement; divided into three sections: Fundamental Skills, Personal Management Skills and Teamwork Skills.

Entrepreneur. A person who starts an enterprise or business of his or her own.

External influences. Values and attitudes that a person receives from family, friends, cultural and religious groups, and society.

Field of work. Grouping of related occupations.

Functional résumé. See **Résumé**.

Globalization. An economic trend toward international trade and competition.

Goal. A statement of intent that is measurable, achievable, concrete and specific.

Graduation requirements. List of achievements, including kind and number of courses completed, that a person needs to earn a senior high school graduation diploma. In Newfoundland and Labrador, these are listed in *On Course: Handbook for Grade 9 Parents and Students.*

Group dynamics. How a number of people working together relate, *e.g.*, how they set goals, plan, assign tasks, share responsibility and negotiate.

Habit. A recurrent pattern of behaviour acquired through frequent repetition.

Hidden job market. Constituting 85 percent of available employment, the jobs in this category are never advertised, and are usually filled by "word of mouth."

High Five. A model for expressing what is key to the career development process. The five points are: change is constant; learning is ongoing; focus on the journey; follow your heart; and access your allies.

Information interview. An interview in which a person is seeking information (as opposed to applying for a job); often used to learn more about a given field of work, occupation or job.

Interest. An area of personal enjoyment, curiosity and ability.

Interest inventory. A quiz or survey that generates a list of personal interests, and is often designed to match your interests with related occupations.

Internal influences. Private values and attitudes.

Inventory. A quiz or survey that results in a list.

Job. A specific set of duties performed for a specific employer in a prescribed location or range of locations for a specific rate of pay.

Job application form. An information questionnaire completed by a prospective employee.

Job interview. A meeting between an employer and a prospective employee in which the employer hopes to learn more about the suitability of the candidate.

Job shadow. Time spent with someone at a job, following the person "like a shadow." In this way someone who is interested in a certain job can get a good sense of what is actually involved.

Knowledge. Information, experience and memory combining in various ways toward the ultimate goal of wisdom.

Labour market information. Information about employment trends and availability. This information can be located by contacting government agencies such as Statistics Canada.

Labour Standards Act. A provincial law that contains Newfoundland and Labrador's basic rules about employing people. Employees and employers both have rights and responsibilities under the Act.

Learning goals. What a person intends to learn—at school or outside school, alone or with others.

Learning style. The primary way a person learns. The three commonly identified learning styles are: visual learner, auditory learner and tactile learner.

Lifelong learning. The notion that learning is ongoing throughout life and that it can occur as a result of any and all life experiences.

Life roles. The roles that an individual assumes throughout life.

Lifestyle. The way an individual lives his or her life.

Long-term goals. Goals that a person intends to reach well into the future (at least 10 years).

Majority rule. When decisions are made based on the largest number in agreement.

Mediation. A process of resolving conflict or difficulties in which a neutral person brings together and facilitates a negotiation between disputants.

Mid-term goals. Goals that a person intends to reach in the foreseeable future (*e.g.* from 3 months to a year.)

Motivation. A reason for one's action(s); the inspiration to act.

Multiple intelligences. A theory that each person has 8 different kinds of intelligence: verbal/linguistic, logical/mathematical, visual/spatial, bodily/kinesthetic, musical/rhythmic, intrapersonal, interpersonal and naturalist.

National Occupational Classification (NOC). A Canadian occupational classification system that codes and categorizes over 25,000 occupational titles according to two basic criteria: skill types and skill levels.

Negotiation. Reaching mutual agreement through discussion.

Network. Connections with other people.

Networking. The process of connecting with other people, often for the purpose of information exchange and support, when searching for work or advancing or changing a career.

Newfoundland and Labrador Human Rights Code. The provincial law that protects individual freedoms.

Occupation. A cluster of jobs with similar tasks and skills performed at a variety of locations. For example, "teacher" is an occupation, but "teacher at Stephenville High School" is a job.

Occupational Health and Safety Act (OHSA). The federal act that governs job safety for all workplaces, defining the rights and duties of everyone in a workplace.

Open job market. Those employment positions that are advertised (15 percent of all jobs).

Options. The various opportunities or possibilities available to a person at any given time.

Opportunities. Possibilities. Chances for advancing toward one's goals.

Organizational skills. A person's ability to arrange tasks, manage time, use work areas efficiently, set reasonable deadlines and meet them.

Peer mediation. A mediation in which the mediators are students trained to help resolve conflicts between other students.

Peer pressure. The influence that a group exerts on its members to conform to certain standards (*e.g.*, of dress, speech and opinion).

Personal characteristics. Those qualities and details that constitute a person's unique personality.

Personal goals. Goals that concern one's self, family, friends and others of importance.

Personal management skills. Skills that people use to manage themselves in relation to factors such as time, goals, money, risk, change and authority. Personal management is rooted in personality or temperament, and includes not only skills but also characteristics (*e.g.*, optimism, independence or persistence).

Personal profile. A summary of self-assessment activities that lists achievements, interests, skills, intelligence types, learning styles and personal characteristics.

Personality types. In the same way that different learning styles and intelligences have been categorized, different personality types have also been categorized (*e.g.*, organizer/manager, social/helper, fixer/builder, creator/inventor and doer/detail type).

Plan. An outline of a course of action designed to achieve a series of goals.

Potential. Unexplored or undeveloped capabilities and possibilities.

Private colleges. Also called "private training schools," these schools offer specialized training for specific occupations. Many offer primarily computer-related courses. Such schools are privately owned.

Professional association. An organization of people who all do the same type of work. Such an organization concerns itself with matters of interest to all its members (*e.g.*, their rights). An example is The Writers' Union of Canada.

Reference. The name of a person who will vouch for someone else's character, job performance and record. On an application form, a reference is a name (with a telephone number) that the employer can contact to ask about the potential employee.

Reflection. To look back at what one has done or thought; to reassess; to rethink.

Resilience. The ability to bend and adapt to change.

Résumé. A personal information document that outlines experience, education, credentials and references.

Résumé (chronological). A résumé that groups education, work and volunteer experiences into lists in reverse chronological order (*i.e.*, starting with the most current information).

Résumé (functional). A résumé that highlights special skills, awards and achievements to target a specific job.

School skills. Abilities or capacities that are acquired and improved upon while a student is in school.

Sector council. An organization comprised of all the business, labour and other interests within a particular industry (*e.g.*, the Canadian Council for Professional Fish Harvesters).

Self-assessment. To consider one's own strengths and weaknesses; to decide how to build upon those strengths, and how to work on those weaknesses; to focus on the person one wants to become.

Self-concept. The way one sees oneself.

Self-confidence. A lack of doubt in one's abilities. This comes from measuring one's self against the world, and having that measurement confirmed.

Self-employment. To be an entrepreneur. To earn money by working for one's self.

Self-knowledge. What one knows about one's self.

Self-motivated. To be encouraged into action by one's self.

Self-talk. The messages one tells oneself in a given situation. These messages may be positive or negative.

Short-term goals. Goals that a person intends to achieve in the immediate future (*e.g.*, next week or next month).

Skills. Abilities or capacities that can be acquired and improved with experience, practice, and training.

Social responsibility. A responsibility to the community and the environment to behave in a manner that is respectful and does not cause harm. In the business world, the term refers to employers engaging in practices and procedures for the betterment of individuals, society and/or the environment.

Social trend. A pattern, style or habit of society in general.

Standardized self-assessment tools. General inventories designed to help individuals survey their interests and skills and to measure them against an established standard.

Stereotyping. Beliefs about individuals or groups that place them in categories and/or in a position of disadvantage.

Stress management. A person's ability to find ways to relax and release tension (*e.g.*, to balance work and leisure).

Success. When action results in a desired outcome.

Teamwork skills. A person's set of "group dynamic" abilities; how a person works and gets along with others.

Technological trend. A pattern or tendency in the overall society relating to technological changes.

Time management. A person's ability to organize his or her time so that all priorities are met.

Trade union. A professional association of workers that provides a common voice with which to negotiate a contract with an employer, that sets out the terms of employment, pay rates, etc.

Transferable skills. Abilities or capacities that can be transferred from one situation or task to another.

Trend. A pattern or tendency or habit in society.

University. A post-secondary institution that offers degrees for theoretical, academic programs of study, using a general or specific approach.

Values. Priorities and beliefs. Private, moral, social, political and spiritual concepts that hold particular importance for a person (*e.g.*, generosity, independence, national pride).

Well-being. A contented state of being happy, healthy and prosperous.

Work goals. A plan that maps a job destination; what a person would like to be doing in the future; thoughts of advancement or job change.

Workplace Health, Safety and Compensation Act. A Newfoundland and Labrador law created to promote healthy, safe workplaces, encourage safe, timely return to work and provide insured benefits to injured workers.

Workplace Hazardous Material Information System (WHMIS). A regulation within the Occupational Health and Safety Act, that specifies rules for labelling goods, providing information, and training workers in the use of hazardous substances.

Index

Y

Credits

This page constitutes an extension of the copyright page. We have made every effort to trace the ownership of all copyrighted material and to secure permission from copyright holders. In the event of any question arising as to the use of any material, we will be pleased to make the necessary corrections in future printings. Thanks are due to the following authors, publishers, and agents for permission to use the material indicated.

Photographs
p. 1: Geostock/PhotoDisc/Getty Images; **p. 2** bottom right: © Donna Disario/CORBIS; **p. 2** bottom left: Photo: Brian Atkinson. Reprinted by permission of Christopher Wabie **p. 3** top left: © Pierre Tremblay/Masterfile; **p. 3** bottom left: Brian Atkinson; **p. 3:** top right, © Chuck Savage/CORBIS; **p. 3:** centre, © Jose Luis Pelaez, Inc./CORBIS; **p. 7:** Photo courtesy of Maidena Welsh; **p. 10:** Sean Murphy/Stone/Getty Images; **p. 16:** top left, CP PHOTO/David Lucas; **p. 16:** centre, Keith Brofsky/PhotoDisc/Getty Images; **p. 16:** centre left, Memorial University of Newfoundland; **p. 16:** bottom right, Ryan McVay/PhotoDisc/Getty Images; **16:** centre right, © Ariel Skelley/CORBIS; **p. 16:** bottom left, © Billy E. Barnes/Photo Edit; **p. 16:** top right, © Charles Gupton/CORBIS; **p. 19:** Comstock; **p. 20:** © Royalty-Free/Corbis; **p. 23:** bottom right, Bob Scott/The Image Bank/Getty Images; **p. 23:** bottom left, © Royalty-Free/Corbis; **p. 24:** centre left, Christopher Tan Teck Hean/Shutterstock; **p. 24:** bottom left, Dennis Brack/Landov; **p. 24:** top right, PhotoDisc/Getty Images; **p. 24:** centre right, PhotoDisc/Getty Images; **p. 25:** © Royalty-Free/Corbis; **p. 26:** bottom right, Geostock/ PhotoDisc/Getty Images; **p. 26:** bottom left, © Royalty-Free/Corbis; **p. 27 (left to right):** CP PHOTO/Brantford Expositor; CP PHOTO/Globe and Mail; CP PHOTO/ Charlie Palmer; CP PHOTO/Kevin Frayer; **p. 29:** Jerry Kobalenko/First Light; **p. 35:** © Royalty-Free/Corbis; **p. 39:** CP PHOTO/David Lucas; **p. 45:** Ryan McVay/ PhotoDisc/Getty Images; **p. 54:** www.comstock.ca; **p. 55:** Jules Frazier/PhotoDisc/Getty Images; **p. 56:** Courtesy of Dr. Roger Tabah; **p. 57:** PhotoLink/PhotoDisc/Getty Images; **p. 64:** Sean Armstrong; **p. 67:** Doug Menuez/ PhotoDisc/Getty Images; **p. 70:** Doug Menuez/ PhotoDisc/Getty Images; **p. 71:** © Royalty-Free/Corbis; **p. 73:** www.comstock.ca; **p.75:** John Wang/PhotoDisc/ Getty Images; **p.77:** bottom left, Risteski Goce/ Shutterstock; **p. 77:** bottom right, Stockdisc/Getty Images; **p. 80:** Daisuke Morita/PhotoDisc/Getty Images; **p. 81:** Corel; **p. 83:** S. Wanke/ PhotoLink/ PhotoDisc/Getty Images; **p. 84:** SW Productions/PhotoDisc/Getty Images; **p. 88:** © Denis Scott/CORBIS; **p. 91:** © Royalty-Free/Corbis; **p. 94:** SW Productions/PhotoDisc/Getty Images; **p. 96:** Santokh Kochar/PhotoDisc/Getty Images; **p. 99:** © Royalty-Free/Corbis; **p. 101:** © Royalty-Free/ Corbis; **p. 102:** bottom right, Corel; **p. 102:** bottom left, TRBfoto/PhotoDisc/Getty Images; **p. 103:** bottom right, C Squared Studios/PhotoDisc/Getty Images; **p. 103:** centre left, Siede Preis/PhotoDisc/Getty Images; **p. 103:** top right, Spike Mafford/PhotoDisc/Getty Images; **p. 107:** Steve Cole/PhotoDisc/Getty Images; **p. 112:** Image courtesy of Indu Ghuman; **p. 115:** Angela Maynard/Life File/PhotoDisc/Getty Images; **p. 118:** CP PHOTO/Jonathan Haywark; **p. 123:** Photo of Stefanie Konkin, Cathie Archbould, courtesy of the Whitehorse Star; **p. 124:** top left, Photo courtesy of Ashley Feltham; **p. 124:** centre left, Photo of Dameion Royes, Connections magazine, Humber College; **p. 127:** © Royalty-Free/Corbis; **p. 128:** © Tom Stewart/CORBIS; **p. 130:** Jason Reed/PhotoDisc/Getty Images; **p. 132:** Courtesy of the Workplace and Insurance Board of Ontario; **p. 133:** poster: "How Safe is Your Job?" Reprinted with permission; **p. 134:** Corel; **p. 140:** Ryan McVay/PhotoDisc/Getty Images; **p. 141:** © Royalty-Free/Corbis; **p. 142:** CP PHOTO/Tibor Kolley; **p. 146:** Ryan McVay/PhotoDisc/Getty Images; **p. 151:** Jack Hollingsworth/PhotoDisc/Getty Images; **p. 153:** John A. Rizzo/PhotoDisc/Getty Images; **p. 156:** Dave Thompson/ Life File/PhotoDisc/Getty Images; **p. 157:** bottom left, John A. Rizzo/PhotoDisc/Getty Images; **p. 157:** centre right, © Royalty-Free/Corbis; **p. 160:** Nick Koudis/ PhotoDisc/Getty Images; **p. 162:** © Royalty-Free/Corbis; **p. 163:** PhotoLink/ PhotoDisc/Getty Images; **p. 165:** Charly Franklin/Taxi/Getty Images; **p. 166:** bottom left, Donovan Reese/PhotoDisc/Getty Images; **p. 166:** centre right, Jack Hollingsworth/ PhotoDisc/Getty Images; **p. 167:** bottom right, David Buffington/PhotoDisc/Getty Images; **p. 167:** centre left, Doug Menuez/PhotoDisc/ Getty Images; **p. 167:** centre right, Kim Steele/PhotoDisc/ Getty Images; **p. 167:** top right, Lawrence M. Sawyer/ PhotoDisc/Getty Images; **p. 173:** © Royalty-Free/Corbis; **p. 177:** © Royalty-Free/Corbis; **p. 181:** C Squared Studios/PhotoDisc/Getty Images; **p. 182:** top left, Steve Cole/PhotoDisc/Getty Images; **p. 182:** bottom left, www.comstock.ca; **p. 183:** bottom, Jeff Maloney/ PhotoDisc/Getty Images; **p. 183:** centre, © Royalty-Free/Corbis; **p. 184:** bottom right, Sami Sarkis/ PhotoDisc/Getty Images; **p. 184:** top, Steve Cole/ PhotoDisc/Getty Images; **p. 186:** Donovan Reese/ PhotoDisc/Getty Images; **p. 188:** Geoff Manasse/ PhotoDisc/Getty Images; **p. 193:** CP PHOTO/Peter Lee; **p. 196:** C. Sherburne/PhotoLink/PhotoDisc/Getty Images; **p. 201:** © Royalty-Free/Corbis; **p. 202:** Teri Dixon/ PhotoDisc/Getty Images; **p. 207:** © Images.com/CORBIS; **p. 209:** Paul Chiasson/CP Photo; **p. 210:** © Swerve/Alamy; **p. 213:** Digital Vision/Getty Images; **p. 214:** SW Productions/PhotoDisc/Getty Images; **p. 218:** CP PHOTO/Wayne Cuddington; **p. 223:** Michael Simpson/Taxi/Getty Images; **p. 224:** centre, Ryan McVay/

PhotoDisc/Getty Images; **p. 224:** bottom left, © Royalty-Free/Corbis; **p. 225:** bottom right, Buccina Studios/PhotoDisc/Getty Images; **p. 225:** centre left, Randy Allbritton/PhotoDisc/Getty Images; **p. 225:** top, SW Productions/PhotoDisc/Getty Images; **p. 225:** centre right, SW Productions/PhotoDisc/Getty Images; **p. 229:** Chad Baker/PhotoDisc/Getty Images; **p. 230:** CP PHOTO/Peter Bregg; **p. 232:** CP PHOTO; **p. 233:** © Royalty-Free/Corbis; **p. 237:** www.comstock.ca; **p. 239:** Thomas Kitchin & Victoria Hurst/First Light; **p. 240:** bottom left, Photo courtesy of Sarah Brown; **p. 240:** centre, PhotoDisc/Getty Images; **p. 241** top left: © Ronnen Eshel/CORBIS; **p. 241** centre left: © Royalty-Free/Corbis; **p. 241** centre right: ©Tony Freeman/Photo Edit; **p. 241** bottom right: John Labbe/The Image Bank/Getty Images; **p. 247:** Tony Hopewell/The Image Bank/Getty Images; **p. 252:** John Labbe/The Image Bank/Getty Images; **p. 253:** Digital Vision/Getty Images; **p. 254:** © David Frazier/Photo Edit; **p. 255:** CP PHOTO/St. John's Telegram/Joe Gibbons; **p. 259:** Ian Waldie/Reportage/Getty Images; **p. 260:** Photo courtesy of Geoff Eaton; **p. 261:** Yellow Dog Productions/The Image Bank/Getty Images; **p. 262:** AP Photo/Ed Gonser.

Illustrations

p. 4: Keri Smith; **p. 6:** Marlena Zuber; **p. 14:** Robert Johannsen; **p. 21:** Heather Holbrook; **p. 30:** Robert Johannsen; **p. 32:** Carmelo Blandino; **p. 34:** Luc Melanson; **p. 41:** Allan Moon; **p. 44:** Jacques Cournoyer; **p. 51:** Robert Johannsen; **p. 60:** Nicholas Vitacco; **p. 63:** Tadeusz Majewski; **p. 79:** Marlena Zuber; **p. 104:** Nicholas Vitacco; **p. 106:** Paul Watson; **p. 109:** Robert Johannsen; **p. 137:** Leon Zernitsky; **p. 149:** Robert Johannsen; **p. 152:** Carmelo Blandino; **p. 168:** Anson Liaw, © 2000; **p. 170:** Marlena Zuber; **p. 176:** Jay Belmore; **p. 180:** Peter Lacalamita; **p. 190:** Carl Wiens; **p. 194:** Leon Zernitsky; **p. 202:** David McKay; **p. 226:** Jeremie White; **p. 228:** Andrew Shachat; **p. 234:** Anson Liaw, © 2000; **p. 235:** Tracey Wood; **p. 242:** Ron Dollekamp; **p. 244** Kveta; **p. 245:** Allan Moon; **p. 248:** Vesna Krstanovic; **p. 250:** Ken Dewar; **p. 258:** Jock MacRae.

Text

Statistics Canada information is used with the permission of Statistics Canada. Users are forbidden to copy the data and redisseminate them, in an original or modified form, for commercial purposes, without permission from Statistics Canada. Information on the availability of the wide range of data from Statistics Canada can be obtained from Statistics Canada's Regional Offices, its World Wide Web site at http://www.statcan.ca, and its toll-free access number 1-800-263-1136.

p. 40: Skills Chart has been reproduced from Canada Prospects 1999-2000. Canada Prospects is published by Canada Career Consortium; **p. 50:** The Far Side® by Gary Larson © 1990 FarWorks, Inc. All Rights Reserved. The Far Side® and the Larson® signature are registered trademarks of FarWorks, Inc. Used with permission; **p. 66:** Employability Skills 2000+ Brochure 2000 E/F (Ottawa: The Conference Board of Canada, 2000); **p. 89:** "Are You Positively Charged?" from Careers 10 by Judith Campbell, Copyright © 2000, page 105, Prentice Hall. Reprinted with permission by Pearson Education Canada Inc.; **p. 36-37:** "The Interest Sorter"; Questionnaire and Summary chart from Canada Prospects 1996-1997, published by Human Resources Development Canada; **p. 41-43:** The Multiple Intelligence Chart and Quiz have been reproduced from Canada Prospects 1999-2000, Canada Prospects is published by Canada Career Consortium; **p. 46-47:** Learning Styles Survey and Summary Chart - adapted from the Honolulu Community College Teaching Guidebook, Learning Assistance Centre, University of Hawaii; **p. 107-108:** Profiles of artists and flow chart - adapted from The Spotlight's On, with permission of the Cultural Human Resources Council; **p. 120:** Profile and photo of Jean-Patrick Balleaux, adapted from Volunteering Works! Be Part of Shaping Your Future, p. 13 and p. 15. Reprinted by permission of Volunteer Canada, www.volunteer.ca; **p. 120:** Profile and photo of Jennie Onyett-Jeffries, adapted from Volunteering Works! Be Part of Shaping Your Future, p. 13 and p. 15. Reprinted by permission of Jennie Onyett-Jeffries; **p. 123:** Profile of Stefanie Konkin. Reprinted with permission from REALM: Creating the Work You Want ™ Fall 1999; **p. 124:** Profile of Dameion Royes. Reprinted with permission from REALM: Creating the Work You Want ™ Summer 1999; **p. 127-129:** Could you Succeed in Small Business? quiz from the Human Resources Development Canada publication, Minding Your Own Business, published 1999.10.15. Reproduced with the permission of Her Majesty the Queen in Right of Canada 2006; **p. 134-135:** "Rights and Responsibilities" from the Employer's Guide to Employment Standards Act. Published by the Ontario Ministry of Labour. (ISBN: 0-778-7632-9); **p. 136:** "She Saw the Symbol" from the Young Worker Awareness Program Student Resource Book. The Young Worker Awareness Program was developed by the Workers Health and Safety Centre (WHSC) and the Industrial Accident Prevention Association (IAPA) and funded by the Workplace Safety and Insurance Board (WSIB); **p. 143:** From *Canada: Our Century, Our Story: Ontario Edition*, Student Text by Fielding/Evans. © 2001. Reprinted with permission of Nelson, a division of Thomson Learning: www.thomsonrights.com. Fax 800-730-2215; **p. 145:** Figure: "Age Pyramid of Population of Newfoundland and Labrador, 2001", from the Statistics Canada website <http://www12.statcan.ca/english/census01/products/analytic/companion/age/nl01pymd.cfm>; **p. 148:** "Skills for the New Workplace" adapted with permission of Janis Foord Kirk from her book SURVIVABILITY ®: Career Strategies for the New World of Work 1996, Kirkfoord Communications; **p. 149:** "Where the Jobs Are" by Jeff Buckstein. Reprinted with permission of the author. Jeff Buckstein is a freelance writer based in Kanata, Ontario; **p. 150:** Questioning Predictions - from Making Career Sense of Labour Market Information, 2001 edition, published by CCDF. Reprinted by permission of The Canadian Career Development

Foundation (CCDF); **p. 155:** Courtesy of the Department of Education, Government of Newfoundland and Labrador; **p. 230:** Reprinted with permission from the November 1998 Reader's Digest; **p. 231:** © Scott Adams/Dist. by United Feature Syndicate, Inc; **p. 231:** FAST COMPANY by BYRNE, JOHN. Copyright 1998 by MANSUETO VENTURES LLC. Reproduced with permission of MANSUETO VENTURES LLC in the format Textbook via Copyright Clearance Centre; **p. 235:** The "High Five" of Career Development, ERIC Digest. Created by the Educational Resources Information Centre; **p. 257:** Excerpt: "Overview of the Voluntary Sector in Newfoundland and Labrador: Quick Facts", data is adapted in part from the Statistics Canada publication "The Daily", Charitable donors, Catalogue 11-001, Thursday, November 4, 2004, available at: <http://www.statcan.ca/Daily/English/041104/d041104b.htm>; **p. 260:** Reprinted by permission of Geoff Eaton.